THE CHANGING NATURE OF THE SELF: A Critical Study of the Autobiographic Discourse

THE CHANGING NATURE OF THE SELF

A CRITICAL STUDY OF THE AUTOBIOGRAPHIC DISCOURSE

ROBERT ELBAZ

University of Iowa Press Ψ Iowa City

International Standard Book Number 0-87745-203-2
Library of Congress Catalog Card Number 87-51135
University of Iowa Press, Iowa City 52242
Copyright © 1987 by Robert Elbaz
All rights reserved
First edition, 1987

Printed in Great Britain

Contents

Acknowledgements

Earlier versions of Chapters 1, 5 and 6 have appeared in *Orbis Litterarum*, *Neohelicon*, and *Europa*. I am thankful to the editors of these journals for permission to use these materials.

My deepest thanks go to George Szanto and Tim Reiss for their encouragement with this project. I am especially indebted to Bina Freiwald for the seminal discussions that have accompanied the production of this text and to Donald and Francien Solitar for their friendship and support. Finally, my deepest gratitude to my wife, Freema, and my children, Maya, Shai, and Shira for their unfailing support.

Preface

This book concerns the slow emergence and gradual consolidation of autobiography as a central practice in the discourse of modernism. It deals concurrently with autobiography as a literary practice evolving in renewed forms over time and with the structuration of subjectivity that these forms attempt to circumscribe. The book's basic assumption is that the concept of selfhood, far from being linear, consistent and continuous throughout the ages, is historically and culturally determined, and as such is given to a discursive analysis to account for its vicissitudes over the ages. It is quite evident that modern autobiography does not subscribe to the medieval religious model and that, in turn, the latest manifestations of selfhood sometimes as fractured and fragmented entity or as performative activity, cannot be said to hark back to the Rousseauist model. A discursive model is therefore needed to account for the mutations that occur in the autobiographical structure. These changes are not gratuitous; they are dictated by particular historical situations and as such contribute to shape the receptive consciousness which grapples with them daily. The book will show how the centralised, territorialised, rational, methodic, self-sufficient, free, responsible and contractual selfhood so essential to the discourse of modernism is born from within the medieval configuration, and how this solidified conception is overturned by what seems to be a new conception of subjectivity as advanced by Malraux.

In his *The discourse of modernism* Timothy J. Reiss elaborates an all-encompassing discursive model which allows for change within the discourse.

The term 'discourse' refers to the way in which the material embodying sign processes is organized. Discourse can thus be characterized as the visible and describable praxis of what is called 'thinking'.

discourse is a coherent set of linguistic facts organized by some enunciating entity . . . any semiotic system as practised, not necessarily a simply 'linguistic' one in any narrow sense (as the term has been generally used). I assert that such a broader definition is essential; language, in other words, is but one of the possible materials through and in which discursive order manifests itself . . . *Entity* is taken here as a meaning produced by all discourse, *a meaning which is at the same time the producer of discourse*. It is, if you will, an empty metaphor marking the production of discourse (at once produced and producing). (*The discourse of modernism*, Ithaca, Cornell University Press, 1982, pp. 9, 27–8)

As the term 'entity' indicates, the dialectical production of discourse *of* and *by* signifying practices cannot be imputed to any consciousness or subjectivity as such for the overall structure of meaning is always moving towards its own optimal realisation regardless, as it were, of the subjectivities which embody it and which in turn it embodies; the subject positions available within discourse evolve and change over time from one discursive space to the next. Further, every discursive space (Reiss terms it 'a discursive class') is composed of three types of practices: residual practices which remain active on the surface of discourse until they exhaust their operative efficacy; dominant practices which constitute the bulk of signifying practices within a social whole (the hegemonic mode, the commonsensical, the thinkable and the sayable, in any given society, if you will); and finally, emerging practices which will solidify over time and come to compose the new discursive space, thus displacing the previous dominance.

This discursive displacement, however, is determined by the fact that every dominance is made up of two sets of practices: the first, a dominant overt theoretical model (i.e. the conceptual tools that produce the commonplaces of a given social space); the second, a dominant covert practice which has a quotidian hold over the phenomena it cannot explain. This dominant occulted practice is 'composed of widespread activities . . . that escape analysis by the dominant model, that do not acquire "meaningfulness" in its terms, that are therefore in the strictest sense unthinkable' (Reiss, p. 11). And from the silence of its occultation it rises up to the surface of discourse and will subsequently constitute the structure of meaning within the following discursive space.

With respect to autobiography, the medieval dominant theoretical practice can in no way explain the emergence of the concepts of equality and contractuality that are germane to the discourse of modernism since the hierarchical structure, which is basically static, allows only for a well-determined and stratified social structure in which every member holds a predetermined place.

However, if we look closely at the inter-human relationships prevalent during the Middle Ages, it becomes clear that contractual relations between equals (of course not the formal equality that we will encounter later on in the eighteenth-century notion of the social contract; this later equality is predated by the contractual equality between lord and vassal or between King John and the Barons in the Magna Carta) are the order of the day.

In effect, as will be shown later on, already in Augustine we have a struggle between freedom and determinism, between the cumulative process of autobiographical data and a metaphysical discourse which transcends them. But the gradual consolidation of the new selfhood which begins to form with the elaboration of methodic rationality (Abelard and later on Descartes constitute points on this discursive itinerary of autobiographical production) will take a few centuries to complete. And if Abelard and Descartes were chosen for our analysis, it is because they both mediate between the medieval self and the modernistic conception of subjectivity à la Rousseau. Malraux, who elaborates a new form that turns upside down this centralised subjectivity, might be said to constitute one of the few first terms of an emerging conception of selfhood, although it would be practically impossible for us to declare what the modalities of such a subject might be, given that discursive analysis can make sense only as a retroactive process, that is, a meaningful process inasmuch as it deals with the extreme limits of an epistemic elaboration, with the exhaustion of a given discursive practice.

1

Autobiography, Ideology and Genre Theory

This chapter will study the ideological presuppositions behind the two prevalent definitions of the autobiographic genre — the 'typological' and the 'dynamic'. The typological view puts the emphasis on the inherent generic dimensions of autobiography, while the dynamic view stresses 'the aesthetics of reception'. Despite formal differences, however, both approaches view autobiography as illustrating the problematic relationship between fact and fiction; that is, an ontological difference is claimed to distinguish autobiography from fiction. Autobiography, it is held, purports to represent a 'truth' about a given reality (through its duplication), while fiction does not. It will be argued, however, that through the processes of mediation (by linguistic reality) and suspension (due to the text's lack of finality and completion), autobiography can only be a fiction. Indeed autobiography is fiction and fiction is autobiography: both are narrative arrangements of reality. The ideological nature of these arrangements in autobiographical writing is the issue of concern here.

Two definitions of autobiography

The typological approach

This position is reflected in most of the existing criticism of the genre.[1] This view rests on the assumption that a genre is born by some act of magic which divides the prehistory of the genre from its history. Thus the typical text, the one that exemplifies autobiography most completely, creates a rupture in the historical process, differentiating itself from the past. This position tends to ignore the historical aspect of generic development; it collapses the past two hundred years into one present. To Philippe Lejeune, for example, Rousseau is the true originator of the genre, and whatever happened after is the mere repetition of Rousseau's venture.

This typological approach, though, rests on a circular argument, for dating the beginning of the genre at a specific point in time is dependent on a prior process of synthetisation. First, one establishes a series of formal conditions through the apprehension of a multiplicity of autobiographies. Then these formal conditions are solidified into one specific text (Rousseau, for example) which hypostatises them all. Each particular autobiography is, in turn, perceived in terms of the model which it has helped establish in the first place.

Typology, of course, relates to the normative aspect of generic development. What one seeks in the separation of one work from the original corpus of unclassified texts is the creation of a new group of texts that conform to the model. In effect, the critical literature contributes a great deal to this process. Canonisation has to do with a series of critical statements that build up through repetition: critics X and Y claim that Text A belongs to the genre, therefore it belongs to the genre until critic Z 'proves' the contrary. Once the model is established critics may differ on classification, for it is practically impossible to measure the gap between the model and its copies, and consequently, problems of inclusion and exclusion result. But let us look at the definition itself:

> Nous appelons autobiographie le récit rétrospectif en prose que quelqu'un fait de sa propre existence, quand il met l'accent principal sur sa vie individuelle, en particulier, sur l'histoire de sa personnalité.[2]

This definition tells us, with irreproachable clarity, that autobiography is a narrative similar to other narratives: it develops linearly from *a* to *n*, following a temporal sequence the logic of which is retrospective. The autobiographer always tells the story of a past and, within that past, the linear development of one's 'own existence': what belongs to the author alone (or is 'owned' by him), his 'individual life' which translates into 'the history of his personality' — a central core which is self-consistent throughout its history. It is clear that this statement assumes the existence of a given and knowable empirical reality, and further assures us that the author of the autobiographic text is in a position of 'authority' with respect to a particular segment of that reality — his own life. Further, the details of this life are to be served up to us as essentially separate from other lives, as having a history and independent existence quite apart from the lives of other men within a communal setting. However, nowhere are we told that such a definition obtains only within a social structure which promotes subjects with 'propre existence', existing as free-floating totalities.

The dynamic approach

This view conceives of genre as a transcendental structure moving with historical fluctuations. Its representatives are Elizabeth Bruss in her book *Autobiographical acts*[3] and Philippe Lejeune in *Le Pacte autobiographique*,[4] whose conceptions of this genre are motivated respectively by John Searle's theory of the Speech Act[5] and Hans Jauss's study of the Aesthetics of Reception.[6] These theories combine to contribute to the latest developments in autobiographical theory; from different angles, each arrives at the contextualisation of the literary text.

To Jauss, context means the social consciousness of the times, whereas to Searle it is the constitutive rules governing literary acts. The link between the two is obvious: the establishment of the constitutive rules of a literary act depends upon its reception by that social group which establishes the rules in the first place.

> Toute œuvre littéraire appartient à un genre, ce qui revient à affirmer purement et simplement que toute œuvre suppose l'horizon d'une attente, c'est-à-dire, un ensemble de règles préexistant pour orienter la conscience du lecteur (du public) et lui permettre une réception appréciative . . . Il s'agit de saisir les genres littéraires non comme genera (classes) dans un sens logique, mais comme groupes ou familles historiques.[7]

A text, then, is not a self-enclosed logical entity; rather, in its being, it postulates otherness, a receptive and dynamic group consciouness. Given different horizons of expectancy, text A might generate, in turn, approval, rejection and shock. When Malraux's *Antimémoires* appeared in 1967, for example, the horizon of expectancy comprised mainly Rousseau's confessional model: this text did not fit the same structure; the genre could not incorporate this new phenomenon. The conclusion is either that it is not an autobiography, constituting a bastard form on the outskirts of the genre, or that it has changed the concept of autobiography and that new criteria are required. Similar changes in the horizon of expectancy make for the demise of old genres, the creation of new ones, the imbrication of the new upon the old. With the *Antimémoires* the horizon of expectancy for autobiography has changed; one can now write within the Malrucian tradition.

The theory of the Speech Act adds a further dimension to the study of literary acts and especially to autobiography, since this form, more than any other, seems to require multiple contractual conditions between producer and consumer. Receptive consciousness faces more challenges when it deals with autobiography because the give and take between dispatcher and receiver is more prominent than in other forms: the autobiographer, presumably, always tells his story to a group of listeners.

> Surrounding any text are implicit contextual conditions, participants involved in transmitting and receiving it, and the nature of these implicit conditions and the roles of the participants affect the status of the information contained in the text . . .
>
> It is only by virtue of the constitutive rules of literature that the features of any given text 'count as' signals of autobiography.
>
> Outside of the social and literary conventions that create and maintain it, autobiography has no features — has in fact no being at all.[8]

It is clear that although each autobiography contributes to the homogeneity of the genre, no autobiography in itself has any inherent characteristics which make it partake in the genre, for the definition of genre is extratextual: it lies in that receptive consciousness. Were the definition not extratextual, the differences between texts would overtake the similarities and each text would exist as a separate class, making classification impossible. The concept of genre itself rides on that thin border between similarities and differences; every text partaking in a genre must keep an equilibrium between repetition and difference to allow at the same time for creativity and homogeneity. The lack of equilibrium between difference and repetition in the text may either threaten

4

the sovereignty of the genre and alter it, or it may quarantine the text as an outcast.

Let us now examine Bruss's constitutive rules:

Rule 1. An autobiographer undertakes a dual role. He is the source of the subject matter and the source of the structure to be found in his text. (a) The author claims individual responsibility for the creation and arrangement of his text. (b) The individual who is exemplified in the organization of the text is purported to share the identity of an individual to whom reference is made via the subject matter of the text. (c) The existence of this individual independent of the text itself, is assumed to be susceptible to appropriate public verification procedures.

Rule 2. Information and events reported in connection with the autobiographer are asserted to have been, to be, or to have potential for being the case. (a) Under existing conventions, a claim is made for the truth-value of the autobiographer's reports — no matter how difficult that truth-value might be to ascertain, whether the report treats of private experiences or publicly observable occasions. (b) The audience is expected to accept these reports as true, and is free to 'check up' on them or attempt to discredit them.

Rule 3. Whether or not what is reported can be discredited, whether or not it can be reformulated in some more generally acceptable way from another point of view, the autobiographer purports to believe in what he asserts.[9]

In principle the idea of 'constitutive rules' is reasonable since they constitute the tools by which a group consciousness apprehends the various mediations of the material world; they nevertheless give rise to some serious questions. Bruss's purpose is clearly the rejection of any static view of the generic structure; indeed, because the constitutive rules move with the changes that occur within the social whole, one can assume that the literary structure undergoes parallel transformations. The emphasis here is on the structuration of the genre, the process of its production. It must be noted, however, that Bruss's conception of autobiography accepts as a basic assumption from the outset the notion of genre; she speaks from within the generic discourse. Her main preoccupation is the adaptation of the concept of genre to a more dynamic view; the concept 'genre' is never put into question. Bruss posits that there is a series of texts labelled 'autobiographies' and these texts must be classified 'dynamically'.

Further, these rules concern the notion of veracity; Bruss's terms are 'verification, truth-value'. But surely factual truth is irrelevant to autobiography, for the meaning of an autobiography — or for that matter the meaning of any literary text — does not depend on its factual veracity. This, of course, raises a more serious problem, that of the relationship between reality and fiction. Is there a difference between autobiography and fiction? Bruss's repeated emphasis on truth-value in the three rules leads one to conclude that empirical evidence constitutes the line of demarcation between autobiography and fiction.

In *Le Pacte autobiographique*, Philippe Lejeune joins Bruss in accentuating the contractual pact between writer and reader; but he stresses the synchronic aspect of the generic structure. Thus, the two views complement one another. Lejeune here (p. 14) recapitulates with negligible changes the definition quoted above from *L'Autobiographie en France*. However, in *Le Pacte autobiographique* he sets out to clarify the principle of identification of author-narrator-protagonist, which he advances as being the necessary characteristic of the autobiographical text. His point of departure is Benveniste's notion of the shifter 'I'. Benveniste's[10] revolutionary contribution, to linguistics in particular and to the social sciences in general, is the point that the shifter's only reference is always found within the discourse. Thus, there is no concept of the person: 'I' always refers to the person uttering it in the act of utterance. The notion of person takes meaning only within the parameters of the discursive event. In other words, the speaker's being depends upon the audience and the nature of the discourse he directs at it, his performance, his role within the social whole. And it is precisely that role which defines the 'I'.

Lejeune, however, uses Benveniste's thesis as a base for his own ideas regarding autobiography. He allows that in the theatrical performance the 'I' has to do with the role being performed;

> Le vertige doit commencer à nous prendre, car l'idée effleure alors le plus naïf, que ce n'est pas la personne qui définit le 'je', mais peut-être le 'je' la personne — c'est-à-dire qu'il n'y a de personne que dans le discours.[11]

Nevertheless, he claims that the text refers to a real name, the

name of the author which appears on the first page of the autobiography. 'Le pacte autobiographique c'est l'affirmation dans le
texte de cette identité, renvoyant en dernier ressort au nom de
l'auteur sur la couverture.'[12] In effect, Lejeune holds that the
declaration by the author on the first page of his autobiography
that indeed this is the 'true' story of his life, and his signature to
that effect, sends the reader back to the existence of a 'real person',
which he coins 'le hors-texte', on which the reader can check.
Lejeune supports his thesis of the 'nom propre' by a difficulty he
seems to find in the following statement of Benveniste's:

> Si chaque locuteur, pour exprimer le sentiment qu'il a de sa
> subjectivité irréductible, disposait d'un 'indicatif' distinct . . .
> il y aurait pratiquement autant de langues que d'individus et
> la communication deviendrait strictement impossible.

And Lejeune adds: 'Hypothèse étrange, puisque Benveniste
semble oublier ici que cet indicatif distinct existe, c'est la catégorie
lexicale des noms propres.'[13] It seems to me that Lejeune totally
misses Benveniste's point. In this passage Benveniste is questioning precisely the notion of 'subjectivité irréductible'. If indeed
each one of us had his own 'indicatif', then there would be no communication. Lejeune distorts Benveniste by taking those lines that
suit him; let us complete this quotation and put it in its proper perspective. The lines that come just before the above passage run as
follows:

> C'est pourant un fait à la fois original et fondamental que ces
> formes 'pronominales' ne renvoient pas à la 'réalité' ni à des
> positions 'objectives' dans l'espace et dans le temps, mais à
> l'énonciation chaque fois unique, qui les contient, et réfléchis-
> sent ainsi leur propre emploi. L'importance de leur fonction
> se mesurera à la nature du problème qu'elles servent à
> résoudre, et qui n'est autre que celui de la communication
> intersubjective. Le langage a résolu ce problème en créant un
> ensemble de signes 'vides', non-référentiels par rapport à la
> 'réalité', toujours disponibles, et qui deviennent 'pleins' dès
> qu'un locuteur les assume dans chaque instance de son dis-
> cours. Dépourvus de référence matérielle, ils ne peuvent pas
> être mal employés; n'assertant rien ils ne sont pas soumis à la
> condition de vérité . . . L'emploi a donc pour condition la
> situation de discours et nulle autre.[14]

C'est dans une réalité dialectique englobant les deux termes et les définissant par relation mutuelle qu'on découvre le fondement linguistique de la subjectivité.[15]

Ils [les pronoms] ne renvoient ni à un concept ni à un individu.[16]

It is, then, through the lack of an 'indicatif distinct' that language and meaning can exist. Language is a vacuous structure in which every speaker engages to assert the existence of the Other, the world and himself. The economy of the shifter, its emptiness, the fact that each speaker can assume language and the Other through the use of the pronoun 'I' conditions the being of social exchange. Benveniste's claim points to the futile referentiality of the extratextual as the 'real' person behind the text. Lejeune conceives of authority as the point of origin of the discourse, for it is clear that in this case the author is the originator and controller of the discourse: he is a god creating the world *ex nihilo*. He speaks the discourse rather than the discourse speaking through him. The extratextual, to Lejeune, is not the social and material conditions that make for the possibility of discourse but the individual author who generates it.

Behind this preoccupation with referentiality is the problem of differentiation between fiction and non-fiction; the fictional would consist, according to this view, in the non-identification of author-narrator-protagonist. The belief is that autobiography recounts the 'truth' about an empirical reality and that fiction, by opposition, does not refer to the real.

Par opposition à toutes les formes de fiction, la biographie et l'autobiographie sont des textes référentiels comme le discours scientifique ou historique, ils prétendent apporter une information sur une 'réalité' extérieure au texte, et donc se soumettre à une épreuve de vérification.[17]

One of the founding myths that informs Lejeune's position as expressed in the above passage is that what one terms 'reality' is a homogeneous, consistent and continuous entity which language, the literary text, describes through its pure transparency. The text's only role is that of direct mediation. History, science, or for that matter any meaningful statement, in no way duplicate reality; they construct it. For language is functional to the ideological position of the speaking subject, and 'reality' is the creation of this same subject. One does not report, duplicate or verify the truth: one makes it.

Thus, the dynamic approach to autobiography as genre, despite its postulation of a non-immanent view of the generic structure, falls back upon the misconceptions of the typological approach. It fails to question the concept of 'genre' itself; it merely adapts it to encompass a more dynamic view of receptive consciousness. That is, it provides a social dimension to the literary structure. It does not put into question the nature of the autobiographical text (which makes up this structure) as a signifying practice, that is, in the larger sense, as an ideological statement.

Fiction and factuality

The problems of classification and of the delineation between autobiography and fiction constitute the major preoccupations of recent criticism of the genre: the issue is of capital importance because it concerns the essence of literature itself. And the problematic of duplication does not restrict itself exclusively to autobiography; it applies to any other text. The question is not whether a given genre can replicate reality but whether reality can be replicated in principle — whether truth is 'found', or 'created' within a social praxis. Let us see what is being said about the imaginative aspect of the autobiographical discourse.

Stephen A. Shapiro chastises Welleck and Warren for excluding autobiography from the literary domain and relegating it to a nonliterary, popular category. To Shapiro, autobiography is an artistic arrangement of phenomena: 'Autobiography is an imaginative organization of experience for aesthetic and for various intellectual and moral purposes.'[18] But while emphasising technique, perspective, dramatic presentation, montage, etc., Shapiro claims in the same breath, 'Autobiography is a literary form but the aesthetic function of autobiography is not its major function: education or reality-testing is its reason for being.'[19] This paradoxical stance is found in most critiques of the genre; autobiography is an imaginative arrangement of the world, and at the same time it repeats experiences as they were lived. This paradoxicality is dictated by ideology, for one cannot concede that the mind — at least the mind of the artist — is a xerox machine, yet at the same time one has to posit, for the sake of the *status quo*, that reality is the same both within and without the text. Only the

9

ideology of sameness can accommodate the myth of autobiographic duplication.

This paradoxical stance is consistent with Roy Pascal's
approach to autobiography; *Design and truth in autobiography*
vacillates between 'design' and 'truth', between fictionality and
factuality. While 'memory can be trusted because autobiography
is not just reconstruction of the past, but interpretation',[20] yet 'the
linear narrative form of the autobiography imposes a distortion on
the truth.'[21] When the notion of factual truth becomes too embar-
rassing to sustain, Pascal resorts to another kind of truth. 'Beyond
factual truth, beyond the "likeness" the autobiography has to give
that unique truth of life as it is seen from inside, and in this respect
it has no substitute or rival.'[22] Roy Pascal, however does not spell
out what 'that unique truth of life' is. Is it a private truth of which
the individual is convinced? Can we compare these private truths
or are they all the same? Pascal sees no inconsistencies in his argument; there exists a possibility of communication through autobiography which has to do with every individual's inner conviction as
to the existence of his own self: 'we do not judge an autobiography
solely upon the evidence of the facts but also upon an intuitive
knowledge of the distinctive character of life as experienced by
ourselves individually.'[23]

The imaginative dimension of autobiography is at the centre of
Louis A. Renza's discussion in 'The veto of the imagination: a
theory of autobiography',[24] which despite its obsession with cate-
gorisation, constitutes a more original attempt in terms of the
questions posed. Renza tackles the problem of classification by
focusing on the writing practice of the autobiographer. 'The
dynamics or drama of autobiographical cognition occurs in terms
of the written performance itself.'[25] This premise leads Renza to
conclude that what is at stake is not the recreation of the past of the
writer but an interpretation of his present, that is, the imaginative
creation of the present of writing. The concept 'persona' is introduced to account for the difference between the present of the
writer and his past — a past which coincides with the real person
adopting the momentary persona of writing. To Renza, therefore,
the task of autobiography is to keep the balance between the
persona and the person. But in effect, Renza does not depart from
the ideology of the self; he posits a person — a self, an irreducible
entity — although this self is not what autobiography is about since
it is limited to the writing performance.

So to Renza the self exists, but outside autobiography, and

autobiography oscillates between its presence and absence.

> Autobiographical writing thus entails a split intentionality:
> the 'I' becoming a 'he'; the writer's awareness of his life
> becoming private even as he brings it into the public domain
> or presentifies it through his act of writing.[26]

This 'split intentionality' is motivated by the vacillation between
person and persona: an 'I' is writing a narrative which through the
'veto of the imagination' is a narrative about an external existing
'he'. This tension between the 'I' and the 'he' forces Renza to
arrive at the impossibility of classification, and to create a new
category of a discourse which transgresses itself indefinitely — in
short, a text that cannot 'be'.

> We might say, then, that autobiography is neither fictive nor
> non-fictive, not even a mixture of the two. We might view it
> instead as a unique, self-defining mode of self-referential
> expression, one that allows, then inhibits, the project of self-
> presentification, of converting oneself into the present pro-
> mised by language. We might also say that its logical extreme
> would be the conception of a private language, though no such
> thing exists as we know from Wittgenstein. At this extreme,
> the autobiographer's life appears like a daydream that at first
> seems recordable, but then, when the attempt is made to
> record it, eludes the word . . . Thus we might conceive of
> autobiographical writing as an endless prelude: a beginning
> without middle (the realm of fiction), or without end (the
> realm of history); a purely fragmentary, incomplete literary
> project, unable to be more than an arbitrary document.[27]

The difficulties expressed in this passage stem from Renza's
insistence on keeping the notion of person parallel to that of
persona. If the 'person' disappears and only the 'persona'
remains, the tension between the two vanishes and 'the project of
self-presentification' becomes a myth. Renza is therefore conditioned by the same ideology he tries to demystify. Indeed, autobiography is a discourse not about the 'I' but about a series of
'he's', because a 'he' does not conform to the mystified consistency and continuity of the 'I': the narrative is made up of a
multiplicity of personae. The narrative is always a 'third person'
phenomenon.

Since I am not myself, I am not the same person I was yesterday or ten years ago; given my relational nature, I cannot be writing my autobiography but the story of a variety of old 'personae' seen from a distance. The autobiographer always writes a novel, a fiction, about a third person. And the question is not whether that third person coincides with the writing 'I' of the autobiographer, as Renza wants us to believe, but rather: What does this third person (or series of third persons) which defies the myth of continuity tell us about the world? What subjectivity, what role, does it incarnate in its relationship to the world?

The usual objective of the autobiographer is to be his own biographer, the narrator of his life story in the first person. The near totality of all autobiographies can fairly be called pseudobiographies, formally distinct from their model by having 'I' where it has 'he' or 'she'.[28]

Claiming that autobiography is not factual does not solve the problem of its classification; it may be non-factual and at the same time be obedient to the ideology which posits the possible duplication of reality. Autobiography may be fictional yet at the same time 'look' factual. At this point there emerge the similarities between the novel of 'characters' — the biographical novel — and autobiography. It matters not in the least whether the narrative does occur in the real world or whether it is narrated 'as if' it occurred in the real world; the ideological import remains the same. What matters is the arrangement of the narrative, for data can be 'made' factual; they can be arranged in a factual way (as in the Realist novel), giving us the same obedience to truth. A sequence of events that is plausible is no different from one which did in fact happen: in the final analysis both sequences are produced by a living consciousness in its apprehension of the material world.

This is why autobiography, contrary to what Renza proposes, cannot allow for the presentification of self; since it is a fiction, it can only inhibit presentification. In no way can it be an 'incomplete literary project' (for no literary project is ever complete), or 'an arbitrary document' (no document is arbitrary). Like fiction, autobiography can only be a beginning, a ceaseless beginning,[29] because that is all there is; because consciousness in its temporal division, in its process of contradiction and negation, allows for beginnings only, for what cannot be completed. And the

12

completion of autobiography — or biography, or any other narrative — is a myth posited within the discursive reality by an engulfing hegemonic mode. Completeness is not a natural phenomenon: time is divisive, by definition.

Suspension and mediation

> About six weeks ago Gertrude Stein said, it does not look to me as if you were ever going to write that autobiography. You know what I am going to do. I am going to write it for you. I am going to write it as simply as Defoe did the autobiography of Robinson Crusoe. And she has and this is it.[30]

This passage is difficult to grasp as a statement about autobiography; unlike the previous two definitions, it offers no firm moorings, much less a clear definition of the genre. But on inspection, it proves to deal with the same issues as the previous two, and to provide us with an equally consistent, if radically different, view of autobiography. The first point to be noted is that the passage should end with a colon, and be followed by the text of the autobiography; it is a preamble to the 'autobiography' of Alice B. Toklas. In fact, it comes at the end of the text; why? Stein is telling us that the beginning coincides with the end and the end with the beginning. The text cannot be completed and it is therefore suspended. The reader must, then, go to the beginning — which is the end — for autobiography (like fiction) is an act of ceaseless renewal: the story is never 'told' finally, exhaustively, completely. The story of a life cannot be laid out in full detail from beginning to end; the significance of that life cannot be exhausted in a single narrative.

The second point to be made about this passage is that it embodies a gap between writing and speaking: the discourse is spoken by a voice which is other than that of the writing agent. The writing 'I' — Gertrude Stein — speaks with the voice of a third person, the 'she' of Alice B. Toklas. The story of Gertrude Stein, her autobiography, is Toklas. This mediation is necessary because, as suggested, the consistency and continuity of the 'I' are mystifications.

The third point follows directly: this third person, this mediator is ultimately a fiction. *Robinson Crusoe*, a fiction written by Daniel Defoe, is, to Gertrude Stein, the autobiography of Robinson Crusoe (whose ontological status is fictional) as written by Daniel

Defoe. And the autobiography of Robinson Crusoe coincides with the autobiography of Alice B. Toklas in that both are fictions: they are both appropriations of selfhood through fictive voices.

Beginnings, then, make for the suspension of the text and reject any notion of completion or finality since the text is in essence a ceaseless process of production of meaning. And this concept relates within the same ideological configuration to the notions of mediation: the text 'begins' through the voice of a third party because language accommodates the Other by adopting the voice of an Other in its movement towards meaning. This process of mediation in turn calls for the non-differentiation between autobiography and fiction; because self-possession is a myth, one can only possess an Other.

Thus everything having to do with language is fiction, the construction of a speaking subject: one always speaks from a linguistic-metaphoric reality. Every discourse is an interpretation. The hope of grasping events in their bareness and immediately as they happen is an illusion which takes strength from the dichotomy 'truth/falsehood' — a metaphysical residue which is one of the bastions of the prevalent ideology.

> There is no textual property, syntactical or semantic, that will identify a text as a work of fiction. What makes it a work of fiction is, so to speak, the illocutionary stance that the author takes toward it, and that stance is a matter of the complex illocutionary intentions that the author has when he writes or otherwise composes it . . . The pretended illocutions which constitute a work of fiction are made possible by the existence of a set of conventions which suspend the normal operation of the rules relating illocutionary acts to the world.[31]

There is nothing in the text itself qualifying it as autobiography: texts do not 'partake' in genres. They are made to 'fit' an existing literary structure. If one insists on the creative construction of the text by critical consciousness then one must do away with the concept of genre. For what is genre if not an ideological grid forced upon consciousness? Generic classification has to do with institutionalisation — canonisation and therefore fetishisation — of literature. The question ought to be not what pre-existing category Text A obeys but in what way do I recreate Text A to widen my consciousness of the historical process. Generic classification is a hegemonic phenomenon which restricts literary practice to approved, institutionalised forms of expression.

It might be argued that classification is natural to man. However, an analysis of the discourse in which classifications are promoted suggests rather that classification is called for when knowledge is conceived of as an accumulation of data to be stored away in little boxes. This trend is related to the development of the empirical sciences; every piece of knowledge must be compartmentalised for fear of losing it. Tables, charts and taxonomies appear, and every object is described in its divisions and subdivisions. Thus, the object is alienated from the rest of the material world. It seems that we are still captives to this process of compartmentalisation, and the compartmentalisation of knowledge leads to the fragmentation of man.

To Walter Ong, classification has to do with a

> shift in sensibility marked by the development of typography. This shift brought Western man to react to words less and less as sounds and more as items deployed in space. Printing made the location of words on a page the same in every copy of a particular edition, giving a text a fixed home in space impossible even to imagine effectively in a pretypographical culture. Printing thus heightened the value of the visual imagination and the visual memory over the auditory imagination and the auditory memory and made accessible a diagrammatic approach to knowledge such as is realized in the dichotomized tables which often accompanied the typographical treatment of a subject . . . Typography did more than merely 'spread' ideas. It gave urgency to the very metaphor that ideas were items which could be 'spread'.[32]

The word, like the chart, and the division into species and genus, has to do with the appropriation of space, with a specific locus on a typed page, and this, to Ong, is a phenomenon which appears in the Guttenberg era. Before type, dialectic and rhetoric, argumentation and persuasion, constituted temporal-organisational principles of reality. Ong argues that this spatial trend is dialectically related to Copernican space, to the abstract space initiated by the paintings of Jan Van Eyck, to systems of thought which saw the mind as a container of object-ideas like the Cartesian or Lockean idea.[33] The word stopped being a process of communication and became (and is) an object, a receptacle 'containing' truth, totally abstracted from dialogue. Print — the first instance of mass

15

production — made of the book a consumer product, which was in line with the spread of the universities as producers of consumer-knowledge. There is no doubt that the ideology of taxonomies has to do with the spatial organisation of reality, with the serial itemisation of phenomena. Hence to Ong, the growing interest in Ramus's methodic rationality in this period.[34] The spread of this kind of knowledge amongst the middle class was motivated by the needs of the commercial mind: itemisation and serialisation allow commodities to be arrayed in space on a page. The knowledge of classification is posed as neutral, made up of the detached bits and pieces on which positivism will later thrive.

Furthermore, with the latest shift in critical theory from the classifiable work of literature to textual productivity, classification has become an exercise in ossification, since it does not answer the need for a dynamic view of the discursive praxis. The 'text' can no longer be classified due to its ceaseless beginning, its endless process of productivity: it exists only to the extent that it produces meaning. Textuality, in opposition to the specific work, the specific genre, is a field of play for an endless process of transformation and metamorphosis.[35]

2
Augustine's *Confessions*

The two styles, in their opposition, represent basic types: on the one hand fully externalized description, uniform illumination, uninterrupted connection, free expression, all events in the foreground, displaying unmistakable meanings, few elements of historical development and of psychological perspective; on the other hand, certain parts brought into high relief, others left obscure, abruptness, suggestive influence of the unexpressed, 'background' quality, multiplicity of meanings and the need for interpretation, universal-historical claims, development of the concept of the historically becoming, and preoccupation with the problematic.[1]

This passage differentiates between the two styles that Eric Auerbach uncovers in classical culture and in the Biblical narrative respectively. According to Auerbach, Augustine makes use of the elevated classical style to express the most mundane human phenomena; Augustine's description of Alypius in the market is indicative of the mixture of styles, of the high and the low.

This chapter will centre on the various relationships generated by this binary combination; of capital interest is the migration of these concepts, the 'sublime' and the 'humble', and the ideological stance they inform throughout the Middle Ages. The hierarchical schema these two concepts denote is at the basis of all sociopolitical phenomena of the low and high Middle Ages. The positive status with which Auerbach endows these two concepts reflects his own ideological bias; nevertheless these concepts provide us with tools that transcend aesthetics. Our purpose is to go beyond aesthetic preoccupations and see how the 'sublime' and the 'humble' are inscribed within the social praxis of the times.

In the process of migration[2] of these concepts, one can identify three major manifestations which seek one another. The first is the mixture of the two styles in Augustine which does not pertain exclusively to the *Confessions*, that is, the types of sentences he uses and their stylistics. The abolition of the division between the two styles is reflected in the relationships between the biographical part of the book and its metaphysical counterpart: God is present in the biographical chapters and Augustine is in the metaphysical treatise. Secondly, Christianity, in its negation of this division between the human and the sublime, introduces the low style into the elevated one; in the Christian narrative, Christ partakes in both realms; he originates in the lowest social group, yet he incorporates the sublime and the eternal. Thirdly, the system of government which prevailed throughout the Middle Ages originates in this hierarchical structure which was presumed to be established by divine providence. It is quite evident that the migration of these two concepts is both synchronic and diachronic. Synchronically, it moves on a horizontal plane from aesthetic to politics and vice versa and, diachronically, on a vertical plane: throughout the Middle Ages, one hierarchical system of government gives birth to another and so on. There exists, therefore, a dialectical relationship between Augustine's presentation of these two concepts in his book and their existence in the material and historical reality in which he lived and, by extension, a relationship between church ideology and the system of government which was structured by it. These basic relationships are genuine to the medieval discursive space.

Autobiography and metaphysics

Augustine's *Confessions* partakes in both the old and the new. The disputatious style found in many pages of this book recalls the familiar rhetoric we encounter in Plato (Augustine himself was an eminent scholar and teacher of rhetoric for many years) and the narrative bears witness to this Platonic and Neo-Platonic influence,[3] and more particularly, to Plotinus; it reflects as well its Scriptural and Christian sources.

The main innovation in the *Confessions* is the creation of a narrative sequence of the biographical facts of an individual human life. With Augustine there appears for the first time a coherent and cumulative account of biographical data which will ultimately develop into what is now termed autobiography. But these data will have to undergo a discursive shift before they solidify and come to constitute the 'modern' autobiography with the emergence of what is now called Neo-Classical discourse towards the end of the Middle Ages.

This is why this innovation calls for a qualification. Augustine goes through a very rigorous process in the selection of his data; the cumulation has a purpose. And the story stops at the moment of conversion; beyond this point Augustine, the individual, disappears to make room for a metaphysical discourse. As most critics point out, the formal unity of the work is jeopardised by the inclusion of Chapters 10–13 which have no relation to the story-line of Books 1–9. Augustine's preoccupation with a 'Philosophy of memory', 'Time and eternity', 'Form and matter', and the 'Creation of the world' has little to do with factual evidence; hence the shorter versions of the *Confessions* in which those final chapters are deleted because of their presumed irrelevance to the concrete life of the Saint. Indeed, some critics claim that the aesthetics of the book is faulty and that one should read the two parts of the book with a different critical eye since the one is a narration, the other a metaphysical discourse. In this chapter we will argue against this approach and claim that the work does not lack unity, provided we take into account the selective process that Augustine followed in the first nine books. We contend that narration of necessity gives way to metaphysical discourse given the essential purpose motivating these confessions.[4]

But despite the narrative innovation, the textual preoccupations in Augustine partake in the residual discursive practices inherited from the Platonic tradition in its concern with the problem of authority — i.e. the reducibility of all phenomena to primary causes. Plato and Augustine share a conceptual ordering of the universe; both postulate an hierarchical system of being. No doubt major differences exist between the two systems, particularly in terms of the generating forces behind them, but the ordering remains very similar in both. Whether the Ideas are self-sufficient and immutable entities or whether they exist in the mind of God, the verticality of the concept of Idea remains the same. Both texts conform to the notion of representation: there is at least a strong parallel between the statement that every Particular partakes in its corresponding Idea and the statement that God created man in his own image.

You are great, O Lord, and greatly to be praised: great is your power and to your wisdom there is no limit. And man who is part of your creation, wishes to praise you, man who bears about within himself his mortality, who bears about within himself testimony to his sin and testimony that you resist the proud. Yet man, this part of your creation, wishes to praise you. You arouse him to take joy in praising you, for you made us for yourself, and our heart is restless until it rests in you.[5]

This is the opening paragraph to the *Confessions*. Augustine does not start with his own story, with 'I was born . . .'; he gets around to his birth only in Chapter 6, after he has dealt with God's greatness, his omnipotence, his immensity, his attributes and a prayer. Nor can one talk of a linear progression in this autobiography; the author does not start with the beginnings of a chronology which presumably led to his conversion to Christianity. Instead he starts with God and only after he has established God's primordiality does he proceed to his personal history. This opening statement lists Augustine's major concerns throughout the *Confessions*. First, God with his greatness, power and wisdom; second, man's fallen condition, his sins and mortality; third, the relationship of dependance between the two, the only solution to this sinful condition being the final rest in God. This is the first glimpse we get of Augustine's conception of history; the *Confessions* can be said to follow the same pattern. The biographical Books 1 – 9 come under the heading 'sin' for they relate to the tribulations of a fallen soul; Books 10 – 13 speak of God and his creation; the link between the two is the theme of a return from sinfulness to conversion and vision.

One cannot therefore speak of chronology in Augustine although it seems to be present in Books 1 – 9 (excepting Chapters 1 – 6 of Book 1).[6] The formal weakness can exist in this book only if we read it as a sequence of events, which is clearly not Augustine's purpose. Rather, in accordance with the Augustinian world view the pattern is cyclical and not linear. And if it is cyclical, wherever one starts, one can always come back to the beginning. This means that there is always a possible return to the Origin; one can move from time to Eternity. And more importantly, history is retro-active; it can be redeemed. This is why the proof of God's existence starts in the material world with man (hence the autobiographical narrative of the first nine books). In other words what counts is the final reading.

Let us take a specific example: the theft of pears from a garden. Very few autobiographers would pay attention to similar acts in their childhood, yet this futile act takes on almost extravagant proportions in Augustine's story. He seems to have selected this little anecdote to make some major gains, and so does he with most other anecdotes. First, he tells us that the fruit was 'desirable neither in appearance, nor in taste' and that he and his friends stole the fruit 'not for our own eating, but rather to throw it to the pigs' (AC 70). Finally, he tells us that he was not in need of the fruit because he had plenty of fruit of his own. So why steal? — 'to go down to death. I loved my fault, not that for which I did the fault, but I loved my fault itself' (AC 71). From here Augustine proceeds to a speech on the causes and kinds of sin, and then on to an analysis of the 'Anatomy of evil'. In between we are told that men sin, perversely, in order to imitate God because they want to acquire the power and pride that God has in his creation. Furthermore, the main motivation for the theft was the association he had with his friends; that is, sin comes with social relations. And this foreshadows the dismal view that Augustine holds of social and political institutions in general.

Throughout the book, a parallelism is drawn between the small facts of a life and the overall meaning of the universe as created by God. Augustine's birth recalls the creation of the world to which the author devotes the last book of his confessions. His problems with the learning of language and control over signs in early childhood gives way to a discourse on the nature of signs in the Scriptures and the meaning of revelation; and the child's mastering of grammar and rhetoric, his quest for earthly knowledge, is measured up against the true knowledge of God, the final vision. Wherever a biographical fact is mentioned there is always an interpretation — a metaphysical one — accompanying it. The end of the story does not lie in the story itself but in its interpretation.

The purpose becomes clearer as one looks closely at those biographical chapters. The scarcity of factual detail in this so-called 'biography' is striking. One can summarise the main events of this life in a few lines: Augustine's birth, his difficulties with language, his studies, his petty thefts, his conversion, his resignation from his teaching position at Milan, his philosophical activities at Cassiciacum, his baptism by Saint Ambrose, his ordination, the death of Monica, his mother, the death of Adeodatus, his bastard son, the vision at Ostia, and his succession to Valerius as bishop of

Hippo. But alongside this story-line runs a commentary accompanied by prayers and incantations. In fact, the biographical details do not hold the centre of this text in line with the parabolic nature of medieval discourse as a whole; these details seem to be marginal insertions between the lines of prayer and commentary: they come merely to provide further support for the main thesis, for a new interpretation.

If the facts are scarce, the elaboration on them, the interpretation, is more verbose. We recall that the *Confessions* is foremost a study of other texts: it inserts between other lines, within other discourses. In itself it constitutes an intertextual space, exploiting the interstices of the medieval discursive space as a whole. The texts which make up this intertext include those of the Manicheans, who constitute a focal point in the book, and Cicero, whose book *Hortensius* inspired Augustine's interest in knowledge; Ambrose's allegorical readings of the Bible as well as Plotinus' metaphysical system, are all essential to the story, and of course the presence of the Bible in the substance of the text is manifest through the numerous quotations. This intertextual relationship is articulated in a negational mode, the proof that the Manicheans, the Astrologers and other heretics are wrong implies that one's past experiences have been wrong, that one's past readings have been faulty. At the same time the truth of the Scriptures is established beyond any doubt. The *Confessions*, then, serves a double purpose: it relates to a concrete life in the world and it presents a discursive reality which is just emerging in Augustine's time, a discourse which will vie for supremacy throughout the High and Low Middle Ages.

One should note the lack of equilibrium — at least in terms of quantity — between the life story and the rest of the text, that is, everything relating to God. The scarcity of personal data contrasts with the proliferation of accounts of God's presence. This lack of discursive equilibrium is essential in terms of the final meaning Augustine wants to impart to his readers. Proliferation here means a reduction of the many to the One; the reduction of the various elements of the discourse to the immutable God. To the modern reader this text is very repetitive; prayer follows prayer, incantation follows incantation. Even the story of one's sins (which presumably consitutes a narrative sequence since, to Augustine, life is sin by definition) turns into the story of Sin because all sins are equal in so far as that they debase man and prevent him from reaching the true Goal.[7]

Augustine's discursive reduction through repetition has one important effect: it annihilates the self-awareness of the speaking subject to the point where only the word-object remains. By extension, this reduction does away with the timeliness of the self and with history. Of interest in this connection is the spatial imagery developed throughout the text. The spatiality of God and the self is expressed in terms of container and contained. 'Therefore my God, I would not be, I would in no wise be, unless you were in me. Or rather, I would not be unless I were in you . . . You fill all things and you fill them with your entire self' (AC 44). To contain God, Augustine must empty himself of everything else; the self must be utterly empty to make room for God; it could not contain God and other things at the same time. Hence Augustine's feeling of emptiness (a real vacuity) when God's presence disappears.

Yet this reduction to the One can only occur when the universal imbues every particular with its presence. Since the name of God is inscribed on every object the eye perceives, the filling of thirteen chapters with the name of God can multiply *ad infinitum*. Augustine is, in fact, writing the name of God on every page in the world *ad infinitum*. The disappearance of the speaking subject in the last four chapters should not come as a surprise because the self is a manifestation of the One Universal. The self disappears to be engulfed in God, the creator. The Verb engulfs all particular verbs; the personal story spills into the cosmic one. Augustine's story turns into biblical exegesis because it has to find its location in the Arch-narrative which includes all other narratives. Once the process of conversion has taken place no room remains for the meanderings and doubts of the soul in the search for Truth. After conversion one's past history can be seen from one perspective only: that of the integration with God. And that famous Book 10 on the multiple powers of memory — a section which seems to belong nowhere — represents the transitional stage from the Universal to the particular. Memory, in its *a priori* recollective dimension, constitutes a bridge between time and eternity, contingency and necessity.

Time and eternity, contingency and necessity, these are only two of the binary combinations permeating Augustine's text and medieval discourse as a whole. Good and evil, truth and falsehood, the one and the many, being and non-being, creator and created, the high and the low, knowledge and ignorance — all these combinations are convertible. Whatever concept one starts with in

Augustine, one always arrives at the same conclusion. One side of the combination identifies with God, the other with wordly creation. One can indeed start the *Confessions* on any page because of the central presence permeating it; every page is both a beginning and an end.

To James F. Anderson,[8] the basic ontological division in Augustine's conceptual framework is that between being and non-being. God — the only entity that *is* full — is the giver of being to all created phenomena through his act of creation. But the amount of being given in the act of creation is not equal in all created phenomena: at the basis of the concept of an hierarchical order lies a quantitative notion of being.

> I beheld other things below you, and I saw that they are not altogether existent nor altogether non-existent: they are, because they are from you; they are not, since they are not what you are. For that truly exists which endures unchangeably. (AC 171)

The apex of being is God; the angels partake in being more than the souls, the souls more than the bodies, and so on down to the inanimate stones. But non-being itself does not mean the total absence of being. For that would entail two coexistent forces fighting for control over the universe. This, Augustine attempts repeatedly to explain in his refutations of Manichean doctrines. Manichean[9] dualism postulates that good and evil are in constant strife to enlarge their respective spheres of influence, and man dangles helplessly between the two spheres. Augustine reacts against this dualism by adopting a vertical concept of order; God could not possibly share the universe with another substance and be, at the same time, the generator of all things. (Hence, 'evil is only the privation of the good, even to the point of complete non-entity' (AC 85)). Also a totally corrupt entity could not be redeemed by God's grace. Every created thing, low and sinful as it is, has a potential for redemption; some have greater redemptive potential than others, depending upon the position they have attained in the scale of being.

Augustine's statement 'My weight is my love'[10] takes on meaning only when we consider the transformation that had occurred in the hierarchical conception of the universe by Augustine's time. Love, a human emotion, has to do with weight, a physical characteristic. True love, the love of God, is functional

24

to the weight one has acquired in one's sinful downslide. The ancient world viewed the universe as an ordered harmony of bodies, the lighter bodies, like fire, climbing higher while the heavier ones, like stones, sliding lower. But on the whole the order is static in its harmony; every object finds the optimal final position which befits it in the order of things. Augustine brings a twofold transformation; first, he finds a correspondence between physical bodies and ethical values: he identifies the high with the good and the true, the low with the base and the false. (This permutation already exists in Plato.) The second contribution to this concept of hierachy is the introduction of energy to the order; things are in constant vertical movement, not by choice but by definition. One cannot stop at any one sinful stage; if you do not move up, you move down. (Certain Judaeo-Christian traditions conceived of further divisions in the realm of the low. The human body itself is seen as made up of a higher half and a lower one, the one coinciding with reason, the other with the animalistic reproductive functions.) Of crucial importance, then, is the fact that this movement upward or downward is not simply a subjective state in man, it is not a question of choice; the movement has an objective ontological status.[11] It is like a physical necessity, a magnetism; corresponding to bodies, souls must go up or down. And if it were not for God's guiding hand, all souls would be moving up and down increasingly.

In order to secure God's total control over everything that is, be it physical or mental, Augustine posited a process of reversibility between his ontology and his epistemology.[12] 'To know the good' coincides with 'to be the good'. One cannot move up the ontological echelons without a corresponding movement in the epistemological ones. In parallel to God, the souls and the bodies, we have intellection, spiritual and corporeal knowledge. One can move up from knowledge acquired through the senses to knowledge acquired by imagination to the true knowledge of reason, which is the knowledge of God, and knowing truly means merging with Him. The vision experienced by Augustine and his mother, Monica, at Ostia comes close to this epistemological level. But complete merger can happen only with the annihilation of the body; to achieve knowledge one must leave this world and move into Eternity. It is consequently clear that human knowledge of whatever kind is merely a temporary tool that must be transcended.

Of facts and values

Augustine cannot make an abstraction of time as a lived experience of the individual consciousness and of history as a dimension which relates among all human phenomena, which connects between the Christian and the non-Christian. He was very aware of the need to redeem the past and thus to provide a new reading of historical contingency. He himself was born to a Pagan father and practised Paganism for many years. How, then, does one account for that in which both the chosen and the non-chosen partake? How does Augustine understand social and private times, external and internal times? He is too aware of his own biases:

> And thus it has come to pass though there are very many and great nations all over the earth, whose rites and customs, speech, arms and dress, are distinguished by marked differences, yet there are no more than two kinds of human society, which we may justly call two cities, according to the language of our Scriptures. The one consists of those who wish to live after the flesh, the other of those who wish to live after the spirit.[13]

The aspiration to one truth[14] must reduce the complexity and variety of human phenomena. The Christian discourse dictates that the apocalyptic view is a retroactive one. It is the future of the past: a final vision that is forced upon the past. Hence when one has reached conversion, the biographical data become meaningless and one moves into a metaphysical treatise. However, these two cities do not exist side by side in the material world; they are supernatural entities in which all humans partake, each according to his choice of salvation or damnation. (The notion of choice itself is contradictory, for man's destiny is predetermined, yet man must will the good if he wants to be saved.) We have no criteria for deciding who belongs where: everything is to be settled with the last judgement. And to the question, why has God created the chosen ones in the flesh and not left them in their ethereal forms, Augustine will answer that the chosen must be 'tried' in order to accede better to eternal life.

In keeping with his opposition to Manicheanism, Augustine does not grant equal standing to both cities. Although this life gives an edge to the earthly city, the heavenly city remains the model to which the earthly one aspires. There is always a promise to be fulfilled in the future. Suffering and misery have to do with that final promise; nothing remains gratuitous, everything has a purpose. This explains why there was no opposition to the corruption of the Empire: everything is pre-ordained and the scheme has been worked out since the beginning of time. The only consolation is that those who suffer in this word will be compensated in the next one and the present winners will be damned. This is, *par excellence*, the politics of 'in the meantime', man is robbed of his present on the assumption that he will get a future if he behaves well enough.

La conception augustinienne selon laquelle le Chrétien, que Dieu fait vivre dans une société mauvaise pendant la durée de l'épreuve terrestre, doit vivre pour Dieu en supportant les cadres, les institutions dans lesquelles il a été placé par la Providence, marque aussi la théorie de la propriété. L'univers tout entier est à Dieu qui le distribue comme il veut. L'état de fait doit donc être respecté comme voulu par la Providence. Idéalement, seuls devraient posséder les biens de la terre ceux qui les géreraient pour le plus grand bien de tous, c'est-à-dire les saints.[15]

The ideological equivalence established in Christian discourse between material objects and their ethical value is of capital importance. In the Judaeo-Christian tradition, Augustine postulates a correspondence between cleanliness and purity; thus a neutral phenomenon is invested with value. Corruption and sinfulness take the guise of empirical phenomena and vice versa. The purpose of the various water rituals is not the cleaning of the body but the purification of the soul. The eradication of predication from empirical reality and its replacement with predicates of value points to the ideological configuration in this tradition.[16]

In effect, one cannot separate the empirical and the moral realms, for value becomes one of the constitutive elements of the material object just like its colour and shape. This provides us with an essential insight into the medieval Judaeo-Christian discursive space. For the abolition of the differentiation between the material object and its ethical counterpart means that there is a superposition of values upon facts; the domain of facts is absorbed by the domain of values.[17]

In Augustine's world there is an equivalence between 'is' and 'ought', between the descriptive and the prescriptive — a distinction which presumes an ideological stance. The statement 'there are very many and great nations all over the earth' and the statement 'there are no more than two kinds of human society' not only are not contradictory in Augustine's logic, but they are equally descriptive. The deontic qualifier is missing in the second one. Augustine does not 'believe' that there are no more than two kinds of human society; it is not his own individual statement; there simply are, *out there*, no more than two kinds of human society. The statement is descriptive and universal whereas it should be prescriptive and particular. This process of universalisation invests the statement with the characteristics of propositional logic and truth value. 'There are no more than two kinds of human society' is a statement based in a belief which makes it as valid as the statement 'the tree is green' or 'it is raining in Montreal now'. It is of interest to note that throughout the Middle Ages, including the later times of Descartes and Spinoza, the existence of God was 'proved' by logical argument. But the Truth of these logicians is very different from that truth (with a small 't') which is conditioned by the logical process of inference, having nothing to do with the empirical world but with premises and conclusions and rules of inference of the ones from the others.

The distinction between facts and values is no less problematic than the logic of propositions which relates to it, and which conceals a static view of the world. Even examples like 'It is raining outside', found in traditional logic manuals, cannot conform to the concept of truth because the statement must be scaled down, sometimes to a pure inanity, in order to be verifiable. 'It is raining in Montreal now' itself depends upon definitions of rain, its quality and quantity, the geography of Montreal (maybe it is not raining two blocks away), a temporal definition of 'now', and a corroboration by a group of rational individuals. However, even these trivial statements take on meaning only when they are inscribed within a wider social text. The 'rain' statement has to do with certain behavioural patterns, like wearing a coat, taking the bus instead of walking, and so on. Similarly, the greenness of the tree means nothing until it is inserted within a social praxis; it might be found in a discourse on the aesthetics of colour, or a discourse on perception, or vegetation. One might even contend that the value statement conditions the factual one, that the prescriptive comes before the descriptive: the coat is essential to the rain; without the coat, the rain would be a neutral entity devoid of meaning. When the weatherman predicts snow for tomorrow, he is talking mostly about coats, driving conditions, transportation, exposure, and so on. In other words, the statement functions less as a referent than as an intertext.

Further, meaningful statements, that is, statements that pertain to the socio-political realities, have nothing to do with truth tables; they have to do with ideological presuppositions and world views, even when they seem to obey factual reality. The traditional division between facts and values rests on the assumption that facts are verifiable while values are not. In other words, reality is assumed to be a homogeneous, consistent and non-changing phenomenon that can be verified — a belief which itself is ideologically motivated. (Descartes's analysis — the breaking down of the problem to its irreducible components — and similar conceptions of knowledge, presuppose that reality can be broken down, that its atomic units exist in a vacuum and can be grasped.) But meaningful statements of fact are defined by ideology (this is true of my own statement that 'every meaningful statement presupposes an ideological position'). The division between fact and value does not allow for the complexity of our sociality. A fact is already an interpretation: interpretability is *sine qua non* to the possibility of language and communication. And even if one accepts the existence of factual statements *per se*, one can still claim that some statements reveal their ideological bias more than do others. However, certain ideologies (and this brings us back to church ideology as well as the ideology of the Enlightenment) disguise their values under the cloak of facts, forget their own particularity and claim universality.

To Augustine, then, the world is what it is because it ought to be what it is, and this by divine providence. But in order to maintain this world view, the medieval Christian discourse (and Augustine within it) must operate a reduction of everything that is to a series of basic credos and erase whatever might threaten its sovereignty — like an objective conception of time, for example, an issue to be dealt with later on. The power and the survival of this discursive operation were conditional upon the taking over of the life world, especially the mental structures, of the subjected. It is not surprising that change took a very long time to come during the Middle Ages despite the fact that the socio-historico-political reality was fertile ground. The discrepancies among the classes were there yet the mental structures necessary for change were taken over by the church. The believer did not live in the world but in the church: 'Le simple fidèle est un croyant, sans toujours savoir ce qu'il croit; il vit dans un monde qui est celui de l'Eglise, et qu'il ne saurait abandonner pour vivre autre part.'[18]

It remains to account for the cohesion of this social whole. If the division into the chosen and the damned is irreducible, then how do these two groups live together in the same world?

> Thus, where there is no true justice there can be no assemblage of men associated by a common acknowledgement of right, and therefore there can be no people, as defined by Scipio or Cicero.[19]

> But if we discard this definition of a people and, assuming another, say that a people is an assemblage of reasonable beings bound together by a common agreement as to the object of their love, then, in order to discover the character of any people, we have only to observe what they love.[20]

Augustine refutes Cicero's definition of a people as a group sharing a common conception of justice on the basis of the Roman example and proceeds to his own definition of a people as a group sharing a common object of love. This does not answer the problem of social cohesion in a given group but it provides the logical differentiation between the two cities. Augustine clearly does not believe that man is political by definition; he does not believe in a social agreement binding all the members of a given group. Man cannot be a political animal if he is to be a Christian one; the two seem to exclude one another. Politics, to Augustine, is necessary to keep the equilibrium of society, to avoid destruction. Sociality is one of the ways given to men to express their needs; it is merely a symptom of human behaviour, not an end.[21] For grace comes before sociality; one is born either damned or redeemed.

> The weakness of Augustine's position is, of course, that it implies a very static view of political society. It is quite content merely to have some of the more painful tension removed. It takes an ordered political life for granted. Such an order just happens among fallen men.[22]

It is interesting to note that Augustine's political theory as expressed in *The city of God* constitutes a rebuttal of pagan claims that the downfall of the Empire was caused by Christian influence: Augustine sets out to prove that Rome was corrupt long before the advent of Christianity. Had it not been for this pagan claim, he would likely not have written a political theory simply because politics as a positive concept does not figure in his basic ideology. Politics and grace do not mix well.

In effect, Augustine's political theory is but a figural re-reading of history. The story of Romulus and Remus, the founders of Rome, is prefigured in the story of Cain and Abel, just as the crucifixion is prefigured in the attempted sacrifice of Isaac. The figural repetition of phenomena goes on until the end of times — the last judgement. This means that a line can be drawn from the beginning of history to its end. Every event finds its copy and explanation in a previous event, in a finite regression to the beginning of time. Such a view necessitates both a beginning and an end as its conceptual extremes, a double closure of the historical process.

> Figural interpretation establishes a connection between two events or persons in such a way that the first signifies not only itself but also the second, while the second involves or fulfils the first. The two poles of a figure are separated in time, but both, being real events or persons, are within temporality. They are both contained in the flowing stream which is historical life, and only the comprehension, the *intellectus spiritualis*, of their interdependence is a spiritual act.[23]

It is clear, then, that the historical event is not considered in its complexity, simultaneity and uniqueness in the historical process; in the figural interpretation it becomes a clear, simple and homogeneous entity closed to further interpretation. There is no logical, causal or temporal connection between the first and the second event; the connection is inherent in the historical process as a whole — or rather, in the view of that process, the *intellectus spiritualis*. The event is transposed whole into another event with which the connections inform this figural world view which is exclusive of all other world views.

In summary, then, to be is to partake in Eternity because time itself is a worldly creation of God. To be is to be out of time because in time one is mutable and given to change. This is the Augustinian process of differentiation between the two histories or the two times, the holy and the secular. Secular history is but a function of the holy one. These two times realise themselves in two corresponding cities — the one, the city of God; the other, Babylon, the sinful city of man. Secular time, or human history, is a makeshift phenomenon that takes on meaning only due to God's grace which is primarily directed to individuals and not groups. Babylon as a whole cannot move up; the cardinal sins of pride and concupiscence are committed either with partners or in a group.

Si l'histoire acquiert une valeur positive, si le temps vécu est l'instrument d'un progrès, ces caractères relèvent non de l'ordre de la nature mais de celui de la grâce. Par lui-même le temps ne peut plus rien produire de bon: seule l'action divine, l'intervention de l'économie du salut peut le racheter, guérir sa blessure et par un redressement paradoxal, faire de ce temps de vieillesse et de mort une préparation et une introduction à la vie éternelle.[24]

Figural time and human time

Within this world view man is left little to do on earth but to hope and wait for his salvation. Augustine attributes only one type of freedom of action to man: the initial will of the soul to commit sin, which brought about its fall into matter; 'You have made him, but the sin that is in him you have not made' (AC 49). Clearly, Augustine refuses to impute to God man's fallen condition; sin remains the only creation of man. By the end of the *Confessions* the reader is left with one certainty: the only agent and actor in the universe is God, and whatever happens in time is devoid of meaning.

Their task [of political and social institutions] was now to minimize disorder. This is the meaning of Augustine's insistence that political authority is not natural to man, but a result of his sinful condition . . . the purpose of the state and of its coercive machinery was to deal with the disorganization and conflict resulting from the fall: to prevent men from devouring each other like fish.[25]

Pertinent to the concept of hierarchy is the notion of mediation. Augustine differentiates between 'the true and the false mediators'. But the concept of mediation presents a major problem in Augustine, which relates to Christianity's hesitation between immanence and transcendence. Augustine's conception of the chain of being is shaped by two major sources: first, Plotinus' theory of Emanation, and second, the Scriptures. He seems to have had difficulty making a choice between the two for both theories appear in the book. The difficulty lies in the fact that the notion of hierarchy connotes a necessary internal relationship linking the stages to one another; the logic of order requires that, by definition, God partake in the order; that is, that He is immanent to it. This would make of Augustine a materialist or at best a pantheist. On the other hand, Augustine insists that God is the prime mover, totally separated from His creation. The reader can assume that Augustine had a predilection for the theory of Creation, for while the theory of Emanation occupies most of the book, he closes it with an exegesis of Genesis Chapters I and II, that is, with a description of the creation of the world, giving thus the last word to the theory of Creation.

'The *Confessions* is no autobiography, and not even a partial autobiography. It is the use of Augustine's life and confession of faith in God as an illustration of his theory of man.'[26] Given the unbridgeable gap between the subject and the mediator, between man and God, one can read the *Confessions* not as the story of an individual, but as the illustration of a type: the man of confession, for the individual story seems futile in a world where grace and eternity are the only criteria for being. The above quotation tends to support Augustine's hierarchical view of things since in a hierarchical structure the individual is of no significant standing. It remains the case, however, that there is a biographical development in the first nine chapters of the book, and there appears to be a sequence to this development. One senses the presence of an individual consciousness in its struggle for Truth. And this consciousness operates by incrementation; it follows certain steps. Augustine no doubt advances the notion of mimesis in that he believes in a correspondence between actual events and narrative sequence. Like the Scriptures, the narrative is here to corroborate certain factual truths. There is little doubt that while the *Confessions* is steeped in the Platonic tradition in its search for a vertical axis to being, it nevertheless promulgates the beginning of subjectivity, albeit a subjectivity steeped in the hierarchical structure of being. The anthropomorphisation and personalisation of God open the door to a definition of man as a relatively independent agent capable of rational decision. (Augustine, we recall, emphasises will over other human faculties.) God is responsible for every individual in his uniqueness, and watches his every act from above. The achievement of confession itself requires a process of interiorisation, the emergence of an awareness of self.

Finally, Augustine's theory of human time, that is, time as the dimension of experience, carries further these flashes of subjectivity. Apart from figural time, the time of God which lasts from the creation of the universe to the last judgement, he advances a theory of human time which encompasses the experiential dimension of the individual consciousness. For one could argue that even given the figural interpretation of history, each consciousness has a separate apprehension of time as a positive experience (which of course relates to the historical process itself) and this cannot be said of figural time. To Augustine, time is a created phenomenon like the universe or any other object; it is not a category in which experience unfolds, for if it were, it would have an objective status that would jeodpardise his system: the notion of objective time in which historical phenomena take place contradicts the theory of creation. Objective time includes a certain element of chance as well as elements of contiguity and simultaneity, which cannot be incorporated within a figural interpretation of history. Chance runs counter to predestination. Augustine shields himself well against any objective notion of time, and although he is aware that figural time unfolds up there symbolically, in God's master plan and therefore cannot account for all human phenomena down here, he nevertheless devises a secondary definition of time which remains in accordance with figural interpretation.[27]

This second definition of time as a created object, interestingly enough, is presented in Book 11 with the sceptical question directed at Augustine: 'What was God doing before he created heaven and earth?' He answers that God is coeternal, without before or after. The next preoccupation is, of course, the existence of 'before' and 'after' in human life, that is, the temporal categories of past, present and future. If the division of time cannot exist within figural history where everything coexists in God's plan, then where does it exist? Augustine claims that these dimensions do exist but only as subjective mental manifestations of every individual.

> But how is the future, which as yet does not exist, diminished or consumed, or how does the past, which no longer exists, increase, unless there are three things in the mind, which does all this? It looks forward, it considers, it remembers, so that the reality to which it looks forward passes through what it considers into what it remembers . . . It is not, then, future time that is long, but a long future is a long expectation of

the future. Nor is past time, which is not, long, but a long
past is long memory of the past. (AC 301)

The subjectivisation and relativisation of time sit well with the
figural interpretation of history. Things can happen either in your
mind — and this is Augustine's necessary concession to temporality, for without it the dimension of temporal experience will
remain unaccounted for — or things can happen in God's time.
And if we experience difficulties in sharing this created time
because of its subjectivist characteristics, the loss is not too great
since all live, willy nilly, in figural time. In short there is no room
for historical contingency.

One should keep in mind the hortatory nature of Augustine's
Confessions, and indeed of all religious autobiographies, the
objective of which is to convince the reader of a certain truth. The
role of the sermon is quite evident in these confessions. The
rhetoric of refutation of all possible alternative truths —
Manichean, heretic, Ciceronian and so on — points to this
didactic purpose, which explains why the completion of the autobiographical aspect of these confessions is necessary. But despite
the break in the narrative sequence, and despite the typological
nature of confessional autobiography, in general, Augustine's
internalisation of the temporal process points to a budding conception of things based on the individual consciousness. This view
constitutes quite a departure from the classical Greek conception
of time as the movement of the heavenly bodies. This trend culmi-
nates in Rationalism and Empiricism (and the various ideologies
they generated) which ground their respective world views on this
same individual consciousness. But of course this discursive
development will have to take its slow course before Neo-Classical
consciousness appears on the surface of the discursive reality.
None the less, the distance between Augustine's experience of time
and Descartes's Cogito, for example, is minimal; in both cases self
is an irreducible agent on which truths can be built. Although
Augustine's purpose is to prove the creation of time by God, since
time is functional to human minds which are created by God, we
can nevertheless conclude that his conception of time remains subjective in essence. In terms of literary history, Augustine initiates
the development of a narrative pattern which subsequently will be
identified in the West as autobiography — the development of an
individual human story through its own irreducible conscious
interpretation.

Contextualising the *Confessions*

One cannot ignore the historical realities which have contributed to Augustine's adoption of this world view; his lack of faith in the political and social institutions of his time no doubt has to do with the precarious overall situation of the Roman Empire towards the end of the fourth century and the beginning of the fifth. This situation clearly influenced the writing of *The city of God* in which Augustine expounds the relationship between politics and evil. Political strife plagued the Roman Empire due to the problems relating to the centralisation of power over the vast spaces the Empire incorporated. By AD 100 the Roman Empire included most of Western Europe and vast portions of the Middle East and North Africa. The control had to be shared with provincial legions which aspired to the central government.

Problems relating to the imperial succession undermined the cohesion of the Empire as a whole. Each emperor was the product of the controlling army faction; civil war was imminent since the preceding emperor had to be got rid of. Also it was the custom of the new emperor to reward his armies and sometimes the Roman people as well, which added a heavy expenditure to an already precarious economic situation. Lack of control in the central government allowed for upheavals in the distant territories and Augustine was well aware of the ongoing warfare which would ultimately bring the Empire to its knees.

By Augustine's time the Empire had become totalitarian to ensure its survival; taxes were raised to meet the mounting costs of army and bureaucracy. The central government took control of the local ones and a new division ensued in the society between the *honestiores* — officers, landowners, bureaucrats — the few privileged by the Empire, and the *humiliores*, the great majority of the underprivileged. This division would persist throughout the Middle Ages. Under such conditions people turned to religion in general, and to Christianity in particular, to compensate for the lack of stability in their political and social structures. Towards the end of the fourth century, there began a shift from paganism to Christianity, perhaps because Christianity postulated the belief in one God responsible for every event in the universe including its creation, a God one can turn to in times of hardship — a personal God. The struggle for spiritual control of the masses was triggered by the setback inflicted upon Christianity by Emperor Julian's reconversion to paganism; Julian reversed the adoption of

Christianity initiated by Constantine in the second century.

More crucial to this hierarchical world view is the impact the Greek way of life had upon the Roman world. With the shift from agrarian collectivities to urban communities and city ways of living, from an agriculture-based economy to a monetary one, there came about a change from the kinship system based on the *patrimonium* to the Polis system. (We recall that Patricius, Augustine's father, was a Polis functionary despite the scarcity of his means; being a member in the Polis gave him the right to raise money for his son's education.) In such a system what counts is 'citizenship', which means that personal traits disappear to make room for the 'public man' who conducts the affairs of the state according to a preset formula. In the Polis every function is a matter of definition and the true man is the one who behaves in accordance with the accepted code. Type or model overtakes the 'irreducible individual'. Further, in the Greek world, personality was conceived of not as an active agent but as a static entity. 'The Greek had no word for person' and believed 'that man is essentially an Idea, a harmony of perfect proportions, a canon of beauty.'[28]

Historians disagree as to when medieval Scholasticism ends and Renaissance individualism begins. Walter Ullman[29] claims that it happened in the thirteenth century and that in fact the Middle Ages contained the seed for the shift from man as subject to man as citizen. The latter notion, he argues, stems from the contractual relationships between lord and vassal in the Middle Ages. Ullman seems to think that equality of rights predated the Renaissance. Colin Morris,[30] on the other hand, claims that the major changes occurred between 1050 and 1200. Both Ullman and Morris use similar arguments, mainly the rise of the cities and the development of cultures and the arts. Paul Delaney will claim that there is 'an evidence against the semi-mystical theory that a powerful, obscure, and widely diffused impulse labelled "Renaissance Individualism" affected all Europeans living between, say, 1400 and 1700'.[31]

However, there is general agreement that the individual's place in society conforms to the hierarchical view of things during the Middle Ages, at least up to the eleventh century. Whether king or pope, the ruler of the Middle Ages became the mediator between the subjects and the divinity; the ruler was ordained by God and all the ruled were expected to obey. Government came from above; the individual had no say in the legal process. Inequality was a given accepted without question. 'The rights' were functional to the person's standing in the hierarchy; society as a whole was seen as a body with organs, some more important and some less. Society was a 'corporation', and the subject was immersed in it, absorbed by it because of the role he had to play in it: 'Society was one whole and was indivisible and within it the individual was no more than a part: but what mattered was the well-being of society and not the parts constituting it.'[32]

It is no wonder that nothing 'personal' remains of the Middle Ages; the cultural product was 'nameless', the artists and writers unknown. The name as signature will be established only when the artist assumes responsibility for his product, when he owns it. (The subject's property belonged to the king at the time.) Furthermore, the prevailing theories of personality were quantitative and not qualitative (which relates to the point that being was a matter of quantity). Psychology was a cumulative phenomenon — that is, the person had a number of traits in various quantities. Personality was an amalgam rather than a process.

> La personnalité . . . pendant la période médiévale semblerait avoir été connue plutôt comme une addition que comme une gestalt, une structure: un ensemble de traits juxtaposés — vices et vertus — qui étaient entre eux, soit compatibles, soit incompatibles, soit en guerre soit en paix les uns avec les autres, mais qui n'avaient pas de relations internes complexes et qui ne constituaient pas un tout organique doué de quelque mystérieuse unité . . . il ne produit ordinairement qu'une transformation en quantité et non en qualité.[33]

Thus the description of a saint, for example, was a question of degree, of how far he was elevated above the human. The human or rather, the natural, was deferred by the act of baptism which in effect elevated the baptised above the immediate concrete life (hence the lack of any science pertaining to nature during the Middle Ages). The archetype and the general rather than the particular and the specific occupied the horizon of knowledge. The individual was individual only to the extent that he took part in the universal of which he was one representation and in which he played a part. And this universal coincided with the hidden order: the material world stood between that order and its meaning.

The task of medieval thought had consisted largely in tracing the architectonics of being and in delineating its main design. In the religious system of the Middle Ages as it is crystallized in Scholasticism every phase of reality is assigned its unique place; and with its place goes a complete determination of its value, which is based on the greater or lesser distance which separates it from the First Cause.[34]

It is clear from this passage that throughout the Middle Ages knowledge of nature coincided with the knowledge of creation, that thought accepted rather than created the structure of things, uncovered the truth rather than made it. This passivity of knowledge will change with the gradual desacralisation of the universe at the point where 'nature' and 'creation' split apart.

The Christian ideology, then, stresses the continuity between self and the world because it guarantees control over the historical process; the passage from self to the world is the passage from self to God; there are no possible transitions between self and the world. There are no ruptures in this synchrony that might open the door to historical becoming; if that were the case the whole system would disintegrate. A linear continuity from facts to values is necessary to the survival of this type of ideology, the only threat to this system being the discovery of a breaking point, the cutting of linearity which might cause the opening up of the system. The double closure of the figural approach assures the church of circular completeness and control over historicity. Augustine was well aware of the necessary establishment of a solid line between the individual consciousness with its temporal experience and the figural historical process, for discontinuity would have meant differentiation, heterogeneity, and therefore the total freedom and multiplicity of historical contingency. Linearity and teleology allow for a secure regression to the origin of the historical process.

Nevertheless, towards the end of the Middle Ages, several factors contributed to make a dent in the hierarchical form of government and in the conception of the person. Ullman claims that 'there were throughout the Middle Ages numerous associations, unions, fraternities, guilds and communities which in one way or another considered the individual a full member',[35] and that the contractual relationship, the mutual obligations between lord and vassal, gave the peasant a say in his own affairs without the interference of the high authorities. Unwritten laws and customs were the guide to daily life. In farming communities as well as in the semi-rural cities, people ran their own affairs according to this unwritten law. The king himself shared in both his role as divinely ordained ruler and his task as feudal head lord under mutual contract of protection to his vassals. (We shall see that the idea of 'contract' itself originates in the economic field where exchange value overtakes the use value of the material object and subsequently brings about the reification of human relations.)

Changes forced themselves upon the medieval situation with the beginning of urbanisation and the coming together of large masses of population. This, in turn, led to the rise of the middle class between the fourteenth and the sixteenth centuries, generating further changes in the social structure. The new middle-class intelligentsia began competing with the church for the control of culture as a whole, and subsequently church and government were separated. Parallel developments took place in the arts and sciences, beginning in the thirteenth century. Drama moved from allegory to real spaces and to people living in recent history: the universal allegory of *Everyman* is replaced by concrete historical figures and characters in the plays of Marlowe and Shakespeare. Similarly, the classical tragedy of circumstance gives way to the drama of character; the tragic flaw overtakes the concept of fate. The flowering naturalism in painting (Giotto is an example) put the emphasis on detailed, realistic portrayals of people. The here and now took precedence over the eternal. There was an upsurge in the development of vernacular literatures, to the detriment of Latin which was confined to liturgy; translations were made of the Bible into most vernacular literatures. The appearance of the university as the centre for knowledge helped promote the new natural sciences. The emergence of the natural sciences, and with them the belief in growth and decay, redeemed man's naturalness, and placed him at the centre of the historical process. The development of anatomy and surgery forced the physician and the priest to follow their separate ways, the one to heal the body, the other the soul. As men coped better with disease and famine the strength of the church diminished and with it the hierarchical world view.

The compartmentalisation of knowledge and its separation from theology, the adoption of the inductive method of inquiry over the formal Aristotelian deductive method, the emphasis on education, the accent on the immediate, the concrete and the specific, the shift from the contemplative to the active life — all these have a bearing on the developing horizontal world view. The Reformation movements with their rebellion against the tyranny of the church had as an unintended consequence the secularisation of the masses. By putting salvation in the hands of the individual, by collapsing the distinction between the layman and the clergy, by abolishing the monastic vocation, by separating church from state, by mistrusting the intellectual theorising of Scholasticism and putting the emphasis on common sense, Calvin had a far-reaching impact on man's view of himself and the world: Protestantism overtook almost half of the European Christian world of the sixteenth century.

With the scientific revolution, Descartes and Newton brought the modern world into a new phase which accelerated the displacement of religion by science. Common-sense knowledge based on the senses was replaced by mathematical reasoning; new experiments were carried out using quantitative methods of measurement. By the seventeenth century the world had become a machine. (Note, for example, the production of clocks and pendulums for the thriving middle class.) The difficult compromise was that between science and religion. Religion was taken out of nature and confined to the expression of beliefs and morals, while science took over in the natural world.

By the eighteenth century, these transformations in the discursive space solidified and no doubt contributed to form Rousseau's conception of the person; but more drastic changes were needed to mould his view of the self. Above all it is the appearance of a new man which encouraged the various changes within the autobiographical discourse. From the start the bourgeoisie did not fit into the Providential scheme which was devised for two classes only, the divinely rich and the divinely poor, each of which corroborated God's will in the universe since both could claim divine guidance. If, throughout the Middle Ages, religion was an expression of class consciousness, by the time the bourgeoisie surges, class consciousness becomes the tool of atheism, for how could the church claim control over a man who created himself, who defied every transcendental authority to establish himself as master of his own destiny? But the total war launched by the bourgeoisie against the church would be tempered in time, as new avenues were found to accommodate this new class which was intent upon the destruction of the old order. Subsequently, the main concepts of the hierarchical world view would undergo a facelift; Augustine's God ceased to be an absolute authority whose subjects were slaves to his whims and became a God who consulted with his subjects, who made concessions to them — a rational God.

Of course this new conception of divinity was not realised without bitter struggles among the various factions. The Jansenists preferred to maintain the old Augustinian credo and accused the Jesuits of taking everything away from God.[36] The Jesuits replied that God was never meant to be a chastiser and that equality was given to all men; all were born equal and worthy of redemption. Men, therefore, were not corrupt by definition. Corruption was no more a state of being, but rather functional to specific acts. Man was not born damned or in a state of grace; he could change the way of things. This was the age in which crime and its counterpart, the judicial system, were enhanced; criminality as a civil phenomenon enclosed in a specific act replaced sin which connoted a general condition of being. Society, then, took over the role of the judge from God, and the criminal was punished here and now for the specific crime he committed; the last judgement was postponed indefinitely because it was useless in the immediate. The duality of the world — the two cities — disappeared to make room for plurality.

> Mais au fond, tous se ressemblent étrangement, et au jour du jugement dernier, il ne sera pas facile de distinguer les justes des méchants, tant il y aura des degrés intermédiaires entre les deux, et tant sera grand le nombre de ceux qui évitant les excès, n'auront été ni trop bons ni trop méchants.[37]

With the birth of bourgeois consciousness extravagance vanishes: the two opposing groups — the chosen and the damned — are no longer on opposite sides of a fence. The differences are tempered; from now on one can be a little corrupt, a little honest, a little damned, a little redeemed. Both corruption and redemption follow the healthy path of moderation. And moderation is the capital virtue of the new order. Further, the tendency to equalise human destiny and to abolish the discrepancies between *cupiditas* and *caritas* runs counter to the old order in which the rich and the poor played a role, the rich being corrupt with a sense of lavish philanthropy to redeem them since they could guarantee their way out of hell by supporting the poor, and the poor to be tried in this life and to exemplify God's humble ways in this universe.

But this new order, in effect, will supplant the old one over time as its discursive operation gradually consolidates. In nature this emerging discursive space is predominantly profane; it negates the providential scheme in which the role-playing of the two groups could be carried out. For in the old order the groups were never taken as aggregates of individuals but as totalities that generated some kind of equilibrium in the universe, in their mutual dependency upon one another. From now on, the collectivities are broken down to their constituent members. There is no universal drama and therefore no need for collectivities to fulfil their divine roles. The emphasis is now put on the specific actions of the individual. Man as individual becomes the sole repsonsible agent in the development of social directives as well as in their deployment. The new rich supplant the old rich and rob them of their salvatory role. A famous priest writes in 1773:

> L'inégalité de ce partage, qui produit l'inégalité des conditions, est ce qu'il y a de plus admirable dans ce gouvernement de l'univers si nous voyons les riches et les pauvres se rencontrer et s'unir par les liens les plus respectables. Le riche regarde le pauvre comme quelqu'un que la Providence a confié à ses soins, et qu'il est chargé de nourrir, pendant que le pauvre regarde le riche, comme l'économe de la Providence, comme l'administrateur des biens que la terre produit pour la subsistance de tous les hommes.[38]

This gradual discursive shift from the old order to the new generated the development of new literary forms to express the new state of affairs. In *The inward turn of narrative*, Erich Khaler describes the transitional points of this movement from the text of the Middle Ages to the new literary forms and in particular to the novel. Khaler draws a parallel between the freedom of the text from tradition and the new-found freedom of man from external powers: 'This liberation was equivalent to man's release from his entanglement with external powers.'[39] *La Princesse de Clèves* is typical of the new literature. The narrative which previously concerned itself with external phenomena now takes an 'inward turn' and preoccupies itself with the psychology of the individual. The independence of the narrative from convention in the Classical age and religion in the Christian one motivates it to seek its identity in the characters it describes who, in turn, now seek their own 'autonomous' definition.

Autobiography is the culmination of this new literature in that it purports to be the most truthful account of the individual; since it repeats life as it is lived, it is more believable than the fictional account. Autobiography is the perfect form to reflect the self-made

man, the man of self-definition. Sincerity is one of the virtues of
the age, and autobiography is the most sincere tale of the genetic
development of the self-made man. For in order to account for all
the steps it took the self-made man to reach his new position, the
story must start with his birth. But the apex of the form, like that of
the novel, will be reached much later, during the nineteenth
century. Lejeune claims:

> La majorité des textes autobiographiques antérieurs à 1760
> ont été publiés avec un ou deux siècles de retard (à partir du
> XIXe siècle); ceux qui ont été publiés ont été très peu lus
> d'abord parce qu'ils étaient médiocres littérairement, ensuite
> parce qu'aucun intérêt spécial ne s'attachait à la lecture des
> vies des particuliers, et que l'on appréciait les mémoires qu'à
> proportion de l'intérêt historique, politique ou social des
> événements racontés. C'est seulement vers 1750, en
> Angleterre comme en France, qu'on a vraiment manifesté de
> la curiosité pour la vie des particuliers écrite par eux-
> mêmes.[40]

Paul Delaney corroborates these facts.[41] The texts written before
1760 were revived two centuries later because the market demand
reached a peak. There is no doubt that the rise of the autobiographic form relates to the rise of the bourgeoisie. Autobiography
is non-existent in primitive societies nor is it found in societies of
non-bourgeois ideology. It is a product of the discourse of
modernism. The question that must be asked at this point is
whether autobiographic discourse undergoes breaking points, or
shifts, in its development. Can one speak of a rupture in the discourse towards the middle of the eighteenth century, or is it just an
imbrication of new ideas upon the old? Is it a displacement of the
same concepts? Is the partial subjectivity that Augustine advances
the same we encounter in Rousseau, or is it a different one
altogether? For it is clear that despite the loosening of the church's
hold over everyday life, religion remains the shaping force of the
mental structures, at least until the Enlightenment. Are the
ideological commonalities of both confessional and secular autobiographies wide enough to put aside any notion of discursive
ruptures? Can one merely say that confessional autobiography
equals the secular one plus the active presence of God? On one
hand, the preoccupations of eighteenth century man differ widely
from those of the Middle Ages, but on the other, the qualities of

God — His intellect, eternity, consistency, homogeneity, uniqueness and irreducibility — are now invested in man.

In order to attempt an answer to this question, we will now consider Abelard and Descartes, key texts that were produced during the consolidation of the autobiographic discourse.

3

Abelard's *Historia calamitatum*

As suggested above, in studying the autobiographical discourse I am not after the deployment of a generic structure over a period of time but rather seek the discursive operation and the ideological confirguration that relate to the mutations of a given concept — in our case, the concept of self. And in choosing specific texts to illustrate my understanding of the autobiographical tradition I am less interested in these as complete statements than as indicators of their respective discursive intertext. A given text is of interest only to the extent that it speaks the discursive reality that generates it; in short, the ideological presuppositional structure that conditions it. For behind what is said rests the anonymous voice of the unsaid upon which the said is functional.

This chapter will therefore deal with the ways in which Abelard's *Historia calamitatum*[1] treats the problem of subjectivity. It seems that this narrative introduces a number of new concerns which do not appear in Augustine despite their common and basic preoccupation with the Scriptures. With Abelard, for the first time man is able to make use of his reason in comprehending the Scriptures. The emergence of the problematic of Universals in the late Middle Ages and the solution contributed by Abelard point toward a new conception of subjectivity; Abelard's crude dialectical method and his development of an ethics based on intentionality rather than activity help shape this new conception.

These concerns will be carried a step further in Descartes's *Discours de la méthode*, one of the most influential texts in modern times (to which the next chapter will be devoted).[2] Of capital importance in Descartes is the relationship between rationality and individuality. By Descartes's time man had become a free agent;

46

although revelation was still the ground of knowledge, man was able to contribute to knowledge as an active operator of this underlying structure. Abelard's *Historia calamitatum* initiates this movement towards the liberation of knowledge and man's increasing operation on the material world.

This narrative, written in 1129, contains the seeds of modern autobiography though its scope is limited to one basic theme — Abelard's sufferings. In its brevity the text does not cover the range and number of events that the life story in the autobiographical tradition will subsequently include. Abelard's autobiography is addressed to a suffering friend (and not to God) that he may be comforted when he compares his woes to those of Abelard. At the outset, the notion of comparison is located in the discourse, not between man and God, but between man and man, not between temporality and eternity but between two temporalities:

> J'espère qu'en comparant mes malheurs et les vôtres, vous reconnaîtrez que vos épreuves ne sont rien ou qu'elles sont peu de chose, et que vous aurez moins de peine à les supporter. (A 15)

But the addressee is problematic in this autobiography since he appears only twice — at the opening and the closing — leaving the reader with the conviction that Abelard is, in effect, addressing himself. Indeed some critics claim[3] that Abelard's call is a mere literary strategy. However, the problematic existence of the addressee raises a more crucial problem, one which has been treated repeatedly by the critical literature: that of the truth or fiction of the events being related. If the addressee is a fiction, then possibly the whole story is a fiction too. Most historians[4] seem to be troubled by the authenticity of these letters. This again reflects the dichotomy — truth/falsehood, reality/fiction — in operation. Such a concern for authority, it seems, has to do with the centralised, Oedipal obsession of Western culture as a whole. The modernistic Western discourse cannot allow the possibility of a fatherless text for the text is said to be created by a single human mind, that mind which exercises authority over it, and authentification means the retrieval of that primary control over the text.

But rather than going back to the origins of the text, the book, the concept, would it not be more meaningful to speak of the text as a field of play of socio-cultural phenomena, as the intertext of a social whole, as an interface of an indefinite set of ongoing dialectical relations? It is certainly more productive to speak of the inclusive text — that is, the space in which all texts occur — of a given socio-cultural entity. Such an inclusive Text, although never fully encompassable given that these dialectical relations form an endless semiotic field, would reveal the various intertexts that contribute to shape the textual production of the social forces which make up the social whole, for the productive forces of a social whole transcend the limit of individuality. Edward W. Said tackles the notion of authority in a refreshing way from the perspective of 'originality'.

> To study literature as given writing, canonized in texts, books, poems, works, dramas, and so forth, is to treat as natural and concrete that which derives from a desire — to write — that is ceaseless, varied, and highly unnatural and abstract, since 'to write' is a function never exhausted by the completion of a piece of writing.
>
> Thus, the best way to consider originality is to look not for first instances of a phenomenon, but rather to see duplication, parallelism, symmetry, parody, echoes of it — the way, for example, literature has made itself into a topos of writing. What the modern or contemporary imagination thinks of is less the confining of something to a book, and more the release of something from a book into writing.[5]

Both those who see veracity and those who see falsehood in the correspondence of Abelard and Heloise look at authenticity in absolute terms. This text is never dealt with in terms of the possible social meaning one might extract from it; the focus on authority clouds the intertext of these letters. As well, the sensationalism and romanticism of the critical literature conform to the same ideology, that which centres on the greatness — read suffering and stamina — of a couple whose love prevails in the face of insurmountable difficulties. Heloise and Abelard have realised a new myth in Western consciousness; they have become the eternal model for true love.

What can Abelard's *Historia calamitatum* tell us about his times? What conception does it advance? The question is not whether Abelard wrote it but why, at this time, the problem of Universals and Particulars becomes a discursive preoccupation. Why is there a need at this moment to write a new ethics? Why insert the concept of interpretation into the discourse? The answers to this series of questions have to do with the material conditions that prevailed in the twelfth century, with the establishment of new universities and a new approach to education, with the spread of urbanisation, with the beginning of a struggle against church hegemony, which will affect its universalisation and generate subsequent fragmentation. The conflicts between Abelard and William de Champaux, or Anselmus, are not disagreements between two minds; they are inscribed within the controversy of 'Universals and Particulars' which arises in this period. The story of Abelard and Heloise is not merely the love story of two individuals, for they are caught in a series of complex relations with all the historical phenomena mentioned above.

The narrative centres mainly on a selection of events pertaining to the narrator's biography in relation to a social reality. There is a sense of developmental continuity in this narrative sequence, in the form of a cause and effect relationship: his birth to a father versed in letters, his predilection for conflicts of discussion over trophies of war, made Abelard choose the career of letters over that of arms. This points to a new phenomenon which could not be found in the Augustinian Text: the insertion of a temporal dimension within the human predicament. But time is not an objective structure in Abelard, that is, a structure which organises phenomena; neither chronology nor temporal duration are applied to the events. Time here is an experimental phenomenon; meaning has to do with the internalisation of external events. Although God still holds control over the affairs of the world, there remains a domain of human activity where God's direct intervention is not needed. Actually, the emphasis in the story alternates between God's guidance of individual lives and the responsibility of man for his own choices; this coincides with the mental structures of Scholasticism which attempted a complementarity between Reason and Revelation. The dichotomies of Revelation and Reason, the private and the public, the marginal and the hegemonic, constitute Abelard's most immediate objects.

> At the center of his *Story of Calamities*, at once its author and its subject stands the autonomous individual who carries his world within, who faces constantly the private decisions and dilemmas, as well as the struggles with his environment, that force him repeatedly to define himself anew, the individual who by choice and action shapes himself.[6]

To McLaughlin, then, Abelard is representative of a trend towards conscious self-affirmation in the twelfth century; the guiding hand of God seems to be disappearing and man faces the world primordially through the assertion of his self as an individual. But the majority of critics differ from this view: Abelard is said to be basing the tenets of Christianity upon reason so that, in effect, there is no contradiction in Abelard between faith and reason. No doubt, Abelard cannot be conceived of in terms of the Cartesian model; we do not have here an all-pervasive rational model which can be applied to all fields of knowledge. (Methodic rationality will appear later on in the works of Peter Ramus.) The tendency in the critical literature is to synthesise reason and faith, and to argue that Abelard is a rationalist with a small 'r'. J. G. Sikes claims:

> Abelard cannot be called a rationalist if we give that term its modern connotation; he was an intellectualist toward the assent to faith. Yet in a restricted sense he was a rationalist . . . He believed firmly in the power of human reason to grasp at least something of reality. Reason was the valid instrument of all human thought.[7]

However, since we are dealing with the slow progression of the discursive reality, we cannot conceive of Abelard as a revolutionary intellectual. He had no choice but to synthesise faith and reason, given that the mental structures of the twelfth century and their dialectical counterpart, the material structures (the scientific revolution will take a few more centuries with the appearance of new methods of inquiry based exclusively on the methodic rationality which is beginning to emerge at this time) did not yet allow for anything but the synthetisation of reason and revelation: theology still permeated all areas of knowledge. We can surmise that by Abelard's time a new rational model, involving the use of mental faculties to apprehend reality in a structural way, is imbricated upon the already existing theological one. Abelard focuses on new concerns which appear in the context of the twelfth century — the possibility of interpretation, the solution of the problem of universals, and finally Abelard's own contribution to a new conception of ethics which supersedes the Augustinian notion of sin, by relating sin to intention and not to action.

By now the discursive shift from Augustine is quite clear. To Augustine, there was one and only one Truth which excluded all others; the struggle took place between the Christian Truth and other external world views (the Manicheans, the heretics). To Abelard, the conflict was within Christianity itself over the meaning it holds. By the high Middle Ages most of Europe embraced Christianity so that dissention took the form of social conflict, albeit centred on the validity of Scriptures. Abelard was persecuted mainly because of his unrelenting conviction that interpretation of the Scriptures is not subject to the authority of the church, while claiming at the same time to uphold and promote Christian values. The issue was whether one arrives at the Truth by blindly accepting the authoritative voice of the church (Abelard's persecutions, we recall, originated in his own masters whom he challenged repeatedly) or whether one can act as a responsible and independent agent in the pursuit of Truth through the interpretation of these same Scriptures. Abelard's book on theology was burnt less because of his specific interpretations than because of the threat to the hegemonic mode of his promotion of the concept of interpretation itself. The challenge to the hegemonic voice came, in Abelard's case, with the introduction of multiplicity into the discourse — the possibility of an open-endedness which threatens the closed, circular, and authoritative Christian discourse. With Abelard, there cannot be two truths — his and the church's; there can be either one or a multiplicity of them. The virtuality of a second interpretation is in its adherence to an infinite series of interpretations. The departure from One necessitates a movement towards infinity. In principle, then, interpretation multiplies *ad infinitum*, and this runs counter to the oneness of truth postulated by the prevalent hegemony. The discursive shift in Abelard is with the new intentional dimension of human action; one must first understand before one can decide upon a course of action.

Je m'attachai d'abord à discuter le principe fondamental de notre foi par des analogies et je composai un traité sur l'unité et la trinité divine à l'usage de mes disciples, qui demandaient sur ce sujet des raisonnements humains et philosophiques, et auxquels il fallait des démonstrations, non des mots. Ils disaient, en effet, qu'ils n'avaient pas besoin de vaines paroles, qu'on ne peut croire que ce que l'on a compris, et qu'il est ridicule de prêcher aux autres ce qu'on ne comprend pas plus que ceux auxquels on s'adresse. (A 41)

If for Augustine rhetoric and the liberal arts must be excluded because they hinder one's mind in the pursuit of true knowledge, which is attainable only at the cost of pure passivity on the part of the individual who is but a receptacle of 'visions', to Abelard there exists a complementarity between the two realms, the holy and the secular, which can allow for the apprehension of the one by the other. In effect, the liberal arts and the holy Scriptures are on the same scale; the secular arts constitute an appropriate tool for the achievement of Scriptural understanding. Truth is not the exclusive domain of the church, for

the reason possessed by man is the recipient of Divine Truth even in the case of pre-Christian philosophers and inspired authors. Abelard frequently quotes them in order to show that they taught Christian truth even before the Incarnation.[8]

The exercise of reason takes a further amplitude with Abelard's postulation of a method of inquiry in his *Sic et Non*. Here we must qualify Walter Ong's statement quoted in Chapter 1; we do not have here a Cartesian method, for sure; nevertheless Abelard conceives of a rudimentary logical tool to promote an easier comprehension of texts. The content itself remains Scriptural but the form is rational. So while we cannot yet speak of the dissemination of methodic spatialisation generated by the material conditions of print, a reductivist method laid out in space already exists in Plato and Poryphry.[9] Poryphry's tree is built on a system where every step is subsumed in the previous one; from the Summum Genus Substance, we move down the tree to Subaltern Genus, animal, and Infima Species, Man, down to Individuals like Plato and Socrates. Substance divides into corporeal and incorporeal, the subaltern genus, body, divides into animate and inanimate, and so on, down to individuals.

In any event, while Abelard's rudimentary method is not universally applicable to all domains of knowledge, it functions as an adequate grid for textual analysis of religious writing. It consists of five steps: (a) the grouping of texts according to a variety of criteria like writing techniques, linguistic style, and so on; (b) the elimination of inauthentic texts and correction of falsified ones; (c) a critique of the writers involved in terms of their other texts; (d) the delineation between universal principles and occasional decisions; (e) a hierarchisation of texts according to authority when the discordances between the texts are irreducible. This method arises from the need to conciliate among the multiplicity of existing interpretations of the Scriptures. But of course it has to do with the availability of an opportunity in the twelfth century, with the need for such a method which ultimately rests in the material conditions of the times.

> Abélard arrivait à point. L'état de l'enseignement appelait enfin une intervention décisive qui brisât avec tout compromis, avec toute timidité: la systématisation des senten-tiaires impliquait un ordre spéculatif; l'accumulation crois-sante d'autorités patristiques plus ou moins disparates rendait urgent un ordre de concordisme; les concepts nouveaux devaient être affinés et critiqués pour entrer dans la construc-tion sans trahir le donné primitif qu'ils devaient traduire; enfin, dans la plus banale scolarité, sinon déjà dans les œuvres écrites, la 'dispute' doctrinale tendait à déborder la simple question textuelle.[10]

Abelard's autobiography must be understood, therefore, in terms of his teaching position and the new educational system to which he contributed greatly. The arguments which fill over half of the text can be understood only in relation to the struggle for a position of prominence in the new profession. Abelard, we recall, made a living out of teaching and was accused of teaching the rich for material benefits. The prestige of a new profession is behind Heloise's initial refusal to marry Abelard; marrying her, he would be unable to devote enough time to compete for a prestigious posi-tion. His boasting and pride over fame have to do with this struggle for professional status. All these phenomena, in turn, relate to the competition between the old monastic schools and the new cathe-dral schools which was brought about by the new urbanisation. 'In this environment, study was given a far wider purpose than it had had in the monasteries, where it had always been subordinate to the spirit of monastic life. This development was strengthened by advancing centralization — around Paris mostly.'[11]

The dialectical bond between reason and individuality, between method and the process of internalisation, is further enhanced by the major controversy, throughout the Middle Ages, between Nominalists and Realists on the question of universals. For the first time a middle way is found between Nominalism and Realism in the form of a new *a posteriori* conceptualisation advanced by Abelard.

Nous avons donc montré pour quelle raison des choses, qu'on les prenne une à une ou ensemble, ne peuvent être dites universelles, c'est-à-dire prédicats de plusieurs sujets: il faut donc bien attribuer cette universalité aux mots et à eux seuls. Est universel un vocable qui a été institué pour servir de prédicat à plusieurs sujets pris séparément, ainsi, le nom homme, qu'on peut joindre à des noms particuliers d'hommes à raison de la nature des sujets réels auquel il est attribué. Est singulier celui qui ne peut être prédicat que d'un seul sujet, comme Socrate.[12]

To Abelard, universals as such are non-existent; he rejects any notion of a univeral essence which permeates individuals. The universal cannot be predicated of the individual as William de Champaux, Abelard's teacher, claimed. Again the Realist movement of the Middle Ages had to do with the material conditions which overlooked the existence of the individual entity; the individual was reduced to an essential structure. The beginning of individualism is marked in the twelfth century by an attempt to erase that reduction of the individual by the subsuming structure — the point at which the feudal and theological models of domination are challenged. This movement is initiated by the perception of phenomena in terms of their constitutive entities, of the irreducible qualities of the individual object. The prevalent Realism of the Middle Ages (at least down to the twelfth century) was functional to the social praxis of the times.

Medieval social ideas were colored with Realism. Corporations were prior to individuals, as the universal was prior to its particulars. Dominating all activities there was the pervasive and unifying activity of the Church. And numerous institutions, the Papacy, the great monastic orders, the ecclesiastical schools, the universities, the town, the guilds, the manors, and many other corporate personalities expressed the medieval confidence in Realist principles.[13]

Abelard, however, does not follow Roscelin's Nominalism, which constitutes an extreme reaction to metaphysical Realism: Roscelin claimed that universals were words, mere physical sounds, without a referent. To Abelard, the word has a referent; it is an individual entity. The universal is therefore extrapolated from an empirical series of objects the existence of which precedes the essence. The universal is an amalgamation of a perceived series of discrete objects on which the mind operates. The extrapolative activity of the mind is the ontological dimension of universals. Knowledge, therefore, is built here and now in a dialectical operation on material reality. And this is a departure from the Augustinian 'vision'. Finally, a universal is 'un vocable qui a été institué pour servir de prédicat'. The universal has to do with a conventional institutionalisation of meaning. But Abelard does not pursue this aspect of the social construction of knowledge. His logic follows the individual perception of phenomena and not the cultural dimension of this perception.[14] Had the cultural dimension of knowledge been his preoccupation (that is, the social input in cognition), Abelard would have organised a group struggle against the church; his marginality is confined to the limits of his own individuality, for the conception of marginality as it relates to hegemony is a creation of the late nineteenth century.

Abelard's epistemology is dependent upon the apprehension of the individual mind for knowledge, at this point of the discursive development, gradually moves from the realm of the miraculous to the realm of the operative efficiency of the human mind. It is an epistemology which presupposes an individual subjectivity; it is the individual subject who perceives discrete objects and extrapolates the universal from them.

Abelard firmly sticks to the consistency of each particular being: individuals are distinguished from one another not only in their accidents, but also in their essence. Universals as such cannot be attributed to particular things, but to words only. As a conclusion universals are immediately related to the perspective of a knowing subject, as far as it is able to express in words some similar features observed in particular beings.[15]

As to the question of sin, again there is a departure from Augustine's understanding of the 'sinful condition'. As suggested in the previous chapter, to Augustine, sin is an overall, almost spatial condition which reaches down to the furthest recesses of the human entity. To Abelard, on the other hand, sin seems to be located in specific areas of experience or in specific parts of the body: for the sin of pride his book is burnt, and for the sin of lechery he is castrated. The punishment is meted out by God but also by man for the specific sins Abelard commits.

Combien était juste le jugement de Dieu qui me frappait dans la partie de mon corps qui avait péché! Combien étaient légitimes les représailles de Fulbert qui m'avait rendu trahison pour trahison! Quel triomphe pour mes ennemis, de voir ainsi le châtiment égalé à la faute. (A 37)

This tit-for-tat approach to sin reveals the extent to which man has acquired a new responsibility for his acts. In Augustine's world men were helpless and dependent on God's grace for their salvation or damnation — mere puppets in God's predestined schemes. In Abelard's world, on the other hand, there is a consistent logic relating between causes and effects, and man, although still dependent on God, is no longer helpless; he can begin to change the course of destiny through his acts. We are not suggesting that the hierarchical structure disappears by Abelard's time; but there are some definite changes within that structure, having to do mostly with the emerging concept of formal equality between individuals. The verticality of the hierarchical structure begins to change the moment a horizontal relationship is introduced among the members inhabiting that organisational structure.

Furthermore, the act of sin itself does not indicate a sinful situation, it is the intention behind the act which makes it sinful. Acts in themselves, to Abelard, are neutral, neither good nor bad; it is the motivation behind them which saves them from neutrality. In effect, one can commit a sinful act with a good intention and a good act with a sinful intention.[16] This division of the act into intention and performance further delineates Abelard's postulation of what appears to be a subjectivity.

And so vice is that by which we are made prone to sin, that is, are inclined to consent to what is not fitting so that we either do it or forsake it. Now this consent we properly call sin, that is, the fault of the soul by which it earns damnation or is made guilty before God.[17]

Thus, although in Abelard's time man's view of his place in the order of things remains attached to the hierarchical systematic organisation — man being but a point in the hierarchy — more is imputed to man's will and reason. Reason as fetishistic 'divertissement' will take amplitude later on with the progress of the bourgeoisie; in the Middle Ages there is no room yet for 'divertissement' (Descartes will be the first one to underline the importance of meditative activity in his famous 'poêle') although asceticism and commitment to *vita contemplativa* over *vita activa* are the practices of the day. The prevailing mode (as the logic of the day can show) is argumentation and rhetoric — the actual debate for Truth, not leisure.

It should be noted that Abelard's conception of self is not merely a universal declaration of human rationality; rather it is inscribed in the changing social structure of the time. As suggested, a professional intellectual elite was forming around the new cathedral schools and Abelard's restless journeys take him from one school to another. This intellectual elite felt it had a universal task to fulfil; Abelard refers repeatedly to his predestined role in human destiny. There is, then, the uniqueness of the human mind in its apprehension of reality and the uniqueness of the professional intellectual. And both share in the formation of the new twelfth-century self, a self which will consolidate with the coming of age of Cartesianism.

There is a most important relationship in Abelard between fame and persecution. Abelard's boastful declarations are motivated by the treatment he receives from his fellow intellectuals, which is but a gradual process of disintegration at the bottom of his act of writing.

Je rapprochais le supplice infligé à mon corps des tortures de mon âme, et je m'estimais le plus malheureux des hommes. Comparée à l'outrage présent, la trahison d'autrefois me paraissait peu de chose, et je déplorais moins la mutilation de mon corps que la flétrissure de mon nom. J'avais provoqué la première par ma faute; la persécution qui m'accablait aujourd'hui n'avait d'autre cause que l'intention droite et l'attachement à la foi qui m'avaient poussé à écrire. (A 49)

The persecution moves gradually from the verbal rebuke of his masters, to the burning of his books, to the open physical persecution of castration and stoning. Persecution here leads to outright madness; his enemies, Abelard feels, are waiting everywhere to rob and poison him; 'je n'apprenais pas la convocation d'une assemblée d'ecclésiastiques, sans penser qu'elle avait ma condamnation pour objet' (A 61). There is, on the one hand, the notion of an individual self aware of its worth and role in society — in conformity with the hegemonic mode for the production of this concept of selfhood permeates the whole discursive space — and, on the other hand, this same self coincides, in Abelard's case, with pure difference which is marked in its body proper. At this point in the history of the Western Text we already have an operational oppositional mode functioning in parallel to the hegemonic mode, and this contradiction between marginality and hegemony will remain unresolved unless we take into consideration the mental structures of the medieval world which allowed for the dissolution of opposition into complementarity. For as we know from the Crusades and the Inquisition, the hegemonic practice of the Middle Ages did not allow for the quiet operation of marginality — although this struggle was concentrated mainly in the theological realm.[18]

The social contextualisation of Abelard's text highlights some of the concerns which will develop further with subsequent marginal voices in the literary discourse; with time, while literature encompasses the hegemonic mode, it becomes the locus of absorption of marginality. Rousseau's madness and his feeling of disfigurement by outside forces vividly illustrate this extreme type of alienation. We are referring here to the materiality of the body as the inscribed sign of pure difference — the marking or branding of human flesh as the locus of marginality. It is becoming clear that the only way to silence the oppositional voice — that is, to annihilate even its mutest murmur — is through the annihilation of its identity and specificity in its material existence. The body as pure difference will manifest itself after Rousseau — for Rousseau is a complementary voice as well despite his repeated efforts to transcend the hegemonic — with the institutionalisation of madness and incarceration.[19] The mental hospital and the prison system are there to allow for the necessary division between the marginal and the hegemonic and the stifling of marginality to a mute silence; that is, they are there to install the fences of differentiation that protect the healthy identity and operative efficacy of the hegemonic mode.[20]

4

Descartes's *Discours de la Méthode*

Descartes's *Discours de la méthode* provides us with an opportunity to investigate the parameters of selfhood as it was understood following medieval Scholasticism. It is unnecessary to outline the impact on modern thought in general of Cartesianism and the relevance of its ideological presuppositions to modern philosophical discourses, such as that of Neo-Positivism. Behind Descartes's seemingly neutral and objective methical tool lie basic social statements indicative of the social climate of his times. Descartes's *Discours*, therefore, is of capital interest not primarily or rather essentially as an epistemological proposition — that is, the nature of the method, the four practical rules by which one accedes to true knowledge, and their impact on the theory of knowledge in general. Nor is the *Discours* of interest in its metaphysical import — the various proofs of the existence of God, the soul and the material world. The two realms of metaphysics and epistemology seem to attract most of the criticism on Descartes; most studies revolve around either the problem of scepticism and certainty or the 'Ontological Argument'. The preoccupation with these two aspects of Descartes in the critical literature points to the positivistic thrust of philosophy in our times; to wit, philosophy as the pursuit of pure knowledge detached from any social relevance.

Of Cartesianism

The ideological biases prevalent in the critical literature are well illustrated by the debate between Alquié and Gueroult — two Cartesian specialists — over the meaning of Descartes's philosophy.

59

While Gueroult puts the emphasis on the rationality of the step-by-step argumentation in Descartes, Alquié sees Descartes as a pure ontologist advancing a non-conceptualisable truth, so self-evident that it defeats reason. Let us put these two approaches in perspective and see whether one can derive any critical understanding from them.

> Lorsque Descartes dit: je pense ou je suis, il invoque une évidence logiquement discutable, et cependant convaincante; il fait appel à cette pure conscience ontologique par laquelle nous sommes tous convaincus que nous sommes des êtres, des pensées, et que nous sommes des 'moi'.

> Ce qui a plus d'être a plus de valeur et de ce fait, le monde se divise en deux domaines: il y a celui du réel physique qui n'a pas de valeur et qui peut être soumis à mon action technicienne, de même qu'il est offert à ma connaissance; car tout cela est du même côté, il y a le domaine métaphysique: c'est ce que je ne comprends pas, c'est sur quoi je ne peux pas agir, et c'est ce dont je ne doute pas: voici mon être propre, qui est liberté, et l'Etre divin, que je ne puis qu'admirer et adorer. (Alquié)[1]

Alquié, then, takes Descartes's dualism to its extreme in establishing two exclusive realms of being, the physical and the metaphysical; he seems to be more Cartesian than Descartes himself, since Descartes postulated some kind of formal relationship between physical and metaphysical knowledge. The method was meant to facilitate human comprehension in all fields of knowledge despite God's ultimate guarantee as to the validity of that knowledge. Further, what Alquié is talking about is a non-conceptualisable and therefore non-communicable experience which is in line with his fixed view of the world: every human being is convinced of his self because Alquié postulates a metaphysical self for every one of us. This conforms to Alquié's ideology of sameness, 'Je crois que toutes les consciences humaines sont semblables, et que dans une certaine expérience fondamentale de l'être, elles se rejoignent.'[2] The problem with this view is that one cannot approach it with critical tools because it purports to uncover a truth which defies all critical faculties; if one questions Alquié's statement, it is out of *mauvaise foi*, for everyone has to have a self — it is so evident that it cannot be refuted.

Martial Gueroult, on the other hand, in his monumental and

meticulous work, *Descartes selon l'ordre des raisons*, approaches Descartes in terms of the logical development of his argument. Descartes's rationalism is seen as the outcome of a step-by-step series of deductions such that every idea in Descartes's system follows from the preceding one.

> L'effort du Cartésianisme s'engage donc, dès le début, vers la constitution d'un système total de savoir certain, à la fois métaphysique et scientifique, système fondamentalement différent du système aristotélicien, puisque entièrement immanent à la certitude mathématique enveloppée dans l'intellect clair et distinct, mais non moins total, et plus strict encore dans son exigence de rigueur absolue. Cette totalité de système n'est nullement celle d'une encyclopédie des connaissances matérielles effectivement acquises, mais l'unité fondamentale des principes premiers d'où découlent toutes les connaissances certaines possibles. (Gueroult)[3]

Gueroult shares Descartes's idea of a non-moving point of departure, so that indeed, knowledge is attained through pure rationality but this rationality has its source in an unshakeable origin. Every concept can be broken down into its logical constituents except that original point of departure which is not a concept but which conditions all concepts. Here we see the unbreakable bond in Cartesian (and Neo-Cartesian) ideology between Reason and Selfhood.

> Le Cogito est lui-même le dernier élément indécomposable auquel bute définitivement l'analyse, il est donc nécessairement une pensée simple et singulière, saisie à ce titre immédiatement dans une intuition instantanée et indivisible.
>
> Ainsi, le Cogito apparaît comme le principe premier de toute science humaine possible, puisque c'est uniquement par lui et par la réflexion sur lui que peut se construire la science comme système de raisons liées par une nécessité rigoureuse. Or, point de science sans cette nécessité.[4]

One wonders at this point what distinguishes Gueroult from Alquié beyond the fact that Alquié was more explicit as to his bias. In the final analysis it is the 'premier principe' which guarantees our relationship to the world. Rationality, in Gueroult's schema, is not an objective phenomenon established within a social praxis;

rather, it is that irreducible basic conviction each one of us is said to hold. Consequently, we must all duplicate one another, otherwise knowledge would not hold, for only the similarity among all those primary selves can guarantee the validity of any general scientific knowledge. If it were not for our basic resemblance knowledge would be the exclusive domain of a private dream world. And this is precisely what Descartes will claim.

The majority of critics on Descartes are Cartesian; that is, they share the same presuppositional framework. And Descartes is of special interest precisely because, as text, he represents a nodal point in an epistemic modality which was initiated with the birth of the Method in Western culture. Descartes as Text gives birth to Cartesianism — a discursive development which has not disappeared from our semiotic space. Hence, the typical study on Descartes will open with a biographical sketch and then take a systematic approach to Descartes's statements; there is always a linear description of Cartesian doubt, the way Descartes overcomes it to prove his existence, the existence of God and the material world. In short, the critiques of Descartes constitute elaborations on his philosophy. Descartes's findings are considered matters of fact that must be interpreted in function of the needs of the age.[5]

Such is the reading of most British logicians[6] who take the Cartesian proposition at face value and try to make sense of it. Jaakko Hintikka's often quoted article 'Cogito ergo sum: inference or performance?' is a case in point. Hintikka suggests that the Cartesian proposition is more valid than a simple inference of the type $b(a) \supset (\exists x) (x = a)$; that is, that being is directly inferred from thinking. To Hintikka, the Cogito statement is stronger in its claim because it is a performative statement of the type 'I promise', 'I warn you', namely a statement which contains its validity in its own utterance. However, Descartes himself would disagree since one does not have to utter the Cogito but to think it: uttering is a physical phenomenon which is not immediately posited with the thinking self, while to all logicians the statement must be physically uttered, that is, communicated.

In Descartes' argument the relation of Cogito to Sum is not that of a premise to a conclusion. Their relation is rather comparable with that of a process to its product.

'Cogito' serves to express the performatory character of Descartes' insight; it refers to the 'performance' (to the act of thinking) through which the sentence 'I exist' may be said to verify itself. For this reason, it has a most important function in Descartes' sentence. It cannot be replaced by any arbitrary verb. The performance (act) through which the existential self-verifiability is manifested cannot be any arbitrary human activity, contrary to what Gassendi claimed. It cannot be an act of walking or an act of seeing.[7]

Hintikka not only accepts the existence of the Cogito but actually makes a stronger claim for it. In this, he joins (in terms of content) the thesis of Alquié, for the Cogito is not a simple performance; it is the performance of all performances — that basic starting point which is beyond logical verifiability. Making of it a logical inference would weaken it. This is why 'I walk therefore I am' is not enough to account for my existence; I must mediate and come up with the irreducible 'Cogito ergo sum' for me to exist. And even if one refutes Descartes's argument, as Ayer does in *The problem of knowledge*[8] by pointing to its linguistic and logical faults, one still speaks from within the same discourse, for a philosophical system — pure, scientific and neutral as it may appear to be — is anchored in the socio-political reality which conditions it. This is most evident in Rationalism and Empiricism where the ideology is patent on the surface of the text. Neutrality, scientificity, rationality as such, are myths for no system can exist in a vacuum waiting for the pure Reason to grasp it.

These preoccupations in Descartes himself — the proofs of the existence of self, God and the world — are obsolete and constitute but an exercise in futility. But the need to prove the existence of one's self and the world from scratch and to make a pure abstraction of every thing that is, through the process of hyperbolic doubt, say something about Descartes's basic postulates. The question that must be asked is: what did Descartes gain from his rational meditation? He himself provides us with an answer in the sixth part of the *Discours*; after he discovered the first causes,

J'ai examiné quels étaient les premiers et plus ordinaires effets qu'on pouvait déduire de ces causes: et il me semble que, par là, j'ai trouvé des cieux, des astres, une Terre, et même sur la Terre, de l'eau, de l'air, du feu, des minéraux. (D 130)

After years of meditation culminating in a philosophical *tour de force*, Descartes discovers the earth, the sky, the stars — in short, the exact replica of the material world with which he started. So why waste time on meditation in the first place? Descartes seems to think that the exercise is worth his while and the circularity of the process is of no consequence to him. His declaration of intentions at the beginning of the *Discours* states the conviction that his philosophical pursuit will lead him to the truth, that meditation will make a big difference in his world view.

> Je ne pouvais mieux faire que d'entreprendre, une bonne fois, de les ôter [les opinions], afin d'y remettre par après, ou d'autres meilleures, ou bien les mêmes, lorsque je les aurais ajustées au niveau de la raison. (D 62)

This statement must be emphasised: Descartes found nothing better to do than undertake once and for all to erase all existing opinions in order to arrive at better ones, or the same ones — and this is what happens in effect — but this time in accordance with the rules of Reason. Descartes believes that existing opinions are relative when compared to the one Truth that Reason can attain given the proper method of investigation. Once that Truth is attained all other truths turn into falsehoods. To us, however, Descartes's venture, as shown by the outcome of his method, is a reaffirmation of the *status quo*, based this time on the tenets of Reason. What is the use of this Reason if one attains the same reality one started with? To Descartes, Reason, as indicated in the first sentence of the *Discours*, is the only thing common to all humans; it is so well distributed amongst them that no one requests more than he is given at the outset. The statement is universal because everyone, Descartes wants us to agree, has common sense; and since all phenomena, complex as they may be, can be broken down to small and simple particles, everyone can grasp them through the mere activation of his intellect.

Descartes as a voice incorporating the discursive activity already lays out here what will be the eighteenth-century conception of the social contract as a binding force among all the members of a given social whole. This statement of the universality of Reason anticipates the development of the social contract that Hobbes, Montesquieu and Rousseau among many others, will delineate later on. The *sine qua non* of the social contract is Reason in its universal dimension. As we will see in Rousseau's theory of the contract, it is man's rationality that determines the transition from the state of nature to the state of culture.

It would be useless to go into the diverse meanings that 'Reason' may hold and whether all humans, including the Barbarians, exercise the same type of Reason. Suffice it to say that Descartes fails to give us an adequate recipe; nowhere does he tell us how one can cultivate reason. Further, not many can indulge in this activity given that it requires a special kind of behaviour reserved for the chosen few. For meditation can take place only in a 'poêle' in a small village in Germany while political upheavals are ravaging France (assassinations of Henri III in 1589 and Henri IV in 1610; an atrocious war in 1563; and the Thiry Years War ending in 1648; the *Discours* was published in 1637).

In this connection we should keep in mind that Descartes's father was a councillor in the parliament of Bretagne, that he was of the Noblesse de Robe, the bourgeoisie of magistrates; that Descartes was well off and never needed a pension to pursue his philosophical career. On the last page of the *Discours*, Descartes says that he would much prefer to be left alone to his 'loisir'[9] (the word 'divertissement' is used as well) than be offered the most honourable position in academia, for any kind of work apart from his philosophical meditations would distract him from his task which is the betterment of all mankind ('le bien général de tous les hommes' (D 128)). His multiple hesitations as to the publication of his works are likewise due to this fear of distraction.

Sameness and difference

Descartes's system as laid out in the *Discours* and *Meditations* can be labelled 'the system of the zero point' — the pure beginning, the *tabula rasa*. The 'poêle' hypostasises this image because the ideal poêle is a tightly sealed room, totally separate from the outside world, which generates its own heat. Insulation plays a double role: it prevents the encroachment of the outside climate on the poêle, and it allows the poêle to reach and maintain its optimal heat. Descartes's first step is the obliteration of the external world in its otherness. While he claims to have undertaken his journeys to seek a difference which would lead him to a comparative study of his own society,

> Il est bon de savoir quelque chose des mœurs de divers peuples, afin de juger des nôtres plus sainement, et que nous

ne pensions pas que tout ce qui est contre nos modes soit
ridicule, et contre raison, ainsi qu'ont coutume de faire ce qui
n'ont rien vu. (D 51)

in the same breath he arrives at the conclusion that journeys constitute distractions: while one is away one becomes estranged from
one's own country. Similarly, Descartes cannot even conceive of
an integration of his knowledge with that of the past — another
distraction — for in being interested in the past one is ignorant of
the present (D 51). One cannot help but acknowledge the existence
of difference, for the Other is there in flesh and blood. This awareness of the Other will in the eighteenth century encourage journeys
to far-off lands. Aside from the missionary quests, there is a new
obligation that forces eighteenth-century consciousness to come to
grips with otherness in its purest forms, i.e. primitive societies.

However, there is also a need to force conformity on that which
is different. This reduction — as we shall see, Cartesianism as a
whole is a series of reductions operated in various realms of reality
— can be achieved only at the price of annihilation of all that looks
different at the outset. This is Descartes's main proposition: whatever one has or does not have, we are all alike. If we scrape away
all the outer layers, the various disguises, we are all the same in the
nakedness of our pure selves, and one naked self equals any other.
The differences are on the surface only, for internally, innately, all
humans are equal. This is precisely the point at which property
coincides with the proper — the piece of land with the self.
Material ownership is but a superficial, external layer: ownership
of self is what counts; hence the equality between self and other,
rich and poor.

The lack of delineation between sameness and difference allows
for a compromise between two contradictory facts in the *Discours*:
Why does the meditation unfold in a 'poêle' in a foreign country?
Descartes could easily have found a poêle in France! But the
relationship between the poêle and the outside does not change
with the change in locus; it holds the same kind of relationship to
Germany, to France, or to any other country.

Je pris un jour la résolution d'étudier aussi en moi-même . . .
Ce qui me réussit beaucoup mieux, ce me semble, que si je
me fusse jamais éloigné, ni de mon pays, ni de mes livres.
(D 57)

However, despite the reduction of the different to the same, the opposition between the two, which cannot be totally annihilated, is a key transformation in the consciousness of the Christian tradition. As suggested, one can argue that Germany is no different from France in the seventeenth century and that we are dealing here with pure repetition. But despite his efforts, Descartes does not make a total abstraction of the diversity existing in the world, as Augustine did.[10] As we pointed out, Augustine's statement of diversity is immediately overtaken by his statement of universality. Cartesianism transforms the Augustinian reduction; the reduction of all phenomena to the Two Cities turns into a reduction to Rationality. In Augustine there is no contradiction because the proposition of heterogeneity is immediately followed and absorbed by the proposition of homogeneity: the Two Cities cancel the multiplicity of nations in the immediate. Not so with Descartes. In the *Discours*, the contradiction between homogeneity and heterogeneity remains apparent despite Descartes's attempt to resolve it by forcing the innate spread of Reason upon all humans: first, because homogeneity does not immediately follow heterogeneity — the Germans and the primitives are still there despite their basic equality; second, because this contradiction between difference and repetition remains open. The Cartesian reduction does not meet with full success since the Other — the primitive, the slave, the marginal — simply refuses to disappear from the surface of the discourse. The marginal cannot be ignored: Descartes was very much aware of Galileo's plight as well as of his scientific truth. (Descartes's repeated obeisance to Christianity is sometimes seen as a ploy to divert the wrath of the church away from him.) By the late Middle Ages, the marginal refuses to budge and the discourse must contend with it. Despite the attempt of the hegemonic voice to stifle the marginal by its own excessive noise, marginality and difference keep cropping up in their bare existence, albeit as a mute presence, refusing to be suffocated.

Descartes's reductivism appears in the heart of the *Discours*, in the four universal rules which repeat on a more abstract plane his situation in the 'poêle'. The first rule is to reject everything that is not certain; all sensual data are unreliable and therefore one must disregard them as well as all commonplaces. Without going into the problems of certainty and reliability, the first rule clearly conforms to the process of 'peeling' which is so crucial to the whole Cartesian venture. The second rule is that of division: Descartes believes that one can take any problem, complex as it might be, and divide it into its basic components — that is, arrive at its

Ultimate knowledge does not take place in time and therefore needs no explanation, its sole guarantee being the power of conviction. (The problem is of course the communication of such an intuition, but Descartes was not concerned with communication.) The immediacy of the Cartesian moment negates both past and future — hence the necessity for God. Were it not for God's guarantee, the continuity of self would be jeopardised; given the unreliability of memory, self would have to be intuited at each moment of assertion and between the intuitive moments it would cease to exist.[11] Without God's guarantee we would have to meditate 'Cogito ergo sum' increasingly.

Clarity means that the self or the idea — the atom — lack any complexity within, and distinction means that the phenomenon is cut off from everything else that is contiguous, below or above it. But had Descartes carried his peeling process one step further he would have reached the exact reversal of his position; the problem is at what layer one can claim to have reached the basic atom, the naked self, for the heart of the onion is but a series of peels and if one follows the process to its logical conclusion, one does not reach a heart, a core, but rather another series of layers. Descartes did not specify at what stage of the process one can be sure of having reached the clear and distinct truth, and the naked self that he claims to have attained at the end of his internal journey is but another layer — an infinite process of mediation that negates the immediate. Descartes refused intentionally to carry his quest further for that would jeopardise the existence of subjectivity, the basis of his whole system; here we see that ideology conditions the superstructure, Descartes's rationalism. Although the atomic self is a myth, Descartes says:

> Je m'avisai de considérer que souvent il n'y a pas tant de perfection dans les ouvrages composés de plusieurs pièces, et fait de la main de divers maîtres, qu'en ceux auquels un seul a travaillé. (D 59)

This statement is reinforced by other examples, making it one of Descartes's basic credos: the buildings built by one architect, the cities designed by one designer, the constitutions written by one legislator, the science elaborated by one scientist, are all better than the ones achieved by a group. The individual, then, is the irreducible generator of all cognitive phenomena. Similarly, the commonplaces of any given society must be looked at with suspicion because of their diversity, and one must reject them, given their sheer numbers, in order to arrive at the one true opinion that conforms to Universal Reason.

The third example regarding the role of the constitutional legislator is of capital importance because it will recur in eighteenth-century social discourse; by the eighteenth century, this concept of the zero point will be transposed from the realm of the individual self to that of the social whole. The zero point of society is common to both the 'naked self' and to the 'man of nature', man before the fall into society. In Descartes's *Discours* a reference is already made in passing to the beginnings of the social structure:

> Ainsi je m'imaginais que les peuples, ayant été toujours demi-sauvages, et ne s'étant civilisés que peu à peu, n'ont fait leurs lois qu'à mesure que l'incommodité des crimes et des querelles les y a contraints, ne sauraient être si bien policés que ceux que dès le commencement qu'ils se sont assemblés, ont observé les constitutions de quelque prudent législateur.
> (D 60)

The assumption that societies have a zero point is without doubt motivated by the ideological presuppositions underlying a conceptualisation of social cohesion; foreign to this conceptualisation is the notion of integration. Descartes, and later the Enlightenment, conceived of cohesion in terms of addition: they believed that society is a cumulation of individual, irreducible, self-sufficient units. In short, there exists a strong relationship between the concept of the 'zero point' and the ideology of seriality; indeed, towards the end of the *Discours*, Descartes produces a coherent image of seriality.[12]

Descartes contends that true knowledge constitutes the return to the unadulterated beginning, to that *tabula rasa* which is in us. But the cost of this return is heavy: one must sever all relations with the material world and abolish the historical process at the same time. One must even operate a split within being, thus putting one's very existence into question. Man, according to Descartes, divides into two exclusive parts, thought and extension, the one characterising the soul, the other, the body and the material world as a whole. This split within the individual extends outward to include all other humans; there is a total lack of communication between self and Other since, by definition, minds are separate and the knowledge of bodies which conditions my possible apprehension of the Other is unreliable. And because minds remain impermeable to one another, knowledge of the Other can at best be attained through a process of inference and introspection. This presupposes that being is homologous in all humans, and that, in turn, there exists a prearranged harmony which makes for the possibility of such homology (as Leibnitz will make explicit). It further presupposes that the naked self is totally transparent to itself, that complete self-knowledge is realisable since self is some kind of reservoir of innate truths, that it is 'full'. This, of course, contradicts materialistic conceptions of selfhood which postulate that self is a vacuum filled from the outside and therefore self-knowledge is nothing but a myth. Also the division of phenomena into thought and extension establishes two histories, the one private, the other public.

'The mind is its own place and in his inner life each of us lives the life of a ghostly Robinson Crusoe.'[13] Gilbert Ryle labels this myth 'the dogma of the Ghost in the machine'; however, he does not seem to be aware of the ideological assumptions behind Descartes's pessimistic outlook on human communication. Descartes does not simply give up on the world; he does not close himself up to meditate out of despair. The act of meditation is intentional, both conscious and wilful. Ryle's claim that Descartes's 'category mistake' is due to the application of the mechanistic model to the affairs of the mind does not provide us with an answer to the question of how one arrives at a mechanistic model in the first place. There is no doubt that the mechanistic paradigm of the seventeenth century relates to the hegemonic mode of the times; the determinism of the machine has to do with the determination of the social structure and vice versa: one sees in the machine what one sees or wishes to see in the social whole.[14]

Descartes's pessimistic determinism, then, goes hand in hand with the lack of dynamism in his view of social organisation. It is of interest to note, however, that determinism is experimented with only in the realm of thought and metaphysics. Descartes never makes a study of the social structure; the hyperbolic doubt is never applied to it. The idea of doubting the social structure remains foreign even to a circular process of investigation; the question is simply never posed because

Ces grands corps [i.e. corps publics] sont très malaisés à relever, étant abattus, où même à retenir étant ébranlés, et leurs chutes ne peuvent être que très rudes. Puis, pour leurs imperfections, s'ils en ont . . . elles sont quasi toujours plus supportables que ne serait leur changement. (D 63)

The images in this passage are quite revealing: the social structure is a mass, a shapeless amorphous body that is bent upon falling, that cannot be helped once its mass pulls it down. (The word 'chute' is quite strong here and carries religious connotations: Adam too 'fell' from grace.) The natural heaviness of the social body creates a lack of dynamism and obstructs any possible amelioration; this is why imperfections are preferable to changes. At the same time the weight and rigidity of the social body confers upon it some kind of stability and this, to Descartes, is already a blessing. And since imperfections are preferable to revolutions, Descartes can only devise a 'morale provisoire' — which remains his final 'morale' for he never wrote another one. To Henri Gouhier, this 'morale provisoire est destinée à ne devenir jamais mieux qu'une sorte de provisoire permanent'.[15] The precepts of this 'morale' are simple: (a) to obey the laws and customs of one's country; (b) to be firm in one's actions; (c) to overcome oneself rather than destiny, change one's desires rather than the order of the world.[16]

What kind of action is meant by the second rule? Could it be action geared toward change? The third rule, however, says that change must be effected internally, on one's desires and not on the social structure, for the first rule accepts without hesitation the organisation of the social body as it is. Action is therefore confined to the 'poêle', to meditation; it bears no relation to the socio-historical process *per se*. Descartes, in effect, refuses man the use of cognition to effect change in the material world.

What are we to deduce from Descartes' first two Meditations? This: that unless acting, that is, bringing about changes in the world, is part of thinking (which Descartes must deny, since acting requires a body and a body cannot be entailed, in his theory, by thought) the essence of man, whatever else it may be, is not action. Could Descartes really have wanted to maintain that it is not part of man's essential nature to be an agent? Could he even have wanted to maintain that it is doubtful whether man is an agent? Yet however broadly we interpret Descartes' cogito, it is difficult to see how we can pass from the claim to be aware, to the claim to do. Our knowledge of our own agency must somehow stand on its own feet, if it in fact is to be knowledge at all. That we are active in respect of our thinking Descartes has no doubt. Indeed, it is precisely by our activity in this sense that we come to know for certain that we exist as thinking beings. But this is not the sense of agency required by the expression 'man (not just mind) is an agent'. Mind can only find out, whereas man can change what there is for mind to find out.[17]

Descartes's upholding of the *status quo*[18] is consistent with the split between self and the world; this in turn generates a division within the historical process between public and private, private history being the history of the naked self, and public, the history of external phenomena. This duality of the historical process constitutes an interface between Descartes and Augustine; Descartes as well believed in the revealed truths which only God's grace can guarantee. Here too we encounter the dichotomy of temporality and eternity — which is to say that discursively speaking some medieval residual practices are still holding in Descartes's time. However, for the first time two homologies are established, between rationality and eternity and between irrationality and temporality. If for Augustine knowledge meant revelation, that is, the pure passivity of the mind on the way to illumination, for Descartes a new element enters into play: more activity is given to man in the cognitive process. Descartes seems to combine both pure intuition — which means that the mind is a mere passive receptacle — and active intellection. Man is a free intellect in the cognitive process of scientific discovery; he is an active agent in the immediate while he is experimenting although, in the end, God is the sole guarantor of all truths.[19]

Le rationnel est intemporel; le temporel est irrationnel. Une société rationnelle serait intemporelle; une société temporelle est irrationnelle.

C'est pourquoi la révolution au nom de la raison est déraisonnable, vouée à l'échec et dangereuse. Elle est déraisonnable car il serait absurde de traiter une société temporelle comme si le temps pouvait en être éliminé. Elle est nécessairement vouée à un échec: elle ne sera jamais la substitution d'un ordre rationnel à un ordre historique; elle n'aboutira jamais qu'à l'avènement d'un ordre également historique. Et après combien de ruines! C'est pourquoi elle est dangereuse par nature: faite au nom de la raison contre l'histoire, elle détruit l'œuvre de l'histoire sans instaurer le règne de la raison; elle est désordre, puisqu'elle renverse l'ordre historique là où l'ordre ne peut être qu'historique.[20]

But social revolution is unwarranted and the *status quo* is upheld because of the prevalent social relations and class structure of the times; from Descartes's perspective any kind of social change would generate a discontinuity between theory and practice.[21] This illustrates that no philosophical system is detached from concrete social relations; the superstructure — Descartes's system — is grounded in the socio-material relations of the seventeenth century. Scientific knowledge, for example, is best achieved, according to Descartes, by the accumulation of self-contained units of knowledge upon a serial line. Descartes cannot conceive of a more comprehensive text which gives birth to and encompasses all the scattered individual voices in the field; the scientific idea or discovery is not picked up from a given discursive reality, but rather, is conceived by a mind which has secured a greater degree of intuition and innateness. Knowledge is attained through the consecutive consumption of the serial units; after one has exhausted a unit one moves to the next, and so on.

> Je jugeais qu'il n'y avait point de meilleur remède . . . que de convier les bons esprits à tâcher de passer plus outre, en contribuant chacun selon son inclination et son pouvoir, aux expériences qu'il faudrait faire . . . afin que les derniers commençant où les précédents auraient achevé, et ainsi joignant les vies et les travaux de plusieurs, nous allassions tous ensemble beaucoup plus loin que chacun en particulier ne saurait faire. (D 129)

'Chacun' here does not mean everyone but 'chaque un', every one. First each scientist contributes in accordance with his private knowledge and abilities and, second, one generation succeeds another generation, and so on; there is a point of conjunction between each generation and its predecessor. Absent is even a hint of a possible interface between two minds. The formula — and the word 'joignant' connotes 'end to end' — is one plus one. And the addition is not merely an addition of discoveries and experiments; it is first an addition of individual lives ('les vies et les travaux') sitting beside one another or rather following one another (as one would join two pieces of material). The time sequence here is not diachronic; it is the static movement within a series. It lacks any notion of dialectics, and has no process of negation built therein. This is the exact formula of Positivism, which is nothing but a pile of positive units, an amalgam of small quantities.

Descartes does point to one social relation that can be engaged in but this relation is not of a concrete, interpersonal nature; it remains external, at the level of physicality. It is the economic use one can make of others, which is at the base of the class structure — the saleability of labour as commodity.

> Il est vrai que, pour ce qui est des expériences qui peuvent y servir, un homme seul ne saurait suffir à les faire toutes; mais il n'y saurait aussi employer utilement d'autres mains que les siennes, sinon celles des artisans, ou telles gens qu'il pourrait payer et à qui l'espérance du gain, qui est un moyen très efficace, ferait faire exactement toutes les choses qu'il leur prescrirait. (D 139)

Clearly, Descartes needs no other human to complete his universal scientific task; the creation of meaning remains his exclusive domain. The Other is there to be used solely as an object, a machine to produce certain material commodities (artisans): abstraction is made of all capacities except the hands, the tools of labour. This abstraction and reification of the Other is made possible by Descartes's conception of the naked self. For if in the realm of public history one is reduced to one's labour value, in the realm of private history one can still entertain the illusion that one indeed holds ownership over one's naked self; introspection and individualism can be conceived of only if historical contingency is divided into public and private. The notion of a naked self is therefore functional to the division of society into classes. For the coming together of public and private histories would enhance interpenetration and social intercourse; it would erase the differences between 'mine' and 'yours'. This reification of the social relation will develop further with the good fortunes of the bourgeoisie in the following two centuries. With the Industrial Revolution the concept of selfhood was already stable and freedom came to mean the saleability of one's labour in the open market.[22]

With the shift in the conception of selfhood, the contribution of Cartesianism to the discursive activity imbricates upon that of Abelard in universalising man's methodical rationality. This new discursive initiative finds a fertile ground in the changing material conditions of the seventeenth century. The new rationality, the reliance on man's faculties to explain the order of things, made for the conceptualisation of laws and causes in nature; things no longer happened gratuitously or miraculously. This shift (or partial shift) relates dialectically to the movement of cartography and navigation and the consequent development of maritime commerce, the discovery of new lands, the creation of banks and movement of money, and colonisation. These phenomena made a dent in the hierarchical conception of things; with Galileo's new astronomy, the earth ceases to be the centre of the universe, and man is no more the centre of God's creation. The centrality of the individual self, though, will take time to develop; thus Abelard's and Descartes's autobiographies are short and do not encompass the wide range of experiences of an individual life. At this time there is a struggle to establish the Cogito on rational grounds, that is, its bare existence. By Rousseau's time, rationality and sub-jectivity are unquestionable givens and the focus is put rather on a wide range of little facts of the daily life of the irreducible self.

5

Rousseau's *Confessions*

This chapter will consider Rousseau's preoccupation with the self as the centre of meaning, and the possible relationship between self and Other as laid out in his social theory. The chapter will also show the consistency of Rousseau's conception of selfhood in his autobiographical venture and in his social philosophy despite the numerous contradictions one encounters in both realms. It will be demonstrated that the refusal of mediation postulated in Rousseau's autobiographical writings is germane to his political writings, and this notwithstanding his emphasis on the social pact as a positive phenomenon, the binding force of the social totality. In defining the social relation as a pact that takes place at a given point in time, Rousseau has come to conceive of the social object as dependent on an act of magic: it is not there before the pact and it is immediately there after the pact. Our conclusion will be that the idea of a pure beginning itself, of a zero degree, can only accommodate the principle of cumulation (i.e. the cumulation of all the individuals who will participate in the social contract).

L'être et le paraître

The eighteenth century sees the introduction of the temporal process into the discourse; thus with Rousseau, chronology is a given. If God[1] is present in Rousseau's confessions, He does not occupy the centre; He exists only as a peripheral entity. Furthermore, God is the 'jugement dernier', the last judge of Jean-Jacques's venture after all human judges have failed to understand him. The introduction of the temporal process into the discourse motivates a new power play, between man and society and no longer between man and his creator. Grace has by now little to do with the meaning of man's life and redemption is to be sought within the human context. If the definition of man is functional, for Augustine, to his aspiration for the transcendental and, for Descartes, to his innate reason, then, for Rousseau, the definition of man has to do with his immanent state of being. If for Augustine and Descartes God is the beginning and the end of all that is, for Rousseau it is man.

> J'achevai ainsi ma lecture et tout le monde se tut, Mme d'Egmont fut la seule qui me parut émue; elle tressaillit visiblement, mais elle se remit bien vite et garda le silence ainsi que toute la compagnie. Tel fut le fruit que je tirai de cette lecture de ma déclaration.[2]

This is the last paragraph of Rousseau's *Confessions*, but it does not follow the narrative sequence, it comes 'after' the story. Rousseau read his confessions to an audience on four occasions; the reading to Mme d'Egmont and her entourage is the fourth and final one. It is the last verdict: silence. And what seemed to be some kind of a reaction, some kind of an emotion is but a mere quiver — not even a murmur, 'un tressaillement', which fades quietly into the silence which engulfs it together with the voice of the *Confessions*. It is understandable why Rousseau related the last reaction to his readings and why further readings are unnecessary. Rousseau has toiled throughout his story to wrest a reaction, a counter-declaration, an answer to his plea, and what he gets is not negative criticism, nor even a statement of indifference — which would be a reaction of sorts — but a mere silence, a non-reaction. We know that after his failure at communication with the *Confessions*, Rousseau will write his dialogues, dialogues with himself, *Rousseau juge de Jean-Jacques*, and his *Rêveries* which postulates no otherness. He remains finally his only judge.

What brought Rousseau to such a hopeless view of human relations? Why can there be no communication? Before arriving at the obvious — his endless physical persecutions, the condemnation and burning of his books, the expropriation of his authorship over what he writes and, finally, the public distortion of his true self — let us see what is at the root of this autobiography. The *Confessions* is not simply a reading of past phenomena; it is an interpretation which mixes the past with the present. This is why the last paragraph is not a careless addition: it provides a key to the whole venture.

Rousseau's interpretation of two early anecdotes constitutes a basic element in his philosophy of man. First, there is the story of the broken comb.[3] While at Bossey, in the heart of the natural paradise, Jean-Jacques is accused of breaking the teeth of a comb which was drying in his room. But he is innocent and the exhortations of everyone around him cannot force him to confess; he is subsequently punished for a crime he did not commit.

> Je n'avais pas encore assez de raison pour sentir combien les apparences me condamnaient, et pour me mettre à la place des autres. Je me tenais à la mienne, et tout ce que je sentais, c'était la rigueur d'un châtiment effroyable pour un crime que je n'avais pas commis. (C 20)

The episode brings drastic changes in Jean-Jacques's view of the world; from now on he is conscious of the impossibility of communicating truth to others, and of the evil this entails. He is for the first time aware of the gap between minds. This story represents his fall from paradise, for after this episode he becomes a thief. In this episode Jean-Jacques is the victim, in the ribbon episode he is the victimiser and draws the same conclusion. While working as a lackey at Mme Vercellis's, Rousseau steals a red ribbon and is caught after the act. He accuses Marion, a young and honest kitchen helper, of the theft, and claims that she gave it to him as a present. 'On ne parut pas se décider absolument, mais les préjugés étaient pour moi' (C 91). Marion is shy and quiet, Jean-Jacques vociferous; Marion is therefore the guilty one. 'Préjugés' and 'apparences' are the key words in these two stories; Jean-Jacques . is conscious of what 'is' indeed, and of what appears to be, 'l'être et le paraître'. In the first case appearances worked against him: he was the only one in the room; in the second, appearances worked against Marion: she 'looked' guilty. In both cases the verdict is arrived at by an audience, a tribunal. Had his crime been exposed in private, Rousseau would no doubt have confessed his guilt (C 94). In other words, the social conditions are responsible for this process of victimisation. Also, the persona, the mask he wore, made for his acquittal. Rousseau says that he undertook to write his autobiography mainly in order to expiate this guilt. But thanks to this event (no doubt filtered through his imagination many times) he arrives at one of the cornerstones of his philosophy: the far-reaching power of appearances. Not only do they work against the innocent, but they twist good intentions: in fact, Jean-Jacques stole the ribbon to give it to Marion, whom he liked; he accused her because he recalled her name when he was caught. 'Ce sont presque toujours de bons sentiments mal dirigés qui font faire aux enfants le premier pas vers le mal' (C 35). Man starts with the 'bons sentiments'; he is good by nature, and the social conditions have twisted his natural innocence.

> Tout le reste du jour, enfoncé dans la forêt, j'y cherchais, j'y trouvais l'image des premiers temps, dont je traçais fièrement l'histoire; je faisais main-basse sur les petits mensonges des hommes; j'osais dévoiler à nu leur nature, suivre le progrès du temps et des choses qui l'ont défigurée, et comparant l'homme de l'homme avec l'homme naturel, leur montrer dans son perfectionnement prétendu la véritable source de ses misères. Mon âme exaltée par ces contemplations sublimes, s'élevait auprès de la Divinité, et voyant de là mes semblables suivre dans l'aveugle route de leurs préjugés, celle de leurs erreurs, leurs malheurs, de leurs crimes, je leur criais d'une faible voix qu'il ne pouvaient entendre: Insensés qui vous plaignez sans cesse de la nature, apprenez que tous vos maux vous viennent de vous. (C 460)

Rummaging through one's past, going over one's periods of innocence coincides in Rousseau with finding the meaning of man's existence as a whole. To uncover the true nature of man before the fall means, for Rousseau, to return to those experiences at Bossey or Les Charmettes, the lost paradise that one must attempt to recapture. (Note, however, that Rousseau does not resort to any metaphysical notion of paradise; paradise is to be found on earth, in this world and not in the next.) If these 'retours' to Bossey or Les Charmettes or the episode with Mlle Graffenried and Mlle Galley, are mentioned repeatedly, it is because they contain experiences that come close to those of natural man. So the discovery of self turns into the discovery of man. Regression here means progression.

Progression and regression

The progression in the regression is attempted in Rousseau's first and second discourses, *Discours surs les sciences et les arts* and *Discours sur l'origine de l'inégalité,* where he shows the flaws of society by resorting to an image of man as he must have been before the process of socialisation took place. It is clear to Rousseau that the present is unliveable: present-day society has destroyed every value in man and one must therefore seek those lost values not in history (for history coincides with the social process) but in another dimension: the realm of the hypothetical. The anecdotes of a biography, the story of a life, are not an end in themselves; their only purpose is to recapture that lost innocence which is obliterated by the haziness of temporal phenomena. In effect, the childhood of humanity is the childhood of the individual; the state of nature is a lived experience perpetuated in infancy. This is why the education of the infant Emile[4] should not be tampered with; nature must do its own work on the infant until he reaches consciousness and can be introduced to the corrupt social order. Looking for man's original innocence means looking into the depth of one's soul; no matter how much society has altered man, no matter how many masks he wears, that innocence is still there, hidden, waiting to be rediscovered. The conceptions of history and of self, then, are similar in Rousseau: events remain a hindrance to the true state of being. One must therefore look beyond the event, transcend the temporal process in the search for meaning.[5]

Rousseau is fully aware of the major contradiction of his whole venture: 'c'est en un sens à force d'étudier l'homme, que nous sommes mis hors d'état de le connaître',[6] for the quest itself involves a process of furthering away from natural man; the first *Discours* argues forcefully that knowledge and reason have lost man.[7] The closer we get to natural man, the farther we are from knowing him: knowledge and reason multiply the processes of mediation and widen the gap; the tools are cultural. This is why the return is impossible, and we must concede that history does not follow nature and that any conception of nature must of necessity be fictional — that is, a particular arrangement of reality.

Rousseau of course found a way around this problematic; in the *Profession de foi du Vicaire Savoyard,* the motto is: 'I feel therefore I am.' In other words, we still possess spontaneous feelings, sensations, that allow us to apprehend the state of nature in the immediate. But even sensation must be expressed in words unless one is content to remain in the woods duplicating the state of nature. And if the conception of natural man is an ideological arrangement of phenomena, it remains to be seen why this specific conception, and not another one; that is, why imagine an animal-like, primitive ancestor? Why go back to the beginning[8] of society and not take society as it is and move on from there?

> Commençons donc par écarter tous les faits, car ils ne touchent point à la question. Il ne faut pas prendre les recherches, dans lesquelles on peut entrer sur ce sujet, pour des vérités historiques, mais seulement pour des raison-nements hypothétiques et conditionnels; plus propres à éclaircir la nature des choses, qu'à montrer la véritable origine. (IN 158)

In order to remedy the ills of society as it is, Rousseau looks to the hypothetical: a conception of what man might have been prior to the social process makes possible a better understanding of what he ought to be. From the logical point of view, this is quite sound, since the *Social contract* constitutes a synthesis of the hypothetical and the real. The 'ought' comes after the recognition of a total incompatibility between the hypothetical and the real. Man cannot be what he is and cannot return to what he might have been; he therefore ought to be what he is on the basis of what he might have been. This, of course, points to a basic contradiction in Rousseau's social theory. If, as will be shown, there is an insurmountable opposition between the state of nature and the state of culture, how can Rousseau hope to synthesise the two? If one says culture, one cannot say nature, and vice versa. But one can refound culture on nature, as Rousseau believes he does in the *Contract*, if one reduces one member of the binary combination culture/nature to the other. If nature becomes culture or culture becomes nature, the contradiction is eliminated. Rousseau was totally unaware of the necessary reductiveness inherent to his system.

The state of nature

As Rousseau describes this hypothetical state of nature it looks like a historical phase since it itself undergoes an evolutionary process: while emphasising the non-possibility of the state of nature, Rousseau describes it in very vivid and realistic terms as though it happened. Rousseau himself is unclear about the ontological status of the state of nature which is so crucial to his system. If vestiges of this state have remained within modern man through some process of archetypal transfer, then the state must actually have existed in the distant past; and if it is not a historical phase, then how can one claim that man still retains some of its original characteristics?

> Car ce n'est pas une légère entreprise de démêler ce qu'il y a d'originaire et d'artificiel dans la nature actuelle de l'homme, et de bien connaître un état qui n'existe plus, qui n'a *peut-être* point existé, qui *probablement* n'existera jamais et dont il est pourtant nécessaire d'avoir des notions justes pour bien juger de notre état présent. (IN 151)

The words we have italicised suggest that Rousseau had doubts as to the hypothetical aspect of the state of nature. Critics have tended to support Rousseau's claim that the state of nature is merely a concept, a comparative tool, a model. Henri Gouhier claims:

> Si l'état de nature n'est pas une époque historique mais une hypothèse de travail, c'est une hypothèse de travail faite pour compendre l'homme historique; si l'état de nature ne représente pas la véritable origine, il se présente comme une origine hypothétique.[9]

The conditional 'si' indicates Gouhier's hesitation as to the historicity of the state of nature. Ernst Cassirer carries it a step further and brings into focus the impact Rousseau has had on recent anthropological and social theories.

> In order to distinguish the 'homme naturel' from the 'homme artificiel', we need neither to go back to epochs of the distant and dead past nor take a trip around the world. Every one carries a true archetype within himself; still, hardly anyone has been fortunate enough to discover it and to strip it of its artificial wrappings, its arbitrary and conventional trimmings.[10]

As opposed to Gouhier, Cassirer conceives of the state of nature as a possible historical phase, for the distant and dead past is within the historical process. This archetypal approach indicates what impact Rousseau (and eighteenth-century anthropological theory) has had on modern anthropological theories such as Jung's. And were we to find that archetype, which is hidden and hard to reach, we would be in a position to abstract the whole historical process since, in essence, no movement has taken place within man. There is therefore a relationship between the concept of 'archetype' and pure absence, to which Rousseau aspires. Lévi-Strauss's 'universal unconscious' bears a strong resemblance to this archetype; hence he sees in Rousseau his mentor. Lévi-Strauss's own bias gives rise to what we believe is an incorrect interpretation of Rousseau.

> La pensée de Rousseau s'épanouit donc à partir d'un double principe: celui de l'identification à autrui, et même au plus 'autrui' de tous les autrui, fût-il un animal; et celui du refus d'identification à soi-même, c'est-à-dire le refus de tout ce qui peut rendre le moi 'acceptable', ces deux attitudes se complètent, et la seconde fonde même la première: en vérité, je ne suis pas 'moi', mais le plus faible, le plus humble des 'autrui'.[11]

The question is whether this 'autrui' is genuinely the Other, whether Rousseau erases his self to espouse someone else. But Rousseau's 'autrui' remains someone hidden within his self; it is not someone outside him that would reflect Rousseau's being-for-himself. Lévi-Strauss posits a Rousseauist dialogue which is simply not there. The fact remains, however, that Rousseau believes modern man to incorporate some of the traits of natural man; his educational theory as a whole is based on his conception of the state of nature and geared to the social praxis of his times. (There were attempts to raise children à la Emile.) Critics prefer to side with Rousseau on this issue, though it was not settled in his own mind, mainly because otherwise they would have to accept Voltaire's criticism that he felt like going on all fours after he read the *Discours*, which would not sit very well with the writer of the *Social contract*. I will indicate later on that the conception of the state of nature is itself ideologically motivated — that in effect, after an adequate analysis, it reflects the social structures prevalent in the enlightened ideology of the eighteenth century. Natural man is an interesting copy of social man but, of course, with some differences: otherwise the concept would lose its mythical appeal.

According to Rousseau, before the process of socialisation, man goes through two stages in the state of nature: first, the stage of each man under his tree, and secondly, the stage of small groups uniting for common interests. The first man interacted with his immediate environment; he was robust, surmounting harsh climates and danger from other animals. Being totally separated from other humans who might harm him, his only enemies were natural: childhood and helplessness, disease and old age. His mental activities were geared to his immediate well-being, his only preoccupations being the hunt and physical survival. Lacking a conception of time, he did not think ahead. If the Other was there, he took the form of a woman with whom natural man had a fortuitous intercourse 'selon la rencontre, l'occasion et le désir . . . ils se quittaient avec la même facilité' (IN 185). Natural man spoke no language except 'le cri de la nature'; he lacked reason, and was amoral because morality comes with standards of justice that society instils. Rousseau summarises the state of nature thus:

> Concluons qu'errant dans les forêts sans industrie, sans parole, sans domicile, sans guerre, et sans liaisons, sans nul besoin de ses semblables, comme sans nul désir de leur nuire, peut-être même sans jamais en reconnaître aucun individuellement, l'homme sauvage sujet à peu de passions, et se suffisant à lui-même, n'avait que les sentiments et les lumières propres à cet état, qu'il ne sentait que ses vrais besoins, ne regardait que ce qu'il croyait avoir intérêt de voir, et que son intelligence ne faisait pas plus de progrès que sa vanité . . . l'homme restait toujours enfant. (IN 201–2)

Thus natural man was, in a way, *sui generis*. That is, he was his own definition. But this definition of self is not mediated by reason. Not only was there no gap between natural men, but also no gap existed in their own being since they perceived themselves in the immediate (that is, each one perceived himself separately — Rousseau, I believe, never thought of natural man in the plural), or rather, natural man 'felt' himself in the immediate. He was 'l'homme du sentiment', hence Rousseau's emphasis on 'sentiment' to the detriment of reason. Natural man lived on the level of the senses and felt no division into matter and mind: he was an absolute whole — not a composite of various elements. Like the infant, or little Jean-Jacques at Bossey, natural man's universe took the dimensions of his own body: the world and self coincide. And this body–mind unit does not even need a language to assert itself; in its irreducible sensual being, it is its own definition.

Most crucial to this state of being is the compatibility between natural man and his environment which rules out any possibility of deprivation. The perfect equilibrium between desire and its compensation, needs and their satisfaction, makes for the absence of lack in the state of nature: everything is full, without gaps, everything continuous without change. Consciousness, Rousseau believes, can arise only at the point where a gap occurs between desire and its satisfaction, which is not the case of natural man. Though he is devoid of consciousness, natural man differs from the other beasts surrounding him: he is not a simple physical automaton. Unlike the other animals, he is free; but he shares with them both an instinct for self-preservation and a feeling of pity for the suffering. And most important, natural man possesses a potential for change, which Rousseau terms 'perfectibilité'. (Here we see the contradiction inherent in Rousseau's system between a theory of evolution and a notion of prehistory.)

However, how can one have a feeling of pity when one is totally separated from fellow humans? Rousseau posits the feeling of pity as active and not virtual in natural man. But if natural man is alone under his tree, he cannot have a feeling of pity for the Other: the Other is simply not there. And if natural man has a feeling of pity, perhaps he is not so natural. Here lies Rousseau's main difficulty: he introduces social elements in the natural order and natural elements in the social process, thus collapsing the distinction between the two. This points to the ideological presupposition which Rousseau shares with the social theorists of his time. The postulation of the order of nature imparts upon a historically contingent ideology the qualities of absoluteness and eternity. Natural man is eighteenth-century man disguised: they both partake in perfectibility and rationality. In effect, then, natural man is non-existent; he is eighteenth-century man (as conceived by bourgeois hegemony) cloaked in the coat of nature to provide him with defence mechanisms against change. (Nature, after all, cannot be tampered with, for natural values are eternal and given to man by birth.)

The question is, what brought about changes in this blessed non-historical state of being? Could it not have gone on for ever due to inertia? Man himself had no reason to alter this paradisiac life, and the shift from this stage to the next remains problematic. First, the primary stage involves some kind of external time in which people evolve, grow old and die. The introduction of decay to the system is nothing new. One might claim, though, that despite this external time, natural man lives internally in eternity. Secondly, what motivated people to come and stay together if they had no reason to do so? The fortuitous relationships could go on forever, with each man under his tree. The answer lies in the concept of perfectibility. Man's potential for change is dormant in the natural state, but external circumstances cause it to awaken. 'Le funeste hasard' takes hold of man's latent faculties and forces change upon them. From here on a gradual evolutionary process takes place.

> Tout commence à changer de face. Les hommes errant jusqu'ici dans les bois, ayant pris une assiette plus fixe, se rapprochent lentement, se réunissent en diverses troupes, et forment enfin dans chaque contrée une nation particulière, unie de mœurs et de caractères, non par des règlements et des lois, mais par le même genre de vie et d'aliments, et par l'influence commune du climat. (IN 209)

These small groups are family cells at first; due to climatic and natural disasters they swell to bigger groups that constitute, in Rousseau's scheme, the ideal society. But this society of the golden age contains the seeds of an irrevesible process of degeneration: agriculture and metallurgy are the sources of all social malaise. The making of tools and the beginnings of agriculture meant that man had lost that primordial equilibrium between his needs and their fulfilment. The cultivation of pieces of land required the acquisition of property which was unnecessary to natural man since food was abundant. The establishment of property, in turn, necessitated some rules of equity for the fighting over land had to be stopped and justice instituted.

Rousseau shares Descartes's ideological predilection for individual achievement over group effort. In the last chapter we pointed to Descartes's preference for the exclusion of the Other, who constitutes a hindrance in any professional task. Rousseau takes this position a step further: perdition is the outcome of collaboration; the minute the Other was needed to compensate for individual weakness, inequality set in.

> En un mot tant qu'ils ne s'appliquèrent à des ouvrages qu'un seul pouvait faire, et qu'à des arts qui n'avaient pas besoin du concours de plusieurs mains, ils vécurent libres . . . Mais dès l'instant qu'un homme eut besoin du secours d'un autre; dès qu'on s'aperçut qu'il était utile à un seul d'avoir des provisions pour deux, l'égalité disparut, la propriété

s'introduisit, le travail devint nécessaire. (IN 213)

As this passage indicates, the need for the help of the Other is followed by the need for one to have provisions for two. The second need (to hoard a double quantity and deprive the Other) does not follow logically from the first need (to make use of the Other's help), yet Rousseau cannot conceive of a group effort for the common good; he seems to think that the need for the Other's help means an infringement on one's territory and consequently a master–slave relationship. In Rousseau's system, the alternative to self-sufficiency is inequality. The social contract is conceived in terms of this same ideological presupposition: men associate in order for each individual to preserve his own territory.

At stake here is the concept of selfhood as denoted by these confessions and the autobiographical tradition as a whole. The *Social contract* bears a direct relationship to the *Confessions*; in effect, the social contract as a discursive production of the eighteenth century is the signified of the *Confessions*. Autobiography as a form is the signifier of the social text which is filtered through Rousseau's mythical beginnings and his conception of the contractual relationship between humans. In short, the reason why Rousseau conceives of himself as a unique individual is found in his social theory which proves to be consistent with his concept of selfhood.

With the gradual development of the second stage of the state of nature, man slowly becomes aware of his own consciousness and of the Other, not as a mere animal among others, but as a being endowed with a similar consciousness. The concepts of relationship and comparison are now established and with them the origins of inequality. Here Rousseau introduces the idea of competition which is based on 'perceptions de certains rapports' (IN 206); that is, artificial criteria are now instituted in order to differentiate between men. Natural equality could exist only in a world without comparison; with the introduction into the social body of principles of difference, civil inequality sets in — an inequality based on 'looks'.

Chacun commença à regarder les autres et à vouloir être regardé soi-même, et l'estime publique eut un prix. Celui qui chantait ou danser le mieux, le plus beau, le plus fort, le plus adroit ou le plus éloquent devint le plus considéré, et ce fut là le premier pas vers l'inégalité, et vers le vice en même temps:

de ces premières préférences naquirent d'un côté la vanité et
le mépris, de l'autre, le honte et l'envie. (IN 210)

'L'être et le paraître' which we have encountered in Rousseau's
early anecdotes are basic to the origins of social inequality.
Rousseau, then, presupposes that man 'is' something but due to
social circumstances he 'appears to be' something else. And since
society encourages appearances in its promotion of competitiveness, men started coveting appearances and left their true selves
hidden behind masks.[12] Again, Rousseau cannot conceive of a
social situation without competition; the minute the Other appears
he brings with him the destruction of my self because I must alter
my behaviour in order to be-for-him. If I am-for-the-Other, I
cannot be-for-myself. Freedom in the state of nature means therefore the total possession of self by self; I cannot belong totally to
myself, my ego cannot be my own centre, when the Other's look is
out there.

This point is crucial to the understanding of the social contract
as a discursive elaboration of the eighteenth century: the source of
inequality does not reside mainly in the material and quantitative
differences between you and me. Although the size of property and
material possessions constitute expressions of social inequality, its
main motivation is the simple existence of the Other out there
threatening my autonomy over myself; the road from myself to
myself has to pass by the Other, who brings with him all social
evils since reason itself develops together with comparativeness,
with the kind of relationship one can entertain with the Other.

The state of culture

Society has come and created civil man; it caused two major gaps
in the being of man. First, the gap within himself: since he has
perfected his reason, civil man must take a distance from himself,
must divide himself in order to perceive his self, not as an absolute
but as a cell in a social whole. So the creation of perspective
through reason has generated a split in the basically spatial self of
natural man. And secondly, there is now a gap between man and
man, with the necessity of appearances and masks in social life.

Telle est, en effet, la véritable cause de toutes ces différences:
le sauvage vit en lui-même; l'homme sociable toujours hors

de lui et ne fait que vivre dans l'opinion des autres, et c'est,
pour ainsi dire, de leur seul jugement qu'il tire le sentiment
de sa propre existence. (IN 234)

Thus the psychological and the economic go together in
Rousseau; the alienation one experiences in society has to do with
material deprivation. The inequality in objects translates into a
gap between minds; the physical barrier is also a psychological
one. Objects constitute a division between consciousnesses, as
though they blur the transparency of self to the Other. Rousseau,
however, does not follow this point through to its logical conclusion, which is that communication comes at the expense of
property, that collective ownership would be necessary to redress
the economic disparities.[13]

It is clear that beyond the detailed criticism of the societies of his
time (the French monarchy and the state of Geneva, in particular),
Rousseau is attempting a more basic criticism. To him, the social
is corrupt by definition. The very existence of the social, and not
merely the existence of a specific society, is here put into question.
The comparison is between the absolute man of nature and the
relative man of culture. Man, then, has lost both unity and
innocence. And Rousseau's purpose in confession is to remedy
these two lacks within being, to recapture his lost innocence and
unity. But though he can return to Bossey, to an individual paradisiac state, the return of man to earlier times ('les premiers
temps') cannot be achieved in time. If there were such beginnings
they would have to be extra-temporal, an immutable stage that
calls for no change, and in such a case the return would be impossible. There is no reason why natural man changed and 'fell' to
become social man; there can be no return because man cannot do
away with the historical steps he has already taken.

So where do we get at least an approximation of these hypothetical beginnings? If natural man never existed, we would have to
create him, or rather Rousseau must create him through fiction.
And if fiction and myth are resorted to, then natural man is given
to interpretation. But that fictional man of nature bears a dialectical relationship to historical man. So, at least, Rousseau believes
and exemplifies in his story. The problem that arises, however, is
whether this process of fictionalisation, this creation of a particular
myth, can precede history. For this would amount to the claim that
essence precedes existence. The very division of history into two
periods, one of which is hypothetical, points to the necessary

failure of Rousseau's venture. No doubt the ideological climate of his times prevented Rousseau from perceiving that any definition of man is an ongoing historical process and that myth itself is historically conditioned; in short, that the virtual is secondary and not primary.

'Le premier qui, ayant enclos un terrain, s'avisa de dire: Ceci est à moi, et trouva des gens assez simples pour le croire, fut le vrai fondateur de la société civile' (IN 205). To Rousseau, the formation of civil society rests on two acts of aggression that combine into one: the enclosure of a piece of land and the declaration of ownership over it. Property, at least in the *Discours*, is the source of all evil because it takes violence to assert one's autonomy over a piece of land which one wrests from one's fellow men in the state of nature, where everything is at the disposal of everyone. From this first 'declaration' on, the hoarding of property continues unabated and a total war ensues which has to be stopped by a social agreement for the preservation of the species. However, the first society that followed this state of war was inequitable since it was formed on the request of those who hoarded a lot of property to the detriment of their fellow men; the rich manipulate the masses to agree to their demands. Rousseau illustrates this manipulation through a monologue spoken by a rich man who lures his fellows with impressive language:

> En un mot, au lieu de tourner nos forces contre nous-mêmes, rassemblons en un pouvoir suprême qui nous gouverne selon de sages lois, qui protège et défende tous les membres de l'association, repousse les ennemis communs et nous maintienne dans une concorde éternelle . (IN 219)[14]

But the pact that followed this agreement was one of submission, not association; natural equality disappeared to make room for civil inequality and the subjugation of the weak by the strong. This, then, is the evolution of civil society down to modern times; despotism is the latest manifestation of this civil tradition, according to Rousseau. And the only way to redress the wrong is through the replacement — at least in theoretical conception, for Rousseau was aware of the gap between theory and practice — of the contract of submission by a contract of association.

Rousseau's view on property, as set forth in the *Discours*, is not his final word on the matter; in his other writings, he seems to have adopted the exact reversal of this position, in line with the general approach to property in eighteenth-century France. We recall that Emile's first lesson out in the world, after he has gained some awareness of external phenomena, is a lesson in property rights. In *Emile* Book II, the key scene is a conversation which takes place among Jean-Jacques, Emile and Robert, the owner of a plot; Emile cultivates the plot to his own taste before inquiring about ownership. Emile subsequently learns that ownership comes with labour, with the cultivation of the land which the stranger should not trespass once ownership has been thus claimed. 'La première idée qu'il faut lui donner est donc moins celle de la liberté que celle de la propriété' (E 89).

This is Rousseau's final position and it is consistent with the crucial role property plays in the *Social contract*.[15] We believe that the whole meaning of the social contract revolves around the concepts of property and ownership — both productions of the Neo-Classical discursive space. Freedom and equality — the other basic ingredients in Rousseau's social pact — are functional to ownership over land and over one's self. The social pact itself, the agreement by which a group of people comes together, has no meaning in a context where everyone comes into the group with no property at all or with equal amounts of property. And the most important point of the contract is the preservation of all the goods each member owns before he enters into the social order and his exercise of liberty over them. The need for an association is itself motivated by the need to keep to one's grounds; we would coin it 'the spreading of selfhood over property'. To have any meaning, the pact must sustain and reinforce all the fences that surround all properties for otherwise there would be no need for a pact since everyone would be entitled to roam freely without threatening the Other. The key word is 'trespassing', or infringing on what we term 'privacy'.

Rarefaction and expansion

Thus, in his process of socialisation man has denied nature; Rousseau's task is to negate what man has negated — a double negation. In opposition to social man, the man of nature did not have to conform to appearances, nor to wear a mask, because his existence was not mediated by another consciousness. But the man of nature still lives within social man. At the level of the individual, we can see how these two periods, or two men, coexist in social man and what kind of relationship they have, at least in Rousseau's case, which is, as he claims in his opening statement to the *Confessions*, 'une première pièce de comparaison pour l'étude des hommes'. This is the point at which autobiography coincides with history in Rousseau's world view. The delineation between the two men, between society and nature, can be achieved best in autobiography because it is the ideal case study. The total knowledge Rousseau has of his own self allows for the differentiation between the states and the rediscovery of that veiled innocence.

Critics have referred to a double movement in Rousseau. Poulet[16] terms it 'movement centrifuge et mouvement centripète'. Burgelin[17] defines it as 'condensation et détente'. Marcel Raymond speaks of 'discontinuité et reconnaissance',[18] while Munteano labels it 'moi-permanent, moi-agent'.[19] All these terms refer to the same reality in Rousseau: on the one hand, the desire to immerse himself in the thickness of the social texture — a tendency to expansion; and on the other hand, the tendency to run away from it all and face himself in solitude — a phenomenon of rarefaction.

This phenomenon of shrinkage has to do with a specific conception of space; that is, one minimises to the limit any kind of desirable object, otherwise it would mean expansion (the coincidence of Narcissus with his self). That minimal space that the self requires in order to stay within its own natural boundaries is the property within which one can move and at the same time meet one's own self to the exclusion of any external stimulation (Descartes's 'poêle' again).

L'idéal du bonheur comme resserrement n'exprime pas seulement un rêve de repos et d'abstention. Il tend surtout à l'unité. Il voudrait abolir toute forme de division: entre l'âme et le monde, entre le moi et les objets, entre le vouloir et le pouvoir. Le drame de l'homme est de se projeter dans une sphère plus étendue que l'étroite zone réservée pour la Nature: l'accomplissement de son moi.[20]

The abolition of the gap between 'vouloir' and 'pouvoir' indicates Rousseau's predilection for non-action; this centripetal movement coincides with the annihilation of desire, with pure stasis, which is Rousseau's main aspiration. In his *Rêveries* he acknowledges the nature of his weakness: 'je m'abstiens d'agir; car toute ma faiblesse est pour l'action, toute ma force est négative, et tous mes péchés sont d'omission, rarement de commission.[21]

Rousseau, however, seems to jump repeatedly from shrinkage to expansion. (In Munteano's words, Rousseau 'oscillates' from one pole to the other like a pendulum.) The one movement takes the form of presence, the other of absence. We also have mixed phenomena where Rousseau experiences presence in terms of absence and absence in terms of presence. In the end, though, the balance seems to tilt in favour of absence in Rousseau's world, for his madness is an extreme form of absence.

From early childhood Jean-Jacques develops the concept of the double; his first experience of the mask comes, not surprisingly, with his exposure to the world of fiction. His father initiates him to books as a child, and in his readings, his self undergoes a gradual change; he becomes someone else, 'je devenais le personnage dont je lisais la vie' (C 9). Later on Rousseau will adopt a model, Venture de Villeneuve, a vagabond friend of his; though ignorant of music, he becomes Vaussore de Villeneuve, a music teacher.

> Me voilà maître à chanter sans savoir déchiffrer un air . . . parisien de Genève, et catholique en pays protestant, je crus devoir changer de nom ainsi que ma religion et ma patrie. Je m'approchai toujours de mon grand modèle autant qu'il m'était possible. (C 164)

On another occasion, he creates his own model and conforms to it: 'Je ne sais par quelle bizarrerie je m'avisai de passer pour Anglais, je me donnais pour Jacobite, on me prit pour tel; je m'appelai Dudding, et l'on m'appela M. Dudding' (C 288). The creation and adoption of the Dudding persona occur while Rousseau is experiencing the most intense love affair with Mme de Larnage; at the same time he is playing the 'malade imaginaire', having decided that he has a heart disease which necessitates an extended cure. The minute Rousseau decides about his 'polype au cœur' nothing on earth can convince him of the contrary; he immediately undertakes a trip to find a cure. In short, Rousseau believes in the models he creates; it takes a long time and many cures to free him of his conviction. A significant statement to this effect is repeated by Rousseau: 'Je crois avoir déjà remarqué qu'il y a des temps où je suis si peu semblable à moi-même qu'on me prendrait pour un autre homme de caractère tout à fait opposé' (C 142).

Role-playing can sometimes become an obsession. When Jean-Jacques decides to become a reader, he cannot stop reading; the activity occupies him to the exclusion of all other occupations. And so it is with chess playing. A momentary whim turns into a manic *idée fixe*. He cannot stop playing chess and the act overtakes all his faculties as long as it lasts. This means that Rousseau wants to extend the whim into a durable present, or a succession of presents that lose none of their intensity. The whim does not fade away, it goes as it comes, in a minute. It disappears in forgetfulness. While it lasts, then, the persona occupies him totally. This phenomenon reflects the lack of consistency in Rousseau's personality, a lack he confesses to and in fact welcomes. Role-playing calls upon the acting self, but all these actions are non-committing since they vanish in no time.

> J'aime à m'occuper à faire des riens, à commencer cent choses et n'en achever aucune, à aller et venir comme la tête me chante, à changer à chaque instant de projet, à suivre une mouche dans toutes ses allures, à vouloir déraciner un rocher pour voir ce qui est dessous, et à l'abandonner sans regret au bout de dix minutes, à muser enfin toute la journée sans ordre et sans suite et à ne suivre en toute chose que le caprice du moment. (C 762)

It is clear from this passage that every object Jean-Jacques turns to occupies him for an intense present; the action itself does not move in time, does not anticipate the future but negates it. This expansive self can collapse the work of ten years into ten minutes, for in those ten minutes Rousseau deeply believes that he is undertaking a ten-year project. In other words, Rousseau refuses temporal mediation to his objects; he becomes a god in a universe without duration. And the transition from one object to the next comes about as an act of magic, as if there were no continuity from one object to the other. This is, then, the expansive self of Jean-Jacques, the self that allows him a social link.[22] Before analysing further these relational acts, let us deal with the other pole of his personality, his solitary self, the self of rarefaction and permanence.

Where does Rousseau get his stability? In what way does he perceive his past and present selves as one and the same? Permanence comes with memory, but this memory is not chronological although it seeks its objects in a past time. 'La mémoire affective', in fact, negates chronology; it aspires to superimpose the present over the past. To Rousseau, remembering Bossey means precisely being in Bossey, in the present and *in toto*. Little Jean-Jacques and the Rousseau of sixty are one and the same in this experience. The recollection of things past in Rousseau is not temporal but spatial, an image that remains 'there', in his imagination, unchanged. But the consistency of such an image depends on solitude, a detachment from the world, and a penetration of nature where the gaze wanders aimlessly. Marcel Raymond refers to Rousseau's reveries as daydreams without specific objects — deliric hallucinations. In nature too, 'recueillement' is possible since the Other's look — which he hates and craves — is not directed at Jean-Jacques. The possession of self comes at the expense of a social exchange. 'C'est à la campagne qu'on apprend à aimer et servir l'humanité, on n'apprend qu'à la mépriser dans les villes' (C 542). Rousseau feels the need for such periods of solitude, his life seems to have been divided between the city and the countryside. His predilection is for nature, and his one aspiration is to move to nature, especially after his reformation. But the city seems to follow him everywhere.

The conviction that there is a centre relating all phenomena in the self motivated Rousseau to provide the reader with all the data necessary to apprehend such a centre. The consistency and unity of the self must be dug out from the rubble of phenomena it experiences; thus all details are relevant, for the more experiences the reader witnesses, the more able he will be to recreate that centre. Similar to 'les premiers temps', self is an irreducible presence that must be unveiled. Although one jumps from object to object, one stays the same; that is, one brings the self to the object; it is not the object that shapes the self, according to Rousseau. 'Je me crois assez observateur: cependant je ne sais rien voir de ce que je vois; je vois bien ce que je me rappelle, et je n'ai de l'esprit que dans mes souvenirs' (C 127). The object is not what Rousseau is facing now but what he faced before; the *déjà-vu* is primary in Rousseau and means stability. Human nature is stable; it remains hidden under the layers of lies and masks which are external to it and force change upon it. Hence the need to postulate one's uniqueness on the first page; the credo comes first, before the proof, for in the process of description Rousseau seems to be aware of a loss of sameness for the benefit of difference.

Je m'applique à bien développer partout les premières causes pour faire sentir l'enchaînement des effets. Je voudrais pouvoir en quelque façon rendre mon âme transparente aux yeux du lecteur, et pour cela je cherche à lui montrer sous tous les points de vue, à l'éclairer par tous les jours, à faire en sorte qu'il ne s'y fasse pas un mouvement qu'il n'aperçoive, afin qu'il puisse juger par lui-même du principe qui les produit. (C 198)

The critic Jean Starobinski builds his thesis on Rousseau's dialectics of the light and the dark, 'la transparence et l'obstacle'. The above passage illustrates this dichotomy in terms of a metaphysical mode of thinking. Key words here are 'causes', 'effet', 'principe' — all metaphysical concepts transposed into the human sphere. Self is a clear-cut entity that can be apprehended easily if one is given the proper light. The reader is supposed to synthesise all the pieces of information and arrive at a basic and simple truth (much like the clear and distinct Cartesian idea). The reader will be the judge of the first principle generating all the effects from the causes. (Rousseau is always facing a court, but his hope is in the court of the future since his contemporaries have found him guilty.) Hence the accumulation of details. Rousseau does not realise, however, that no accumulation of biographical data can possibly exhaust the complex reality of life and that, contrary to his wish, the reader will at best be able to reach an approximation of Jean-Jacques. Also he seems not to have considered that a multiplicity of detail entails multiple selves and not unity, and that details are given to interpretation.

In the *Rêveries*, Rousseau is aware of the problem of veracity, that is, of the irrelevance of factual data to truth. With regard to his confessions, he says:

Je les écrivais de mémoire; cette mémoire me manquait souvent ou ne me fournissait que des souvenirs imparfaits et j'en remplissais les lacunes par des détails que j'imaginais en supplément de ces souvenirs, mais qui ne leur étaient jamais contraires. J'aimais à m'étendre sur les moments heureux de ma vie, et je les embellissais quelquefois des ornements que de tendres regrets venaient me fournir. Je disais les choses que j'avais oubliées comme il me semblait qu'elles avaient dû être, comme elles avaient été peut-être en effet, jamais au contraire de ce que je me rappelais qu'elles avaient été. Je prêtais quelquefois à la vérité des charmes étrangers, mais jamais je n'ai mis le mensonge à la place pour pallier mes vices, ou pour m'arroger des vertus. (R 55)[23]

Let us now deal with phenomena that combine both rarefaction and expansion. We have referred to the silence Rousseau encounters after the final reading of his confessions; an internal inhibition seems to counterbalance this exterior silence. Critics have emphasised Rousseau's physical ailments and particularly the urinary problems which made him shun society. In this connection, two small but very symbolic physiological details must be noted: Rousseau is both short-sighted and hard of hearing. In other words, he can see best what is closest to him and hear best his own noise.

Un grand bruit d'oreilles . . . et ce bruit était triple ou plutôt quadruple . . . Ce bruit interne était si grand, qu'il m'ôtat la finesse d'ouie que j'avais auparavant, et me rendit non tout à fait sourd mais dur d'oreille. (C 262)

Rousseau hears a continual 'bourdonnement', and internal noise that hardly leaves room for an external message. Interestingly enough, this internal noise forces him to stay up at night and write his books. The inner noise hampers any communicative dispatch that comes from the outside. The internal noise, as it were, conditions the external silence that he meets at Mme d'Egmont's.

Now what are the actions Jean-Jacques undertakes in the world? His worldly acts illustrate in many ways the problematic of mediation which, we believe, is central to Rousseau. After the episode of the comb, Jean-Jacques discover theft and becomes a kleptomaniac. But he is never tempted by money, because money stands between the subject and the object. The mediating effect minimises the power of immediate possession that one can have in the theft of an object (C 41). However, indulging in theft entails punishment. Indeed the purpose of the theft is not the object only, but the punishment that follows as well, for crime and punishment go together. Jean-Jacques enjoyed the beatings administered by Mlle Lambercier at Bossey, and actually encouraged them because they satisfied some childish eroticism in him. This first encounter with the Other seems to be repeated throughout Rousseau's life. Mlle Lambercier can be replaced by Jean-Jacques's critics and contemporaries, those who persecute him. The sado-masochistic form of the relationship is common to both experiences; in both cases, Rousseau asks for the punishment. The *Confessions* constitutes an apology; Rousseau is asking for forgiveness, if not from his contemporaries, at least from the future reader. 'Je jugeais que me battre comme frippon, c'était m'autoriser à l'être. Je trouvais que voler et être battu allaient ensemble' (C 37). Being defined as a criminal by the Other gives one the right to be one.

At the beginning of Book III, Rousseau describes the agitation caused by sexual deprivation, but instead of finding an object to remedy the erotic lack, he resorts to exhibitionism. The exhibitionist exposes his nudity in dark alleys but close enough to be seen by the other sex. On the face of it, this seems to be a transitive act, since the exhibitionist challenges the look of the Other. But, as Starobinski suggests:

L'exhibitionisme représente la limite extrême d'une action qui se porte vers le dehors sans néanmoins consentir à s'engager aggressivement parmi les obstacles du monde extérieur. Il s'agit bien d'atteindre les autres, mais sans se quitter soi-même, en se contentant d'être soi et de se montrer tel qu'on est.[24]

Such an act stands for the expression of a minimal presence to the world; it remains intransitive because it does not reach out. Rousseau wants to be seen on his own terms, not on the terms of the Other.

Rousseau's love affairs are significant in respect to their mediating factor. We find that love, the epitome of communication, of reaching out, is intransitive in Rousseau's case.[25] Jean-Jacques never concludes his love, and rarely consummates it. He can take pages to describe a look or a kiss, and drive as much pleasure from them as anyone who takes them as starting points (C 154). 'Je ne suis pas heureux dans la conclusion de mes amours' (C 104). Why? Possession means total presence to the Other, and this is in opposition to Rousseau's mode of loving: in order to love, Jean-Jacques must be absent.

Je me souviens qu'une foise Mme de Luxembourg me parlait en raillant d'un homme qui quittait sa maîtresse pour lui écrire. Je lui dis que j'aurais bien été cet homme là, et j'aurais pu ajouter que je l'avais été quelquefois. (C 207)

In absence, Rousseau creates a love that meets his heart's desire without being challenged by the Other. Other instances of Rousseau's refusal of mediation are seen in his being an auto-didact — negating the teacher; submitting his five (or seven) children to Les Enfants Trouvés — refusing parenthood; and rejecting a pension offered by the king. Neither the teacher, his children, nor the king can define Rousseau.

Rousseau's story is marked by numerous trips. Travel is a major activity, not only towards the end of the book when Rousseau is apparently forced to run for his life, but right from the start when he leaves Geneva. The trips he enjoys most are the ones he takes on foot. In fact an ambulatory mania seems to have a hold on most of his faculties: he cannot think without walking, and most daydreams come with wandering. 'Je ne peux méditer qu'en marchant; sitôt que je m'arrête je ne pense plus, et ma tête ne va qu'avec mes pieds' (C 486). (Starobinski claims that Rousseau's walking involves a process of self-hypnosis.) The main characteristic of such wandering is its aimlessness; one goes everywhere and in all directions. It is also an action that forgets time: one does not wander for an hour. Both daydreaming and wandering are occupations with no end, devoid of moorings in reality. 'Chose extrêmement remarquable, Rousseau arrive à se tenir sur le seuil, à la limite idéale de l'existence et du néant.[26] B. Munteano has also noted Rousseau's aspiration to non-being. One important anecdote from the *Rêveries* further supports this thesis; on one of his promenades, Jean-Jacques is knocked over by a dog and suffers a head injury. Subsequently,

> Je naissais dans cet instant à la vie, et il me semblait que je remplissais de ma légère existence tous les objets que j'apercevais. Tout entier au moment présent je ne me souvenais de rien; je n'avais nulle notion distincte de mon individu, pas la moindre idée de ce qui venait de m'arriver; je ne savais ni qui j'étais ni où j'étais. (R 17)

This amnesia brings an erasure of the temporal process (he even forgets his name); the vacuity and absence within the self coincide with the spreading of self over all perceived external objects. Munteano points to pantheistic elements in Rousseau which at the same time indicate both the dissolution of presence and the recapture of selfhood through expansion. However, Rousseau's pantheism is different: he is not part of the whole; rather, the whole is part of him. That is, the cosmos takes the size of his self.[27]

Rousseau, then, must be absent in order to be present. But the absence is not the distance the artist takes from his object to achieve perspective. The absence to the object is total; perspective entails a divided consciousness which would not benefit Rousseau's quest to possess the immediate through sense perception. 'Si je veux peindre le printemps, il faut que je sois en hiver; si je veux décrire un beau paysage, il faut que je sois dans des murs; et j'ai dit cent fois que si j'étais mis à la Bastille, j'y ferais le tableau de la liberté' (C 154). So closeness to the object is attained by wiping it out and recreating it anew though the process of fiction. Fiction seems to be the only mediator between Rousseau and the world. This equation becomes alarming when we realise that, in Rousseau's case, the ontological gap between fiction and the world is trespassed to the point of madness.

How does Rousseau live the greatest love of his life? Neither he nor Sophie d'Houdetot are present in this relationship, because Rousseau defined her long before he met her.

> Elle vint; je la vis; j'étais ivre d'amour sans objet; cette ivresse fascina mes yeux, cet objet se fixa sur elle; je vis ma Julie en Mme d'Houdetot, et bientôt je ne vis plus que Mme d'Houdetot, mais revêtue de toutes les perfections dont je venais d'orner l'idole de mon cœur. (C 521)

First, there is an objectless desire; then he meets Sophie, but he meets her in terms of Julie, the heroine of his *La Nouvelle Héloise* — the fictional fulfilment of his real desire.

Writing and hiding

Les Confessions is, in fact, the gradual development of a transposition of reality into fiction. As mentioned above, Jean-Jacques penetrates the world of books at a tender age, and identifies with his heroes. Over the years this identification becomes internal, through the creation of his own fictional universe. Towards the end Rousseau cannot cope at all with the Other who becomes a pure anonymity, an omnimous hand lurking in the shadows. The Other remains transfigured through the process of fiction. But sometimes, in moments of lucidity, Rousseau catches himself at his own game: 'après avoir eu peur des Jésuites, j'eus peur des Jansénistes et des Philosophes' (C 672). He is sometimes aware of his exaggeration in the portrayal of the Other. Diderot, Grimm, D'Holbach seem to spread their wings not only over the people Rousseau comes in contact with, but over all the spaces he lives in. The old friends become despicable enemies: they lose their names and identities; hence the plot that is being woven quietly in the dark.

There has to be some tension between shrinkage and expansion, between self-possession and social relation, but the permanent self takes meaning within the social context, to the extent that the subject assimilates the Other. Otherwise, the Other loses existence and must be created *ex nihilo* as a composite entity — all the enemies group into the One, an entity which in Rousseau's case, threatens the very existence of the subject.

This alienation is generated by one major act, the only mediation for Rousseau, the act of fiction. Again, *Les Confessions* is the most comprehensive portrayal of this act. Although Rousseau's literary career is relatively short, its preparation and aftermath seem to take the parameters of his life. Writing has a beginning in childhood, but it seems to have no end, since writing is not an activity Rousseau undertakes at the table facing a blank sheet; he writes 'in his brain'. 'C'est à la promenade, au milieu des rochers et des bois, c'est la nuit durant mes insomnies, que j'écris dans mon cerveau; l'on peut juger avec quelle lenteur, surtout pour un homme dépourvu de mémoire verbale' (C 126).

It is the act of fiction which gives rise to the insoluble paradox in Rousseau's life: the expression of negation through a positive act, saying 'no' to the world through the book which is pure affirmation, writing for public consumption while one craves absence, which in itself is a curse since assertion becomes functional to negation. Rousseau gives a tragic qualification to his vocation: he 'fell into it' unawares. One day in the summer of 1749, while reading the *Mercure de France*, 'Je tombai sur cette question proposée par l'Académie de Dijon pour le prix de l'année suivante: Si le progrès des sciences et des arts a contribué à corrompre ou à épurer les mœurs' (C 415). Rousseau wrote an essay, entered the competition and won the prize. A few lines further down, he says: 'Je le fis, et dès cet instant je fus perdu. Tout le reste de ma vie et de mes malheurs fut l'effet inévitable de cet instant d'égarement' (C 417). Rousseau imputes all his misery to his assumption of the act of writing.

J'aimerais la société comme un autre, si je n'étais sûr de m'y

montrer non seulement à mon désavantage, mais tout autre
que je ne suis. Le parti que j'ai pris d'écrire et de me cacher
est précisément celui qui me convenait. Moi présent, on
n'aurait jamais su ce que je valais. (C 119)

To write and to hide: two acts that combine to make Rousseau
what he is, the only acts that define him.[28] One should say 'to-
write-and-to-hide', for indeed these two verbs are not consecutive:
they are simultaneous, constituting one integrated act. To be
present involves not only a disadvantage (we recall that Rousseau
is awkward in society, cannot talk properly, looks stupid — 'sot' is
his term, is never taken seriously and fails all tests requiring a performance) but a disfigurement as well, a metamorphosis of one's
features, a total alienation.

But the discourse itself is problematic, for Rousseau holds the
conviction that the immediate is speechless. In the immediate, the
sign does not stand for the object but rather, the sign is inscribed in
the body of the object; sign and object are one. In the immediate
one can never be out of place, look awkward, or be at a disadvantage. Speech is replaced by a non-verbal sign language.
Rousseau would have liked to be mute, to point to things rather
than speak them. Repeatedly he indicates the limits of language
and its inability to express meaning. We know of Rousseau's
aversion to social verbiage; 'babiller' is a damaging occupation
(C 232). Further, 'le vrai bonheur ne se décrit pas, il se sent, et se
sent d'autant mieux qu'il peut le moins se décrire' (C 271). Only
the body can express meaning: meaning is literally squeezed out of
the body through its immediate presence. A magnetic force causes
the attraction of subject to object and vice versa. This is the level at
which the body becomes text — hence exhibitionism. Or writing.
Exhibitionism and writing are identical: to-write-and-to-hide constitutes an act of exhibitionism that calls for silence. The parade of
one's words coincides with the parade of one's body.

How can one communicate in a language that erects walls, a
language of divisions?[29] But perhaps one can avoid the alienating
word — lay down the pen and resort to an immediate mode of
communication. Maybe one can carry a message through the
language of the body! It is not without reason that Jean-Jacques
starts his reform with his outside appearance. In discarding his
watch and sword he performs two magical acts: he negates time,
because in the immediate time is of no consequence, and he rejects
his social status. The Armenian robe completes the a, b, c of his

body language. Rousseau declares over and over that he was persecuted less for his literary fame than for his personal reform. But he seems to ask for it. For the change of clothes, the negation of the external definition, the postulation of difference, is achieved with pomp. He wants to retire to the woods but he makes enough noise for everyone to notice it. He plays the game of hide and seek.

In consequence, Rousseau is a double loser. Not only is he unable to communicate through his body, through the virtues he seeks in the act of reform, but the choice to retire is taken away from him: retirement is forced on him through persecution. Wandering turns into running, to the point where Jean-Jacques asks for imprisonment in Ile Sainte Hélène; 'j'osai désirer et proposer qu'on voulût plutôt disposer de moi dans une captivité perpétuelle, que de me faire errer incessament sur la terre, en m'expulsant successivement de tous les asiles que j'aurais choisis' (C 769). The attack on his world coincides with the physical attack on his body.

The persecution Rousseau asks for is, to Starobinski, the panacea for all his troubles. For being persecuted, disfigured, alienated in voice and body, encourages one to seek inaction. 'Circonvenu de toutes parts, il n'est plus le maître de l'espace où son action aurait pu se déployer.'[30] By altering his words and feelings, by making him other than he is, the persecutors force him to enter the immediate. But since no kind of regression is possible in history, and since Rousseau of necessity was anchored in reality, the immediate becomes the realm of impotence and masturbation. For the only thing Rousseau can do is look at himself. (His first work is *L'Amant de lui-même*; 'Je me suis amusé à voir tomber mes larmes dans l'eau' (C 169).) The domain of action is restricted to fiction, not fiction as a mediation of the real world, but fiction as an end in itself. Deliric verbiage replaces social small talk. 'Dès lors j'étais seul; car il n'y eut jamais pour moi d'intermédiaire entre tout et rien' (C 388). Fiction assumes the role of the mediator 'entre tout et rien'. This is the only compromise Rousseau is able to afford, but at what price!

L'impossibilité d'atteindre aux êtres réels me jeta dans le pays des chimères, et ne voyant rien d'existant qui fut digne de mon délire, je le nourris dans un monde idéal, que mon imagination créatrice eut bientôt peuplé d'êtres selon mon cœur . . . Oubliant tout à fait la race humaine, je me fis des sociétés de créatures parfaites, aussi célestes par leurs vertus que par leurs beautés, d'amis sûrs, tendres, fidèles, tels que je n'en trouvais jamais ici bas. (C 506)

The logic of seriality

To reconcile the antagonism within man between the natural and the civil, Rousseau proposes a re-evaluation of the social whole and the refounding of society upon the tenets of nature. The practicality of such a venture is hopelessly limited for no society would agree to change its status for an unfamiliar structure. But despite the theoretical nature of his contract, Rousseau had in mind the possibility of such a realisation; otherwise he would not have attempted to draw up constitutions for Poland and Corsica. Even if one doubts the possible application of his social theory, one must consider his statements at face value and look for the coherence of the system as well as the ideology which generates it.

In the *Social contract*[31] Rousseau departs from the view of the social that he advanced in his *Discours*; he believes that one can find a form of association in which the fusion of natural freedom and civil obedience is non-contradictory. Indeed he attacks Hobbes so forcefully in the *Contract* because Hobbes[32] put the emphasis on the natural state of warfare to which the pact must put an end; in submitting themselves to a powerful authority by the contract of submission, men safeguard their lives and property. Hobbes's absolute monarch constitutes a kind of referee with an iron fist. Rousseau, on the other hand, denies the natural corruption of man as well as the natural state of war. 'The war of all against all' makes no sense to Rousseau, since in the state of nature man is free; he has no inclination to compete given that in his dispersion and isolation he has no contact with the Other.

The idea of struggle in Hobbes is fruitful but not in its ethico-metaphysical context; Hobbes seems to think that there is an innate evil in man, for the war of all against all connotes the existence of a predetermined moral essence in man before he appears on the social scene. In any case Hobbes is more of a realist than Rousseau and a correct reader of social phenomena. Struggle as a positive concept is inherent in the social object; in order for the body politic to achieve its ongoing realisation it must do it within the context of a moving contradiction. Contradiction is inherent to the structure of the social body itself; the movement in the dialectic from one stage to the next hypostatises this conception of the social dynamics.

If Rousseau negates Hobbes's postulate of natural war, he must find a reason for the social pact. The social pact is conceived to counteract civil inequality and to devise a means to recover man's lost natural freedom.[33]

> Trouver une forme d'association qui défende et protège de toute la force commune la personne et les biens de chaque associé, et par laquelle chacun s'unissant à tous n'obéisse qu'à lui-même et reste aussi libre qu'auparavant. (CS 360)

> Chacun se donnant à tous ne se donne à personne, et comme il n'y a pas un associé sur lequel on n'acquiert le même droit qu'on lui cède sur soi, on gagne l'équivalent de tout ce qu'on perd, et plus de force pour conserver ce qu'on a. (SC 361)

This formula rests on a cold calculation; in giving oneself and one's property to the social whole, one in effect loses nothing because one gains on the Other the rights he loses through the act of association. Rousseau assumes that his basic act itself is indicative of man's maturity, his willingness to do away with natural rights and to opt for an artificial order based on the tenets of reason. With evolution (one of the basic concepts of modernistic discourse consolidated in France mostly in the eighteenth century) man has developed to the stage where he can encounter and accept the Other of his own free will and be accepted in return. And in creating an order of exchange with his fellow men, civil man in no way subjects himself to them, for that primordial act of association is voluntary and intentional. The total dependence of man on the state guarantees his independence from his fellow man. Rousseau's notion of freedom in submission is that, in partaking in the body politic, man adopts a new identity which asserts his initial act of participation and an ongoing free renewal of that primary act as long as the social body exists. The body politic is sovereign, one and indivisible, and expresses itself through the General Will. Rousseau differentiates clearly between the General Will and the will of all, that is, the sum total of all wills within the body politic. The General Will deals with the shared common interests of the whole whereas the will of all deals with the sum total of private interests.

> Chacun de nous met en commun sa personne et toute sa puissance sous la suprême direction de la volonté générale; et nous

recevons en corps chaque membre comme partie individuelle du tout. (SC 361)

The second part of this statement emphasises the qualitative difference of this contract from any other contract between two individuals. The social contract is not between every individual and every other individual — that would be merely a series of contracts without a binding element connecting all the contracting parties; the contract is between every member and the totality of the group. The body politic as a whole is taken as a party to the contract as if it were one person. This points to Rousseau's assumption that all civil identities cohere into one entity.[34]

This illustrates what Rousseau claims to be the collective nature of the social body, so that the General Will 'is' or 'is not'; it is inalienable; it cannot be divided for then we would fall back on a pact of submission and not one of association: certain elements of the body would be subjected to others because private interests never coincide. To Rousseau, everyone wants what everyone else wants; a moral imperative drives the collective body to seek its own welfare.[35]

However, sometimes the general welfare is not fully understood by the collective body and the latter, according to Rousseau, might need some assistance in meeting its moral imperative. And when the social body is not fully aware of its intended goals due to collective ignorance or failure, it must appoint a Legislator, an enlightened man with the qualifications of a god because, although his will is private, in its perfect knowledge of the ethical directives of the body politic it coincides with the General Will. Rousseau will be criticised for this notion of the Legislator which clearly opens the door to totalitarianism.

'Ce qui généralise la volenté est moins le nombre des voix que l'intérêt commun qui les unit' (SC 374). Sovereignty is inalienable by definition, for when it disappears, the body politic as a whole disappears as well: if a people gives up its political authority it ceases to be a people. It is clear that there is nothing quantitative in the notion of sovereignty, nor is the General Will some kind of synthesis of the sum total of particular wills. The General Will coincides with each particular's membership in the social body. We have here a double identity: first, every man is seen as an individual subject and this identity is quantitative; second, we have the will of every citizen as member of the sovereign, that is, as embodying the General Will. Every one in his membership in the collectivity coincides with the sovereign.[36] Although sovereignty is indivisible in principle, it is divisible as to its objects. Here Rousseau separates the executive from the legislative: no one can legislate but the body politic as a whole. Rousseau advocated direct participation over representation because the law is the purest expression of the General Will; hence his predilection for small states where direct participation can be realised. But the sovereign can appoint an executive body which will constitute a mere intermediary between individuals and itself, that is, between the subjects as private men and the subjects as the collective members of the sovereign (SC 396). In short, the institution of government is not a contract — there is only one contract, that of association — but a law of the social body.

Despite the theoretical and absolute nature of the *Social contract*, Rousseau believes that three kinds of political system are viable: democracy, aristocracy and monarchy. And these forms of government depend, among other things, upon natural causes and climate. Forms of government are therefore relative and the same one does not suit all peoples. One cannot doubt Rousseau's bias for democracy; he cannot be accused of supporting an absolute monarchy. 'Pour être légitime, il ne faut pas que le gouvernement se confonde avec le souverain, mais qu'il en soit le ministre; alors la monarchie elle-même est république' (SC 414).

Rousseau's social theory constitutes a big step forward over any theory of submission. His grouping of political authority in the people themselves and his conception of equality among them deal a blow to the theory of authority by divine right which prevailed within the medieval discursive space. The *Social contract* can provide a stepping-stone to an ideal and equitable society; indeed the bulk of the critical material on Rousseau sees him as the father of the modern democratic state, the reformer of society, the man of reason and order, and sometimes, even, the instigator of the French Revolution. This dominant trend in the critical tradition counteracts another trend which finds in Rousseau's notion of the General Will and his concept of the Legislator, as maker of constitutions, the basic ingredients for the totalitarian state.[37] John W. Chapman analyses both sides of the coin and sees the possibility of a dual interpretation: 'Emphasis on his concern for moral creativity makes Rousseau a liberal. If his willingness to impose order and value on human life is brought to the fore, he becomes a totalitarian.'[38] Rousseau's own famous phrase 'on le forcera d'être libre' accentuates the totalitarian aspects of his theory; freedom, he claims, can be forced upon any private will which is not in harmony with the General Will. The dominant rationalist-liberal critical tradition — which is at the centre of the discourse of modernism together with the production of self-hood — is best exemplified by the works of Cassirer and Derathé on Rousseau. According to Cassirer, the *Social contract* proposes the absolute unity of the social body: in alienating their individual wills to the absolute power of the General Will, men join in a collective endeavour based on their autonomy and ethical reasoning. The state comprehends all its members and merges them into an indissoluble unity.

> To him freedom did not mean arbitrariness but the overcoming and elimination of all arbitrariness, the submission to a strict and inviolable law which the individual erects over himself. The state claims the individual completely and without reservations. However, in doing so, it does not act as a coercive institution but only puts the individual under an obligation which he himself recognizes as valid and necessary, and to which he therefore assents for its sake as well as for his own . . . It is not a question of emancipating and liberating the individual in the sense of releasing him from the form and order of the community; it is, rather, a question of finding the kind of community that will protect every individual with the whole concerted power of the political organization, so that the individual in uniting himself with all others nevertheless obeys only himself in this act of union.[39]

Cassirer argues that Rousseau postulates integration in nullifying the contradiction between law and freedom; far from cancelling one another, in effect, law guarantees freedom, for without law freedom would disappear and chaos would prevail. Again,

> Law in its pure and strict sense is not a mere external bond that holds in individual wills and prevents their scattering; rather, it is the constituent principle of these wills, the element that confirms them spiritually. It wishes to rule subjects only inasmuch as, in its every act, it also makes and educates them into citizens.[40]

Law, then, is part of the constitutive structure of the individual and therefore cannot be opposed to will; a harmony prevails between man's spiritual demands for order and his aspiration to freedom. It is clear that Cassirer is talking about law in the absolute and not about law as historical contingency. He also presupposes that what he terms freedom and order are in man before he is social; civil society, as it were, synthesises these two existing tendencies in man. This indicates Cassirer's bias and his own contribution to the tradition of the Enlightenment.

Derathé follows a similar line of argument: both reason and sociability are potential drives in man that develop with the termination of the natural state of isolation. In *Le Rationalisme de Jean-Jacques Rousseau*, Derathé gives an overview of the polemic surrounding Rousseau's rationality or lack thereof,[41] which constitutes a preparation for his approach to Rousseau's political theory. It seems to us that the argument over Rousseau's rationality or irrationality is of little importance given that Rousseau himself was never consistent: he tilted back and forth from feeling to reason and vice versa. Certainly, the first *Discours* is a strong condemnation of reason. Nevertheless, Derathé's analysis is interesting in that it lays out Rousseau's division of the age of reason into three phases: (a) the prerational which is limited to the passive recording of scattered sensations without connecting between them; (b) sensitive reason, which means the conception of simple ideas which compare between sensations; and (c) intellectual reason, or the generation of complex ideas on the basis of simple ones. Emile's education exemplifies movement from one stage to the next. This, then, places Rousseau in the Empiricist tradition: he conceives of reason in sensual terms, since even the final stage of intellectual reason is based on the previous stage which is sensitive reason.[42]

While Derathé tends toward a compromise between the two realms (not followed through in his second book on Rousseau's political theory):

Il n'y a point chez Rousseau, nous voulons dire chez Rousseau penseur, de primat de la sensibilité. Ce qu'il a toujours affirmé, c'est le primat de la vie morale sur la vie purement spéculative, mais il a cru trouver la solution du problème moral dans une sorte d'équilibre entre la raison et le sentiment, plutôt que dans le règne exclusif de l'instinct.[43]

Cassirer, on the other hand, rejects the irrationalist thesis altogether: 'this supposed irrationalist ended up with the most belief in reason. For Rousseau, the belief in the victory of reason coincided with his belief in the victory of the genuine "cosmopolitan constitution" '.[44]

> La raison et la sociabilité qui sont les deux principales de ces virtualités ne pourront se manifester qu'au moment où l'homme sortira de l'isolement de l'état de nature, et elles se développeront solidairement. Car la sociabilité ne pourra devenir un principe effectif de la conduite humaine, que lorsque les 'facultés virtuelles' de l'homme, l'imagination et la raison, entreront en action.[45]

> La sociabilité, selon Rousseau, est un sentiment inné, tout comme la raison est une faculté innée, mais en puissance.[46]

In order to achieve a proper perspective on his political philosophy, the mystification surrounding Rousseau[47] and his social theories must be overcome. The question is not whether Rousseau is totalitarian or liberal but whether he believes altogether in the possibility of the social object; for Rousseau to posit a social being, he must first accept the existence of the Other as an external consciousness with whom he must interact. And as we have indicated, he negates mediation in his autobiographical venture: the Other is there to rob him of his identity. It remains to be seen whether this holds true in his social theory, whether Rousseau is consistent throughout his writings.

The *Social contract* is based on a logical circularity; we have said that an act of magic separates the pre-contract from the post-contract phases, but Rousseau posits in the pre-contract phase elements of the post-contract one. The reason for coming together is a social one actively and not potentially, which means that there is a social contract before the social contract. This logic would carry us backwards in infinite regression.[48] On the other hand, if man has lost the natural goodness of the pre-contract phase, how could he perceive the benefits of the post-contract phase?

Let us suppose for a moment that this contract does take place and see how equality works in its context. Freedom, we recall, is functional to equality. But Rousseau never meant material equality which is, in effect, a contradiction in terms. In the first version of the *Contract* he says:

> A l'égard de l'égalité il ne faut pas entendre par ce mot que les degrés de puissance et de richesse soient exactement les mêmes, mais que, quant à la puissance, elle soit au-dessous

111

de toute violence et ne s'exerce jamais qu'en vertu du rang et des lois, et quant à la richesse, que nul citoyen ne soit assez opulent pour en pouvoir acheter un autre, et nul assez pauvre pour être contraint de se vendre. (SC 332)[49]

Who is to decide how much disparity it takes for slavery to come about? Is it a quantitative measurement? It is certain that the act of association preserves the *status quo* of the individual participant; the pact is one act by which I give everything I own to the state and at the same time recuperate immediately everything I give. The alienation and recuperation of my goods constitute one single act. In other words, I do not first alienate myself and my possessions to the state and then receive from the state an equitable share of all the accumulated common good. Rousseau repeatedly stresses the fact that the individual, in the end, obeys no one but himself. The individual never disappears behind the General Will; rather, it is the General Will which manifests itself in the individual will. Ideology enters the picture at this point, for the alienation of all individual goods to the social body should entail a collective ownership of all goods. Logic necessitates that if I give up something, I cannot claim to own it, for somebody else owns it, and in our case it should be the social body. Rousseau clearly does not follow this logic through.

Ici éclate le divorce entre la liberté de détermination, qui n'est que participation à la souveraineté dans l'expression de la volonté générale, et la propriété — au lieu de n'être que la participation à la propriété commune est possession individuelle.[50]

Considering the formal side of the concept of equality, we end up with the exact reversal, and formal equality means inequality. For in saying that the same principle applies under the law to all citizens alike, one abstracts the basic differences among them and, in effect, reinforces the natural inequalities. If the purpose of society is to supplement natural inequalities which cannot be avoided, then it should rather consider the concept of inequality. By applying different standards to different men, society could compensate for the natural inequalities.[51] Furthermore, Rousseau's concept of equality, as a discursive phenomenon in eighteenth-century political discourse, takes hold only within the existing class structure, that is, in a situation where the gap between the classes must be minimised. It is not a concept which attempts a radical transformation of the class structure itself; it merely attempts to modify the *status quo*. The transformation of the social structure was not the problem but, rather, how to raise the living standards of over 80 per cent of the population to a more humanly acceptable level (at least from the formal-abstract perspective of Enlightened Humanism).

This is in line with the passage relating to material equality quoted above. Rousseau was not indifferent to the masses; on the contrary, he was probably the only one among the philosophers of the Enlightenment who identified openly with the poor. We have already mentioned his dislike for high society and its manners. But regarding possible solutions to the social problem, he remains captive to the hegemonic mode within which he produced. Rousseau, indeed, typifies the struggle between a subject's search for meaning and the mental structures of the period. In the end hegemony overcomes his lonely voice to the point where the only remaining solution was an individual one — madness — which he adopted with a vengeance.

Equality, then, means the value every self attains in its exercise of autonomy over property and not the well-being of the individual in his contribution to the welfare of the social body as a whole. Rousseau's dream must therefore be the exercise by every individual of sovereignty over his own piece of land, the only guarantee that the individual will not become enslaved by the rich.

Il croit que toute richesse vient de la terre; mais encore il ne conçoit pas qu'une satisfaction du besoin d'égalité puisse être apportée par le sentiment d'être partie du corps social qui possèderait toute chose: comme s'il voulait rêver au lopin de terre qu'il aurait dans son idéale cité.[52]

But equality can reside only within a social body. If we look closely at his social theory we see that he does not depart from the view of the Other that he espoused in his autobiography. Here we see the interface between autobiography and social theory for the conception of subjectivity is germane to the conception of a social structure in any given discursive matrix. And Rousseau is but one voice, albeit a lucid one, within the Enlightened discursive matrix. If Rousseau rejects the Other, no room is left for the social body and the pact of association is nothing but an artificial construct.

Natural man exists for himself in a radically different way

from the way in which others exist for him, for he possesses an identity for himself and yet does not recognize other men as similarly endowed with self-consciousness. Natural man in not being aware of others as centers of consciousness in the world, cannot be aware of having an existence in their consciousness, of being somebody for them. Man's consciousness does not merely happen contingently to be non-social, while it could be social, but is necessarily non-social, for it is defined in such a way as to be incompatible with a social consciousness.[53]

This is true of man both before and after he participates in the social contract; we recall that the fall of man, in Rousseau's vision, is due to his being perceived by the Other, to his being attributed certain characteristics from the outside: that is, to his dependence upon the opinions and judgements of the others. Therefore, in wanting to refound society on nature, Rousseau does not synthesise between the natural and the social but, rather, introduces his conception of natural man — as totally independent and self-sufficient — into the social, and this is a contradiction in terms.[54] If in the social order there are not enough trees to accommodate everyone, a feeling of independence must be fostered in every consciousness and this can be done through a proper approach to education.

> Il se considère sans égard aux autres, et trouve bon que les autres ne pensent point à lui. Il n'exige rien de personne, et ne croit rien devoir à personne. Il est seul dans la société humaine, il ne compte que sur lui seul. (E 244)

This is Emile before he falls into the social order (although he was born in it). Rousseau differentiates between the education of man and the education of civil man in correspondence with the two identities of man. *Emile* is mostly a treatise on education of the first identity; towards the end of the book, when Emile is twenty-two and ripe for full social relations, he is given a talk on civil education and the laws of government. Rousseau's assumption is that contact with the corrupting effects of the social order must be delayed until the child has built up his natural defences. Until that point the child or adolescent is sheltered from the judgements and opinions of others in order not to hinder the development of his own natural view of himself.[55] Rousseau's fundamental credo with regard to the education of man is liberty; however, liberty is not total since the child is dependent upon his mentor (who looks very much like the enlightened legislator of the *Social contract*) until he reaches the ripe age of twenty-four when he is ready for a wife. But even the educator does not interfere with the work of nature; authority is never exercised directly on the child through threats or punishment. The teacher never comes to a confrontation with Emile; he controls him negatively, by creating a climate in which Emile comes to the right conclusions. This negative approach, to Rousseau, will enable Emile to develop, first, a feeling of material independence and, second, a definition of self that does not lie outside himself.

This type of education is in line with the instinct of natural man for self-preservation, that is, 'l'amour de soi' as opposed to 'l'amour propre' which one acquires with the social mask. But what about the second natural tendency in man, to abhor suffering in others? Is not pity a form of intercourse with the Other? If so, then perhaps Rousseau does posit the necessity of an external consciousness for self-definition.

A seize ans l'adolescent sait ce que c'est que souffrir; car il a souffert lui-même à peine sait-il que d'autres êtres souffrent aussi; le voir sans le sentir n'est pas le savoir, et, comme je l'ai dit cent fois, l'enfant n'imaginant point ce que sentent les autres ne connaît de maux que les siens: mais quand le premier développement des sens allume en lui le feu de l'imagination, il commence à se sentir dans ses semblables, à s'émouvoir de leurs plaintes et à souffrir de leurs douleurs. (E 260)

A question must be raised here: if the child has developed all along with a feeling of total independence as to his identity, how is he going to identify with the Other in his suffering? Rousseau seems to suggest that the work of the imagination is needed here; the child, as it were, abstracts the otherness of the Other and reduces it to a series of cries or pains to which he lends his body. The feeling of pity, then, is not aroused by identification with the Other in his pain but by identification with his pain after he has been abstracted from it.[56]

The negation of mediation can also be found in Emile's affective education. Again, we are exposed to a relationship which involves no genuine mutual exchange between the partners; each partner attributes to the Other qualities that exist in his imagination only. The love object is met above the real; its real traits are abstracted and replaced by a new love object which better answers the demands of fiction. The correspondence between Rousseau's love story as exposed in his *Confessions* and his theory of love in *Emile* is quite evident.

> Tout n'est qu'illusion dans l'amour, je l'avoue; mais ce qui est réel, ce sont les sentiments dont il nous anime pour le vrai beau qu'il nous fait aimer. Ce beau n'est point dans l'objet qu'on aime, il est l'ouvrage de nos erreurs.' (E 495)

In human relations of any kind, in Rousseau's world, the Other is met exclusively on the subject's terms; there is no duality or exchange between self and Other. The feeling of possession itself which might involve some kind of commitment on the part of the subject is done away with. Towards the end of *Emile*, Rousseau suggests to his disciple that to be genuinely involved, to relate properly, means to be able to lose the object of one's love; 'l'homme ne jouit que de ce qu'il sait perdre.' (E 569) This is why Emile cannot realise his love for Sophie immediately after he falls in love with her; he is forced to take a long trip abroad and come back to marry her. In the social contract as well, the relationship with the Other is tailored to the subject's own monopoly; in joining the social body, in effect, every one joins his own self. The social pact enlarges the sphere of the individual through all the barriers, physical and mental, it creates in order to differentiate between self and Other. In short, 'Rousseau rêve d'une action qui saute les intermédiaires, force les lois des choses, supprime les résistances du réel.'[57]

As suggested in the opening paragraph, the conception of a social contract as a starting point for the social order, and the redefinition of society in terms of what might have happened before that starting point, involve a rejection of man's exclusively social nature. And this hypothetical fictionalisation of his beginnings points to the ideological presupposition behind the idea of the 'pact', which was so prevalent in enlightened thought. The pure beginning must, by definition, accommodate individualism; the social pact postulates a cumulation of scattered individuals who, through a process of addition, form what amounts to a group. The notion of the pact implicates the idea of aggregation. Seriality is at the roots of this system of thought for seriality follows

necessarily from the conception of a beginning. The series starts
with zero, one, two, and so on. Given its inherent individualism,
the Enlightenment could not conceive that any system of social
reformation must postulate the existence of the social body and not
put that existence into question. The alternative to a social form
evolves from its previous form; the social is already there and one
does not join it by choice; one *is* the social form one does not come
to it.

It is clear, then, why Rousseau and the social theorists of the
Enlightenment could not conceive of integration, for integration
does not conform to the notion of a starting point. Integration
demands that the social body be in temporal and dialectical movement, that it be in history, which the theory of the pact refuses.
Integration implies that the historical process is ongoing, and
negates the possibility of a beginning in time. The conception of
the zero point stresses the heap, the pile of units and not the solid
bond among them.

The impetus to autobiography at this point in the development
of the discourse of modernism is therefore not gratuitous; the
Rousseauist formal culmination finds a fertile ground in the social
text of the times and the conception of selfhood therein. It is not
surprising that with the division of man into two exclusive
domains, the public and the private, through the promotion of
ownership of self and property, there ensued a privatisation and
internalisation of human phenomena. Just as the ownership over a
piece of property could not be debated so the ownership over the
self was unquestionable and society had nothing to do with it.
Man's social dimension was now reduced to the market dealings
that were to be made; apart from formal contractual relations in
the social body, the self was the exclusive domain of its owner. The
self was not a dialectical entity created within a social praxis but an
object to be owned like any other material object. Moreover, the
private experience of the self-object makes its narration a matter of
inalienable conviction because, knowing it from the inside, the
subject could not possibly lose control over its transparency: the
self is totally clear to its owner. Hence the story of the self can
never be a fiction. Autobiography, according to this ideology, is by
definition a truth since it deals with the most unshakeable conviction of the subject whose self is his exclusive laboratory. From
now on, whatever is of the self is the truth and whatever is not of
the self is fiction. The liberation from this limiting conception of
autobiography will come with the abolition of the distinction

6

Malraux's *Antimémoires*

In *Antimémoires*,[1] André Malraux offers us a new conception of the autobiographic text, a conception indicative of a discursive shift which will take time to come to its maturation. For in *Antimémoires* Malraux transgresses the basic tenets of the autobiographical tradition: he postulates a redefinition of selfhood which negates the concepts of truth and veracity by abolishing the distinction between reality and fiction, and which promotes the fictional dimension of the self. Malraux's autobiographical venture can be understood only if it is inscribed within the complete text of his fiction; its coherence depends upon our rejection of the differentiation between fiction and non-fiction. For every text, be it autobiographic or not (if we accept for the moment the existing classification), constitutes a narrative — a story, and the meaning of this narrative lies between story and history. Meaning is the metaphorisation of history by the story. Malraux's self as presented in *Antimémoires* as well as in his fiction arises in the relationship — that irreducible bond — between story and history. Malraux's autobiography takes meaning in contributing to the production of a socially oriented literature: with the rejection of psychologisation and the promotion of a language of action, Malraux places himself and his protagonists within historical transcendence. Subjectivity as a self-contained entity disappears to make room for a sociohistorical consciousness in its ongoing search for historically determined roles and their fulfilment.

Of repetition

Antimémoires is looked upon by the critical literature as a collection of essays duplicating in various ways Malraux's fictional works.[2] It is nowhere referred to as an autobiography mainly because it satisfies none of the existing definitions of the genre. But if our point of departure is the ideological presuppositions of the genre as it evolves at the moment, then the demystification of the genre can lead to a new conception of autobiography and concurrently to a new conception of selfhood. Indeed, our purpose is to indicate in what way Malraux produces a text which makes room for a new literary form that we may term 'antimemoirs' as well as a departure from the ideologies of the 'centre'.

How does one read Malraux's *Antimémoires*? The reader of autobiographies is baffled by the chaos of this text for chronology does not seem to be a guiding factor in its organisation. Clearly, it is not a story of a life, although here and there we encounter fragments of biographical data; nor is it a transcription of historical data since there is no obedience to historical fact. It cannot be a pure work of fiction: many characters in the book are real people. One is tempted to define these 'memoirs' as a random accumulation of unrelated pieces, but we know that Malraux has achieved a considerable degree of cohesion in his fiction. A careful scrutiny of the text leaves us with the conviction that this chaos is intentional, that it is conditional to the meaning of the text. Indeed Malraux seems to be postulating that autobiography, the story of the self, is a combination of a number of disorders. The confusion, however, is only apparent; in fact the text advances a new and coherent view of the self, the world and the relationship between them. Malraux's text suggests that self is not and cannot be defined, and therefore no narrative can encompass it; it constitutes an ongoing process of redefinition dependent upon the transcendental-historical phenomena which shape it. And autobiography, the story of the self, will therefore have to be the story of the phenomena which continually give birth to that self.

The first issue the reader must contend with in *Le Miroir des limbes* (of which *Antimémoires* is the first half) as a whole is the problematic of repetition; key scenes and passages from Malraux's fiction seem to have found their way into his autobiography either verbatim or with minor transformations. Malraux's concern in *La Tentation de l'Occident*[3] as embodied in the dialogue between the Chinese Ling and the French A.D. — that is, the dialogue of East and West — is, this time around, Malraux's own dialogue with the Nehru of reborn India. The expedition to Cambodia of Perken and Claude, the adventurers of *La Voix royale*,[4] is now retold by Clappique, a hero from *La Condition humaine*,[5] to Malraux himself in a café in the form of a film scenario about Mayrena,[6] a real-life adventurer who led some native tribes to insurrection. 'La Condition humaine' is the title of both the novel and one of the sections in *Antimémoires*; this time, however, we do not witness the Chinese Revolution in the making but rather the aftermath of the Revolution in a cerebral dialogue between Malraux, the French Minister, and Mao tse-Tung, the embodiment of the Chinese Revolution. Kassner's nightmarish flight to freedom from his Nazi torturers in *Le Temps du mépris*[7] is now atttributed to Malraux himself as he goes looking for the kingdom of the Queen of Saba in Yemen. The tank scene and the colloquium of Altenburg from *Les Noyers de l'Altenburg*[8] reappear in part VI of *La Corde et les souris* when Malraux, in his hospital bed, rethinks the gas attack. This same section of *La Corde et les souris* recalls Katow and his cyanide from *La Condition humaine*, *Le Temps du mépris*, pieces from *L'Espoir*,[9] the tank scene again, and the Nazi camps.

In effect, then, key passages of Malraux's fiction reappear in his autobiography, crowding out portrayals of his childhood or his formation as a writer (the most common theme in literary autobiographies). He seems to have forgotten himself with a vengeance. As an autobiography, *Antimémoires* in no way satisfies the reader in search of biographical curiosities. But this is a new education in reading; Malraux refuses us his biographical data because he wants us to look for something other than his self, and also because those facts, if they do exist, are inscribed within a narrative, a fictional discourse calling for interpretation. Interesting in this connection is Malraux's own lack of corroboration or negation of critics' and biographers' accounts of his own deeds, for the simple reason that André Malraux, the individual, is also a fictional creation, one protagonist among many others in fictional narratives.[10] What is Malraux's purpose behind a seemingly random re-collection of fictional chapters from his novels? In what way do these chapters constitute his autobiography? For there is not doubt that he wants us to take these accounts as the story — or stories, for there is always more than one story to a life — of his life.

The reader's concern ought to be for the intentionality behind Malraux's repetitive process. Malraux is not short of words; he could very well have written 'new' texts. He certainly cannot be said to be promoting his novels; if that were the case, they would have been kept whole, not fragmented and collected into a hybrid unit. Repetition here is an ideological configuration, the purpose of which is the creation of an equation between fiction and non-fiction. Malraux is suggesting through this process that his fiction is his autobiography and his autobiography is his fiction. *Le Miroir des limbes* is not a remembrance of things past as lived by an individual but a remembrance of created fictional worlds which coincide with the story of the remembering — creating consciousness. The emphasis is not on linear memory but on creative imagination, intentionality and action.

Antimémoires is written in 1965 when Malraux, on his doctor's advice, undertakes a world tour. This journey brings back to memory other trips to the same places: Egypt, India, China. The voyage backwards, that is, the telling of the trips of 1923, 1929, 1934 and 1958, constitutes a description of historical events that changed the face of the world and the Third World in particular. One should note, however, that these expeditions to India, Egypt, and China are not only trips to the immediate past; they are also voyages into the cultural and artistic heritage of these nations, dating back millenniums (in contrast to the relatively short span of Western Christian culture which, in Malraux's view, has met a dead end).

Apart from the parallel trips (to Ceylon in 1923, to the holy cities of northern India in 1929, the political mission of 1958 on behalf of De Gaulle to strengthen relations with India, and to the French colonies of Guadaloupe, Haiti, and Martinique to promote a French cultural commonwealth following their independence), there is another journey to the scenes of the Second World War, its destruction and atrocities filtered through the fictional accounts of the battles of the French Maquis and the real account of concentration camp survivors.

If *Antimémoires* constitutes the narration of major historical events that have shaped the twentieth century, it is also the story of certain personalities who have shaped these events. Again, it is not the story of the lives of these personalities but the story of the relationships between these men and the events they helped shape. Attention to physical traits is minimal — in contrast to Rousseau, for example. It is not mere chance that three major dialogues are central to the book: they constitute one of the many centres of the book. De Gaulle, Nehru, Gandhi, Mao tse-Tung and Senghor, among others, are real characters but not in the Balzacian sense of the term; they are central to the extent that they have an impact on the destiny of the world in fulfilling a role presented to them by history. These characters in themselves are of no interest to Malraux; we are not exposed to anecdotes that might shed light on their personalities; they are answers to situations. They meet their respective vocations — the call of destiny.

Of simultaneity and juxtaposition

The reader must try to understand in what sense Malraux's life story is the story of Mao, De Gaulle and Nehru. In what sense it is also the story of the Sphinx and the pyramids of Egypt, the story of Madura, Ellora, Benares — the holy cities of India, the story of the Lascaux caves, the story of Nazi survivors, and so on. One cannot ask the question of Malraux's presence in the *Antimémoires* for he is everywhere and nowhere. Everywhere because dispersed and spread over all the phenomena he relates and describes, and nowhere because the entity André (Malraux) is non-existent. It is replaced at best by fictional characters or performers: the Minister of Culture undertaking the clean-up of Paris and the restoration of museums, the tank commander showing solidarity with his crew, the archaeologist and thief of art works, the Maquis commander.

Of crucial importance is this last role of the Maquis commander. Malraux wrote about Colonel Berger before he lived the life of Colonel Berger, the Maquis commander whose name used to be André Malraux. Malraux lives the life of Colonel Berger first in fiction and then, in 1944, in real life when he assumes the command of the Alsace-Lorraine Brigade. Fiction foretells life but it is not forced upon life (à la Rousseau). Fiction in (with) Malraux comes before life, prior to the immediate, in the consciousness of a relationship to the world. Fiction is the explanation of reality because it is a relationship to that reality, a mediation of it, and *Antimémoires* is the spreading out of an infinity of complex relationships. *Antimémoires* is pure juxtaposition and simultaneity. The present shapes the past; the trip of 1965 filters all other phenomena and translates them.

Ce qui m'intéresse dans un homme quelconque, c'est la condition humaine; dans un grand homme, ce sont les moyens et la nature de sa grandeur; dans un saint le caractère de sa sainteté. Et quelques traits qui expriment moins un caractère individuel qu'une relation particulière avec le monde. (AN 20)

'Une relation particulière avec le monde' is precisely what Malraux achieves in the *Antimémoires*. The relationship to the world comes with the intention — 'anti-mémoires' — and with the description of that intention. 'J'appelle ce livre Antimémoires parce qu'il répond à une question que les mémoires ne posent pas, et ne répond pas à celles qu'ils posent' (AN 20). The *Antimémoires* consitutes a negation of memoirs; it counters unity with dispersion. But dispersion does not mean chaos; it means mainly the replacement of a particular conception of unity by another conception of unity. In Rousseau, for example, unity means particularity and uniqueness, separateness; in Malraux, it means being one with the world, being in relationship to the world. The preoccupations of this text transcend the immediate; the *Antimémoires*, by extension, reach to the infinite in all directions of time and space, since every relationship multiplies into a variety of relationships. The book, of course, contains a limited number of relationships; it is finite in its 600 pages, but it postulates an infinity of relationships and transcendence. Malraux seems to want to include the history and prehistory of all civilisations and the relationships among them.

The trip to India, for example, is not told from A to Z: in opposition to the Rousseauist model, it does not follow a linear sequence. The second and third sections of the book deal with the various trips to India but criss-crossing these trips are major events that occur in other parts of the world. The section 'Antimémoires' starts with Malraux's trip to India in 1965, past trips emerge: the 1923 voyage to Ceylon, the 1929 trip to the holy cities of India, the 1958 political mission to French Guyana. By association this political mission raises memories of Malraux's first meeting with De Gaulle in 1945. The dialogue with Nehru covers most political issues of the modern world but following it is a flashback to 1944 when Malraux, or rather Colonel Berger, is captured by the Nazis; this flashback is motivated by a line from Ghandi, 'La liberté doit être cherchée dans les murs des prisons.' The third section of the book, 'La Tentation de l'Occident', starts with the visit to Benares, Ellora, Bombay, and especially their museums and temples; there follows a meditation on the ancient cultures of India. The section ends with a comment on the concept of transmigration. Malraux then transcribes the tank scene from *Les Noyers de l'Altenburg*: the scene deals with the solidarity of a tank crew facing the enemy and the anxieties they undergo as a group when their tank crashes in a trap. Malraux then returns to his meditation about the eternity of Indian cultures, followed by a long chapter on Nehru, Ghandi and the non-violent Indian Revolution which brought about the freedom of India.

> A multilayered time-space network, a multilayered itinerary, a multiplicity of narrative voices, the universe of the *Antimémoires* is, from a literary point of view, a whirling prism of color, form, sound, in which legend and reality, fiction and fact, past and present, memory and dream, mingle and fuse.[11]

Times and places interrelate, criss-cross and interpenetrate one another, the only guiding factor being the power of relationship or association — the workings of a living consciousness and not an artificial ordering of events. Malraux's imprisonment by the Nazis is relived in terms of Ghandi's imprisonment and his statement about the relationship between imprisonment and freedom. The tank anecdote follows a segment on the meaning of death in India in opposition to the meaninglessness of life as a result of the war. Following the tank anecdote Malraux tries to imagine an Indian counterpart to Pradé, Bonneau and Leonard, the members of his tank crew. On seeing the religious crowds of India, Malraux remembers other crowds: that of the metro and that of the war. 'Ce qui s'évoquait en moi, n'était pas une foule chrétienne: c'était la foule du métro, et surtout celle que j'avais le mieux connue, celle de la guerre' (AN 293). The purpose of this text is not to portray the divisibility or separateness of the event but its comprehensiveness.

> Tous ces mondes mineurs se mêlent, les ruines de Mareb à celles du stade de Nuremberg, aux deux jetées qui portaient les feux entre lesquels Hitler invoquait l'Allemagne dans la nuit, aux grandes flammes des anciens autels des Mages dans les montagnes de Perse; à la chambre funèbre de Cleops dans la pyramide, et à la mort embusquée là-haut dans ses steppes d'astres, qui me fit apparaître le lacis des veines de la terre des vivants comme les lignes de la main de ma mère morte. (AN 105)

This passage is typical of Malraux's intentions in this text. It deals with the multiple relationships between what seem to be limited worlds. The ruins of Mareb, which Malraux discovers on his search for the kingdom of Saba, relate to the ruins of Nuremberg after the war; the flames in the Nuremberg stadium evoke the flames on the altars of ancient Persia; the funerary room in the pyramid recalls Hitler's underground quarters in Nuremberg: the 'same' staircase seems to be leading to both; the veins formed by water on the earth as seen from a plane recall the disappearing lines on the hand of Malraux's dead mother. What strikes us in this paragraph (as in the rest of the book) is the complexity of the material world that Malraux tries to impart to the reader, and the way a consciousness experiences such a complexity.

The simultaneity and juxtaposition of events prevails throughout Malraux's writings, demonstrating that an individual life does not exist in a vacuum and does not order the world around its centre; rather, the individual is enmeshed in historical contingency. The complexity of phenomena and the irreducible multiplicity of dimensions come through forcefully in a passage from *Hôtes de passage* in which Malraux dialogues with Senghor on the revival of Negro-African culture, its music and dance, as well as the recent revival of the Third World with its anxieties over Western hegemony. The dialogue ends on Senghor's note: 'Bonne chance avec le tiers monde, il peut coûter cher . . . Nous n'aurons pas trop de tous les moyens, y compris les vôtres' (AN 534). The dialogue is followed by this passage:

> Dans les fenêtres montent les courts gratte-ciels de Dakar, les mêmes que ceux du Caire, de Bagdad et de Bombay. Sur la cheminée, il y a une petite pendule. Elle me semble marquer midi vingt-neuf pour l'éternité. Midi vingt-neuf, au temps de la naissance de la nouvelle Afrique et de la nouvelle Asie, au temps de la reine de Sebeth, des klaxons au-dessous de nous . . . Nehru aussi, et Ghandi, et Mao, et tant d'autres, ont regardé les aiguilles qui marquaient l'époque où l'Europe cessait d'être maîtresse du monde. J'écoute le président du Sénégal, je pense que César n'avait jamais vu une horloge, je pense au siècle où les horloges ont substitué leur aiguille encore unique à l'ombre sur le cadran solaire; aux heures qui allumaient les vitraux, et les éteignaient avec la nuit de Dieu . . . Dans cent ans, dans deux cents ans, peut-être devant cette petite pendule, un homme rêvera de l'époque où se

réveillaient les continents endormis, l'époque de la première
bombe atomique et des camps d'extermination. (ML 534)

No analysis of this passage can exhaust it; it resists any kind of
closure. The suspension periods Malraux inserts between the lines
point to the text's irreducible openness. We would venture to say
that the lines are inserted between the suspension periods, that suspension encompasses the text. For suspension means the endless-
ness of the historical process, only an infinitesimal part of which a
text can cover. Suspension throughout Malraux's text — be it
suspension periods, the elliptical language of action, the absence of
narration and characterisation — is omission, not a given omission
but pure omission. It is not the elliptical omission we encounter in
the detective novel, for example, that can be filled to restore the
completeness of the text: it is not the omission the writer provides
for the reader's pleasure. The omission is total; the text can never
be completed due to its relationship to historical transcendence. A
text, any text, divides itself from the world by a process of selection
and negation; in its finitude, it can include a,b,c, but not x,y,z.
However, it ought to be open to all that it negates because the
material world has no end in its friction against the creating consciousness. And that creating consciousness, in its discursive
productivity, ought to posit the world in all its complexity and
infinity. So unless one falls back upon a metaphysics to fill all gaps
and give an illusion of continuity and consistency amongst all
phenomena, the text, in its ceaseless movement towards a future,
in its ever new beginning, can never be completed. Completion is
a myth: the story never ends simply because the material world
never ends.[12] The economy inherent in Malraux's langauge of
drama and action is therefore not primarily an expression of
literary craftmanship, not a gimmick or a puzzle directed at the
reader: it constitutes Malraux's world view. The gap is of all that
cannot enter into the text but which the text must hypostatise in its
openness. Suspension, then, coincides with an ongoing process of
interrogation — the open-endedness of consciousness grappling
with the world.[13]

The passage quoted above incorporates the temporal dimensions which represent the complexity of the event; it approximates
the workings of a living consciousness. Malraux, or a given
presence, is in a room, in Dakar, the capital of Senegal, a Third
World nation, looking through a window similar to other windows
in blossoming Third World capitals. The look passes from the

outside to the inside of the room, from the short skyscrapers to the clock on the mantelpiece with all the connotations it brings forth. The time metaphor is then filtered through the gaze of those who were obsessed by the historical process, the Nehrus, the Ghandis, the Maos. The clock moves us backwards in time to Caesar, to the times when no clocks existed, to the transition from solar time to mechanical time, to the Middle Ages and the play of light and shadow on stained glass windows in medieval churches. The passage ends with a movement forward when someone gazing at the clock, or a similar one, recalls Malraux's present, that is, the atomic bomb, human torture and degradation in concentration camps. With one flickering present which a clock forces upon a consciousness, we are exposed to an infinity of complex historical relations in the present, the insertion of this complex present in a three-dimensional temporal structure of past, present and future, and the infinite series of ramifications to which it points. This is merely one tiny moment in the endless centrifugal movement of a human consciousness. The limitless horizons suggested by this passage oppose any attempt to reduce a life story to a single plot, for such a plot abstracts the historical process of which it is a minute part.

This negation of closure is prevalent throughout the text even in passages describing a given synchronic slice. The dialogue with Max Torrès, Malraux's friend from the Spanish Civil War, for example, takes place on Monday, 6 May 1968, (ML 581–611). In the foreground there is a dialogue of intellectuals exposing some interesting ideas on the relationship between drugs and creativity; in the background, however, this dialogue of intellectuals is criss-crossed by a number of telegrams portraying the progress of the May 1968 student revolution in France. These telegrams in themselves unfold the tragic turn of events and constitute some kind of chorus to the dialogue on creativity. At the same time Malraux glances at the newspaper on his desk; the headlines tell of the student revolution, the Vietnam peace talks and Dubcek's visit to Moscow. In effect, the Malraux–Torrès dialogue takes meaning only in relationship to Vietnam, Dubcek, the student revolution and an infinity of other events which a book in its finitude cannot contain.[14]

Complexity, then, accounts for the denseness of Malraux's language, for the aim is to introduce into the text as much of the material world as possible. The comprehensiveness of the event, the juxtaposition and multiplicity of events show how a consciousness apprehends reality more faithfully than would the telling of the individual event. To return to the above passage relating the palm of a dead hand to the veins of the earth, a realist writer might have reduced the event (by which Malraux attempts to approximate the complexity of reality) to personal grief, centring on it as if it were the only thing happening in the world at the moment; the world would be reduced to the parameters of a hand. Malraux enriches the event by making it more comprehensive: the relationship between the veins of the earth seen from a drifting plane and the palm of a dead hand gives a further dimension to both phenomena; it integrates both in a more complex universe. This complex process of 'relating' reduces divisiveness and separation and promotes solidarity.

Of comprehensiveness and dialogue

The comprehensiveness of the historical event makes for Malraux's basic postulation of otherness and his rejection of individualism, both the ideology and the novelistic form which incorporates it. His concern with man's place in the historical process is already apparent in his first novel, *La Tentation de l'Occident*; on the one hand, 'mesurer toute chose à la durée et à l'intensité d'une vie humaine' (TO 66); on the other, 'ne concevoir la vie que dans son ensemble' (TO 44). But the temptation is twofold and the dialogue stands for the shift from one culture to the other: it is the temptation of the West to forget its individualism and espouse the Eastern merger with the universe, as well as the temptation of the East for Western ways to accede to modern history. This dialogue ends with no definite adoption of either one of the two views of selfhood, rather making each conditional upon the other; that is, it hypostatises the mutual dependence of both. The insertion of an 'other' world view as a counterbalancing force to the Western one emphasises Malraux's departure from an exclusive literary tradition. It emphasises as well his postulation of otherness as the overall ontological structure which conditions being and a corresponding dialogical structure which produces a new literary form. Hence the absence of a protagonist who exists for-himself; hence too the absence of a life story — dialogue requires at least two life stories. There are only situations and human beings interacting within these situations.

De Gaulle, for example, to whom Malraux devotes an entire

book, is present only as an incarnated voice in the dialogue;

> Il exprimait un destin, et l'exprime lorsqu'il proclame son divorce avec le destin. L'intimité avec lui, ce n'est pas de parler de lui.
> Le Général est inséparable des forces qui semblent moins les siennes que celles du destin. (ML 620)

One ought to differentiate between the two almost contradictory meanings of the word 'destin' which Malraux uses throughout his writings. The first is the meaning we get from the phrase 'the call of destiny'; that is, the availability of an opportunity within the historical process, i.e. a subject position the historical process provides for a given consciousness — the role to be enacted. The second meaning is the opposite; destiny in this case is what cannot be helped: the forgetfulness that man must oppose with intentionality, the nothingness he must fill with being. The term 'anti-destin' which recurs in the Malrucian text coincides with the first meaning of 'destiny'. The two sides of the coin are dialectically related for freedom, volition and action of mind fit the placidity and indifference of matter. Further, 'destiny' and 'anti-destiny' correspond respectively to what we term 'event' and 'non-event': whatever is acted by consciousness, on the one hand, and what cannot be helped, on the other.

If De Gaulle and Mao and Senghor have no biography, then what are they? They are simply what Malraux coins 'les héros de l'histoire'. The role pre-exists the man who fills it; the historical process is filled with such roles, as they arise in specific situations. The dream is already there to be realised. Interestingly enough, Malraux attributes a common predicament to both the historical personage and the fictional protagonist because he posits that history in its process of productivity as text, is a fiction, an intentional relationship to the world incarnated by a given subjectivity.

> Son action ne vient pas des résultats qu'il atteint mais des rêves qu'il incarne et qui lui préexistent. Le héros de l'Histoire est le frère du héros de roman . . . Et le Général De Gaulle le devient en cessant d'être Charles. Un personnage n'est pas un 'individu', en mieux. (ML 631)[15]

De Gaulle, the historical personage, exists in the Other, in dialogue, and the dialogue is both a dialogue of cultures and a dialogue of individuals. The Malraux–De Gaulle exchange is inscribed within a structure of dialogue which comprises the Malraux–Nehru, the Malraux–Mao, the Malraux–Senghor exchanges, and a multiplicity of other exchanges. These names can be replaced by other names; what remains is the dialogue between two consciousnesses in their confrontation with a given historical reality, be it Black Africa, the Chinese Revolution, the Indian Revolution, the Fourth Republic in France and so on. The dialogical dimension inherent in Malraux's text is the repeated performance of two 'characters' on a stage exchanging views, two characters with no specific individualities. The absence of physical description, or for that matter of narration which has no bearing on the action, points to the non-pertinence of the biography of these individuals. Mao means to the extent that he fulfils the role of 'Mao tse-Tung', the leader of the Chinese Revolution, Senghor, to the extent that he is 'Leopold Senghor', the speaking voice of modern Africa. The dialogical nature of Malraux's text as a whole posits the absence of selfhood in its particularity; it rejects mediation and introspection as the apprehension of self and advances a language of action as the historical dimension of consciousness which creates and is created in its friction against the world.

The dialogues of Altenburg, one of the main axes of *Les Noyers de l'Altenburg*, centre on the definition of man. The three key positions of the colloquy as represented by the narrator's father, his uncle Walter Berger and Rabaud, while arguing against one another, seem to complement one another in their search for a more comprehensive definition of man.[16]

— Et d'ailleurs, [says Walter Berger] que savoir jamois? Pour l'essentiel, l'homme est ce qu'il cache. Un misérable petit tas de secrets.
— L'homme est ce qu'il fait! répondit mon père avec brutalité. (NA 89)

— Tout de même, mon cher Rabaud, dans tout ça il y a quelque chose qui me gêne! En somme vous admettez certaines lois de l'homme; vous acceptez l'idée d'un homme constant, d'un homme éternel.
— Je crois à un homme éternel, dit le comte, parce que je crois à l'éternité des chefs-d'œuvre. (NA 113)

131

Is man eternal? Is his nature eternal? Is he a heap of secrets, something that must be dug out? Or is he simply what he acts? Malraux
opts for the latter position, which both Rabaud and Walter Berger
ultimately endorse. Rabaud's eternal human nature becomes 'son
aptitude à mettre le monde en question' (NA 146), that is, man's
ongoing act of interrogation. And to Walter Berger, the heap of
secrets has a deeper implication:

> Le plus grand mystère n'est pas que nous soyons jetés au
> hasard entre la profusion de la matière et celle des astres; c'est
> que dans cette prison, nous tirions de nous-mêmes des images
> assez puissantes pour nier notre néant. (NA 98)

Malraux's predilection for action implies a rejection of any
definition of man in which destiny overtakes intentionality.
Rabaud's and Walter Berger's early positions constitute expressions of two ideologies that look backward for a definition of the
future. And if the future is to be transcendental and not figural,
man's unconscious or his eternal nature cannot lead to the
freedom necessitated by action. Indeed, Rabaud's human nature
and Walter Berger's unconscious posit man's definition before he
acts on the historical scene; they indicate man's helplessness and
lack of courage in the face of destiny, whereas the definition of
man as action is an anti-destiny, an ongoing intentional transformation of the material world, a ceaseless metamorphosis.
Intentionality and anti-destiny motivate Malraux's main metaphor in this book; the trunks of the walnut trees of Altenburg stand
for man's unfailing will to metamorphose the universe: rather than
attempting to free themselves from the earth which is intent upon
subjugating them, the roots of these trees impose their presence
and rectitude on it; they subdue the earth with their massive will.

> L'épanouissement en feuilles de ce bois, si vieux et si lourd
> qu'il semblait s'enfoncer dans la terre et non s'en arracher,
> imposait à la fois l'idée d'une volonté et d'une métamorphose
> sans fin. (NA 151)

There prevails in the critical literature a contradiction between
those who see Malraux's concerns as being primarily socio-historical and those who place him within the Pascalian metaphysical
tradition.[17] Often enough the phrase 'the absurd' is mentioned,
and man's struggle is said to be against the natural elements rather

than against the rigidity of the social structure; some kind of cosmic force tends to subjugate man, and the Malrucian hero is victorious in his fight against this anonymous force.

On the whole the liberal-humanistic vein of criticism on Malraux tends to support the metaphysical claim while the historical-material trend supports the opposite thesis. A typical example of the liberal trend is Joseph Hoffman's *L'Humanisme de Malraux*,[18] as well as all those who focus on the problematic of death as the centre of Malraux's concerns. Kline,[19] for example, claims that Malraux's primary preoccupation with death is expressed through insect, erotic and water images which do prevail throughout his fiction. Malraux himself does accommodate such interpretations; in his introduction to *Le Temps du mépris*, he speaks of Kassner as being a hero in the tragic tradition:

> Le monde d'une œuvre comme celle-ci, le monde de la tragédie, est toujours le monde antique; l'homme, la foule, les éléments, la femme, le destin. Il se réduit à deux personnages, le héros et son sens de la vie. (TM 8)

However, we understand this 'sens de la vie', with Malraux, as taking place within a specific historical situation like that of Nazi Germany. We side, therefore, with the analyses of Goldmann and Greenlee; the latter says: 'Malraux's reinterpretation of history is one of the strengths of his fiction. Its importance has been largely overlooked by those scholars who find in his novels a continuing elaboration of the basic tragedy of mankind abandoned in a hostile universe.'[20]

Sometimes even Malraux's fictional techniques are attributed to his (so-called) metaphysical preoccupations:

> Since its endeavour is to lay bare the meaning of metaphysical destiny, his achievement as a novelist need not conform to the literary and humanist norms of the well ordered narrative, although he expresses his intentions via a story and an adventure quite concretely situated in a particular historical reality . . . Not only the general intention but the actual phrasing and structure of the novel exemplify 'abridgment': the writer's breathing does not maintain its steady rhythm in some finite human environment, but pants in infinite space.[21]

We have already touched upon the problem of suspension, or as

Alberes terms it 'abridgment'; we will return to the narrative techniques later on. The 'infinite space' recalls Pascal's fears of infinite space in Pensée 91. The phrase 'la condition humaine' is also taken from Pascal, but it would be erroneous to conclude that they share the same preoccupations. Though Malraux deals with death in most of his novels, he is not concerned with its metaphysical meaning. If death holds any meaning in the Malrucian world, it is in relation to action, for death is the state of non-action. Death is the non-event, *par excellence*. 'Ce que redoute le personnage malrucien dans la mort, c'est avec l'effacement et l'oubli, l'irrévocabilité du destin. La mort enferme l'homme dans son passé, le réduit à la somme de ses actes, sans possibilité de rémission.'[22]

If indeed man is defined by action, he cannot be an artificial construct made up of a heap of secrets, nor can he be a series of well-ordered events, for he is as he acts and action negates cumulation and linear order. Action does away with chronology which is the main operational concept of the prevalent ideologies of the West. Events do not happen within chronology; actually, they defy it: they are the asperities which spring up upon a rugged historical terrain. Chronology follows the logic of the series which in no way can encompass the complexity of the historical process. Events make up the historical process while threatening its unity and continuity, since they stand up against the background of the non-event, that is, the event which is not intentional, the event which occurs despite itself, the event that cannot be helped.[23]

Of roles

Malraux's fictional world accommodates a variety of actions; there is the action of the individual as in *La Voix royale*, and the action of the collectivity as in *L'Espoir*. There is the action of the adventurer (Perken, Garine) and the action of the socially committed man (Kyo, Manuel, Katow). There is action geared towards being something, to wit, action directed towards self-fulfilment, and action aimed at social amelioration. Most striking among a plurality of roles are the roles of the adventurer, the revolutionary, the militant, the drifter and the artist. These roles partake in the historical process in qualitatively different ways since they incarnate different ideologies.[24]

An important role in Malraux's fictional gallery is the role of the drifter-dreamer; that is, the escapist as portrayed by Clappique in *La Condition humaine*. Clappique is the gambler who risks both money and life; in choosing to live on the border between dream and reality, Clappique wears a variety of masks which he presents to others in order to escape any definition. If 'rien n'existe: tout est rêve' (CH 36) then neither the Other nor Clappique himself exist. Clappique likes to indulge in narcissistic sessions facing a mirror; 'il transforma son visage en samourai de carnaval . . . il commença à grimacer, se transformant en singe, en idiot, en épouvanté, en type à fluxion, en tous les grotesques que peut exprimer un visage humain' (CH 210). The risks he seems to be taking with the shipment of arms do not constitute a commitment to the revolutionary cause. Rather, the revolution is a precarious situation to be exploited in terms of the money that can in turn be spent at the gambling table where destiny is played out. 'Il découvrit que le jeu est un suicide sans mort' (CH 197). Life is a carnival and Clappique is the clown; he exits the novel in the attire of a sailor after gambling away his fare. 'Non les hommes n'existaient pas, puisqu'il suffit d'un costume pour échapper à soi-même, pour trouver une autre vie dans les yeux des autres' (CH 239).

Despite Clappique's important part in the revolutionary events he is not a positive voice in the novel. The novel is made up of Clappiques as well because the fictional world, like the real one, in its complexity includes Kyos, Katows, Ferrals and Clappiques.[25] Clappique is a mythomaniac who negates life because he lives in a situation to which he refuses to contribute. Clappique is Clappique because he interacts with the revolutionaries, the militants, and the Chinese masses in terms of an intentional ideology of escapism.[26] Clappique is not forced to be Clappique; he 'acts' Clappique.

The adventurer is one of the prime movers in the fight for the new order; indeed, Perken and Garine are committed to the establishment of a new society based on equality and justice, and to a certain extent they succeed in their endeavour. Garine does awaken the proletarian masses, gives them hope by orchestrating the strike in the port of Hong-Kong; he transforms propaganda into a weapon. Perken also attempts to give a sense of identity, as well as weapons, to the tribes he supports against foreign domination. The adventurer is not a dreamer but an active man with a goal. But does this goal coincide with social amelioration? It seems as though the revolution itself is not the end but a means in the hands of the adventurer to realise his own self-fulfilment. The search for power is never the promotion of the social cause: the cause is but a by-product of the adventurer's drive for self-assertion.

Although he ultimately contributes to the revolution, the adventurer restricts his commitment exclusively to his own self which he seeks, in action, after having failed in the bourgeois society from which he originates. The eventual future of the new order for which the adventurer fights is of no consequence: the frenetic present of action is what attracts him. Perken's defining characteristic is 'son indifférence à se définir socialement' (VR 16); as well, 'l'absence de finalité donnée à la vie était devenue une condition de l'action' (VR 39). As to Garine, he is more explicit:

Je ne tiens pas la société pour mauvaise, pour susceptible d'être améliorée. Je la tiens pour absurde. Absurde. Je ne veux nullement dire déraisonnable. Qu'on la transforme, cette société ne m'intéresse pas. Ce n'est pas l'absence de justice en elle qui m'atteint, mais quelque chose de plus profond, l'impossibilité de donner à une forme sociale, quelle qu'elle soit, mon adhésion. Je suis asocial comme je suis athée, et de la même façon.[27]

But the adventurer is bound to fail because, in the end, he does not realise the self he thought he had when he escaped the solitude of his bourgeois culture. His commitment to action does not lessen his feeling of isolation, because he does not want to create a new self but to keep the old one with all its old values. Rather than letting the situation dictate his role, he dictates his own role to the situation. The adventurer drags his old self with him, and his failure is echoed in his physical downfall. Both Perken and Garine end their lives sick and helpless, and while the defiance of sickness gives them a greater sense of power (in controlling, as it were, their own death), they finally become conscious of their failure. This realisation, however, occurs at the point of no return, when the course of events can no longer be reversed. The true tragedy of the adventurer is in the realisation of his failure and in his struggle with destiny. Both Garine and Perken, ironically enough, become self-conscious not through 'l'emploi le plus efficace de sa force' (CO 57), but through the look of the Other. Garine and Perken are thrown back to their own lonely, diseased bodies by whores who refuse to be made into objects.[28] Perken has an urge to kill

Claude at the end of the novel, because his existence is not his own but is dependent on Claude's look, a look which condemns him to death.

> Pour la seconde fois, il rencontrait sa mort dans le regard d'un homme; il éprouva furieusement le désir de tirer sur lui, comme si le meurtre seul aît pu lui permettre d'affirmer son existence, de lutter contre sa propre fin. (VR 191)

The exclusion of the Other in the realisation of self is further elaborated by the revolutionaries[29] who carry the action of the adventurer to its extreme. Self-possession becomes the only drive of Tchen and Hong who forget the cause for which they are fighting; their action is mere terrorism, bordering on anarchism in its negation of the principles and ideas of the parties they so enthusiastically joined in the first place. Both Hong and Tchen represent Western consciousnesses in their obsession with their own self and with the realisation of self through a totally destructive action. To Hong, 'seule l'action au service de la haine n'est ni mensonge, ni lâcheté, ni faiblesse: seule, elle s'oppose suffisament aux mots' (CO 146). In his incessant search for being something, Hong becomes blind to the complexity of social phenomena: 'il n'y a que deux races, dit-il, les misérables et les autres' (CO 144).

As for Tchen, 'l'action dans les groupes de choc ne suffisait plus au jeune homme, le terrorisme devenait pour lui une fascination' (CH 51). The entanglement with self, and the fascination for terrorism to realise it, bring about a feeling of alienation in Tchen; 'il n'était pas des leurs. Malgré le meurtre, malgré sa présence. S'il mourrait aujourd'hui, il mourrait seul' (CH 74). Tchen's pursuit of his self finally drives him to self-destruction; his final act is not a heroic one since his true purpose is not the murder of Chang-Kai-Shek but an extreme form of self-possession. Tchen wants to be his own God in giving himself his own death; but even self-possession in death is unrealisable for the final release of the trigger is barely a conscious act, if at all intentional; 'il tira sans s'en apercevoir' (CH 191). The revolutionary, then, is an adventurer taken to the extreme; they both negate the cause for which they struggle, and must therefore be transcended if social change is to take place; they both die or disappear from the scene of the novel.

The roles of the adventurer and the terrorist are counterbalanced by the role of the militant. The action of the militant is determined by the social principles which pre-exist him and which he contributes to bring about; the militant is a tool in the hands of a social movement. Kyo and Katow are motivated by social principles which transcend them; their death as individuals in no way affects the course of history and the fight for these principles.[30] The militant struggles for a cause, not his own. 'Sa vie avait un sens, et il le connaissait: donner à chacun de ces hommes que la famine en ce moment même, faisait mourir comme une peste lente, la possession de sa propre dignité' (CH 55). The militant is not concerned with the immediate since he constructs a building which takes time and planning; the militant rejects the Apocalypse and builds for the future.[31]

Jean-Paul Sartre provides us with a substantial analysis of the Malrucian dichotomy between being and doing, between those who seek self-definition and those who seek social amelioration.

Un ordre s'établit: la fin existe d'abord et c'est elle qui définit le parti comme l'ensemble concerté des actions qui permettent de l'atteindre. Chaque action à son tour se cherche son instrument et par là définit une personne. Le militant ne demande pas à son acte de le justifier: il n'est pas d'abord pour se faire justifier ensuite. Mais sa personnalité enveloppe sa propre justification puisqu'elle est constituée par la fin à atteindre. L'entreprise qui le définit excède de loin la durée d'une vie; il travaille donc sans cesse au-delà de sa propre mort et sa disparition ne modifiera pas le processus historique, pas plus que son apparition ne l'a modifié; sa volonté lui survivra, que le parti lui avait un instant prêtée, elle continuera l'ouvrage sans lui.

Mais pour le jeune bourgeois qui tente de communiquer avec les hommes, c'est l'action qui est la fin parce que c'est elle qui doit réaliser cette communication. L'ordre est renversé: il agit pour se sauver et choisit une fin pour agir; toute fin est bonne en principe: il suffit qu'elle justifie l'action qui le justifiera. Toutefois son projet fondamental est négatif. Il ne saurait envisager, en effet, de recevoir des hommes une personnalité: il voudrait le salut de celle qu'il a.[32]

The ultimate failure of the adventurer points to Malraux's postulation of selfhood as the product of a situation which, in the case of the militant, coincides with the ideology and subjectivity with which the party, the social cause, invests the individual. The committed man exists in a network of relationships; he is for-the-others whereas the adventurer seeks self-definition and fulfilment in the arrangement of his own biography. Heroism (the traditional hero) constitutes a chronological laying out of autobiographical facts in a series; that is, the performance of an autobiography. Rather than living out a life-in-situation, in relationship, the adventurer (and the hero) acts out his autobiography.

These roles, it should be noted, are dictated by a historical situation, be it the Chinese Revolution, the Spanish Civil War, or the Second World War, and they are assumed as such by the individuals who embody them. Whether the role is of the escapist, or of the militant or adventurer, they all relate to a situation of social change. This view differs from prevalent theories of role-playing such as Erving Goffman's in *The presentation of self in everyday life*. Goffman views everyday life as a stage on which players act out their roles:

> In analyzing the self we are drawn from its possessor, from the person who will profit or lose most by it, for he and his body merely provide the peg on which something of collaborative manufacture will be hung for a time. And the means for producing and maintaining selves do not reside inside the peg; in fact these means are often bolted down in social establishments. There will be a back region with its tools for shaping the body, and a front region with its fixed props. There will be a team of persons whose activity on stage in conjunction with available props will constitute the scene from which the performed character's self will emerge, and another team, the audience, whose interpretive activity will be necessary for this emergence. The self is a product of all these arrangements, and in all of its parts bears the mark of this genesis.[33]

This in itself makes more sense than theories which impute behaviour to the individual's inner qualities and flaws, to his so-called nature, and is no doubt an adequate portrayal of the social dynamics, but Goffman's theory is confined to role playing as it is practised in the daily life of Western society. The setting is always 'any place surrounded by fixed barriers to perception in which a particular kind of activity regularly takes place.'[34] The values of this society as well as the roles, or subjectivities, with which it provides individuals is never put into question. Goffman's approach is that of a neutral observer, the objective scholar — a role which is itself dictated by the hegemonic mode. Goffman's lack of commitment to the values which his own examples connote is indicative of his critical weakness. Sartre's famous example of the waiter in the café playing at being a waiter is quoted by Goffman as being an adequate instance of role playing. The waiter is indeed overdoing it, and this has to do, according to Sartre, with the ceremony the public demands of all tradesmen: 'there is the dance of the grocer, of the tailor, of the auctioneer, by which they endeavour to persuade their clientele that they are nothing but a grocer, an auctioneer, a tailor.'[35] Goffman ignores the fact that these roles are often fake roles forced on a subject who has no choice but fulfil them, that these roles are dictated by a specific market situation, and that they, in effect, negate a sane social praxis. This is precisely the context in which 'l'enfer c'est les autres' because the public, the others, imprison one in a role which promotes the dialectics of victimiser and victimised. As Sartre indicates: 'there are indeed many precautions to imprison a man in what he is, as if we lived in perpetual fear that he might escape from it, that he might break away and suddenly elude his condition.'[36] And Goffman's examples of role-playing conform to the mechanics of fact and not to the enhancement of value.

Malraux's conception of the role is different in that while it cannot describe the role within that future society, it at least points to the possibility and the direction of these roles in a sane social praxis. After all Malraux himself is a product of a well-defined historical period in which the 'adventurer' is still a possible role. Also, the roles of the adventurer and the escapist are residual roles originating in the West. (Discursively they hark back to the Neo-Classical era when the travel and the escape were new productions, for all the literary thematics of the period centre on travel and escape down to the end of the romantic period.) In conformity with the notion of the historical personage, Malraux's conception of role is historically conditioned; it is a meeting place of a social definition and an individual consciousness which chooses freely to incorporate that definition. The role is not a ceremony: it is a genuine social performance geared towards the improvement of the social body as a whole.

The new autobiography

L'homme ne se construit pas chronologiquement; les moments

de la vie ne s'additionnent pas les uns aux autres dans une accumulation ordonnée. Les biographies qui vont de l'âge de cinq ans à l'âge de cinquante ans sont de fausses confessions. Ce sont les expériences qui situent l'homme. Je crois que l'on peut trouver une vie à travers ses expériences, et non pas énoncer l'expérience comme le couronnement du récit . . . Les *Antimémoires* refusent la biographie avec préméditation. Ils ne se fondent pas sur un journal ou sur des notes. En partant des éléments décisifs de mon expérience, je trouve un personnage, et des fragments d'histoire. Je raconte les faits et décris le personnage comme s'il ne s'agissait pas de moi. De temps à autre, des épisode me reviennent en mémoire, je les rajoute simplement.[37]

This passage clarifies some of the motivating ideas behind Malraux's autobiographical venture. It informs both a technique and a world view. In terms of structure, this text opposes the cumulative process of traditional autobiographies where one event follows another as if things happen in a linear sequence. Linearity is an artificial construct totally alienated from the event itself. Instead, Malraux proposes a cluster of experiences around which one can situate a self, but his self does not limit phenomena to its own parameters. It is 'relationship' and as such must be considered as an element within a whole. This is precisely why Malraux encounters a personage, for in every relationship the role is primordial. The personage, the persona that is formed from the outside through the combination of a situation and another consciousness is described with detachment; from an angle one can have a perspective on one's acts. Malraux describes the act as if it were not his; this is the point at which fiction and life become one. Those fictive roles coincide with the contingent entity labelled 'André Malraux'. The episodes from the past — and this is a secondary process — are brought back by memory and Malraux simply adds ('rajoute') them to those basic experiences that define him.

Memory is a secondary process — a simple addition — because it is not the primary organising principle of experience. The organising principle is that cluster of experiences to which all other phenomena are functional. The small biographical details attach to those central experiences: they do not constitute an end in themselves. And if they can be done away with, so much the better. The story of a childhood becomes futile since it does not contribute to the basic relationship Malraux wants to establish with the world. But memory does not run in opposition to imagination; it is merely subordinate to it, for certain acts of memory are necessary in the creation of relationships and juxtapositions. Malraux is negating a specific kind of time, not time *per se*. In the writing of *Antimémoires* he is rejecting an individual time which developed in the classical age.[38] But while negating individual time Malraux promotes historical time. Rousseau, we recall, in his rejection of time, gives the effect of a frozen moving picture for he advocated the superposition of the past over the present in the sphere of the individual consciousness. The achievement of eternity in Rousseau — stillness — is the outcome of a transformation of time into space: the frozen image becomes a spatial entity. Not so with Malraux. We are presented in this text with an indefinite series of tableaux interconnecting and interpenetrating one another. It is a horizontal movement, but with an inner dynamic. Time, in Malraux, means the dimension which consciousness achieves in its spreading of itself over the surface of things — a 'counter-memory'. The act of spreading itself is a moving present for, while it moves, consciousness creates itself together with the world — the effect of a series of movies running on the same screen in synchrony.

In effect, then, Malraux achieves two important goals. One is the creation of a new form within the autobiographical tradition (a transformation conforming to a definite discursive shift which Malraux embodies) which has to do with the structure of the book. The other is a rejection of a world view in which the world is reduced to the self. The refusal of chronology in *Antimémoires* means the rejection of introspection, for beyond Malraux's expressed hatred for his own childhood, there is a philosophical statement about the recapture of childhood in general. The introspective process functions on the assumption that one can corner one's self, that one can go back to a basic truth, to something that is there although not apparent at the moment. But in effect one encounters only an image of one's self, and a fleeting one at that. This image cannot be consistent since it changes as time goes on. Catching one's centre is similar to the dog's futile attempt to catch its tail. The recapture of a past individual life that finds meaning in its own irreducible and immediate uniqueness as an entity abstracted from the historical continuum (or in most cases as an escape from that continuum) is what Malraux is attempting to negate in this text. In classical autobiography self is less a negation of the world than an affirmation of its power against the world; self always remains the last resort against all external odds — especially, the Other. This is a conception of self that promotes competitiveness and divisiveness, and opposes integration.

Malraux is offering us an integrated self, a self within-the-world, a self which is pure exteriority. To Malraux, self-knowledge, self-discovery, is an illusion. Self cannot be discovered since it is not there; it is a vacuum to be filled from the outside. It has to be created. Hence the necessity for fiction: there is no truth to be found or discovered in the story of a life; truth must be created. Truth remains a future process, something to look forward to. And if Malraux cannot find his central self (because it does not exist) he must seek his identity in the various fictional selves which he creates. The various masks mediate one another in turn; and each mask is mediated by the outside world — that is, the existing situation and the other consciousnesses partaking in it — while it is enacted.

This conception of self gives a perspective on Malraux's views of Freudianism and the Surrealist movement which he espoused at the beginning of his writing career. Both Freudianism and Surrealism share one basic belief: that one can go back to a primordial reality inherent within the human consciousness. Freudianism, in its early manifestation, postulated the discovery of a truth, or rather, the return to an experience hidden under the thick layers of the unconscious, of which the patient is ignorant. The hidden truth must be sought and discovered for the patient to regain control of his self. Interestingly enough, self-discovery in the mental patient comes with a confession, the patient's recalling and verbalisation of that basic traumatic experience. This 'something' that one goes back to is shared by the Surrealist movement as well, for the Surrealist must enter a previous state of innocence if he is to be creative. This belief lies at the heart of 'Ecriture Automatique'. Malraux left the Surrealist movement early in his career (after the writing of two Surrealist texts, *Lunes en papier* and *Royaume farfelu*) because it did not answer his call for meaning. He subsequently sought meaning in art and revolution — both activities of affirmative negation.[39]

The New Literature and the 'signifying personage'

With Malraux there is nothing to go back to and definition

143

becomes a transcendental movement towards the future. If action replaces introspection, it is because action is the dimension of hope (*L'Espoir*). The man of action, the artist, does not drag a self with him wherever he goes; he creates a fresh one as he moves.

> Agir n'est pas seulement exprimer une personnalité qui existe déjà, c'est véritablement créer sa personnalité, l'acte étant le moment où le magma informe des éléments constitutifs du moi se regroupent, s'organisent afin d'atteindre un but précis.[40]

This 'magma informe' is the external ongoing feedback which makes up the self, the vacuous structure which has existence only to the extent that it awaits opportunities, that it holds its breath in its aspirations to realise a role within a given socio-historical reality. The refusal of chronology also means the negation of resignation, and of any kind of completion or satisfaction. The traditional autobiographer 'accepts' himself and undertakes to describe a totality he is satisfied with (see Edward Gibbon's autobiography and the details of his gentlemanly upbringing). Not so with Malraux. The fact that he wrote the book in his seventies does not make him a summariser of past events for Malraux never planned to write his autobiography. He wanted to complete another work of fiction stated early in his career, *La lutte avec l'ange*, but instead, the *Antimémoires* came to him. To Malraux one does not plan an autobiography not because one cannot plan one but because there is nothing to plan, nothing to arrange. Self, then, is the dimension of imagination and not of memory, an entity that must be renewed ceaselessly. The creation of fiction coincides with the remembrance of an imaginary act which is, in effect, an autobiographical act. And those critics who claimed that Malraux was unable to create independent characters and that all his heroes are extensions of his self missed this crucial point.[41]

Denis Boak, for example, claims that 'Malraux has deliberately attempted to create his own life as an artistic entity in its own right',[42] and that 'in all Malraux's characterization the one constant factor is intellectual conception. He does not achieve such richly human characters as Proust or even Martin du Gard.'[43] These statements clearly indicate where Denis Boak stands; his comparative tool is the novel of 'character', the biographical novel. Indeed, if we compare Malraux's heroes to the traditional hero of the Realist novel, they certainly lack substance. But is this

an adequate basis of comparison? Forcing this comparison on
Malraux's text means inserting it in a literary tradition he rejects,
a tradition he writes against.[44] So Tchen, Garine, Perken, Kassner
are naked not because Malraux could not grant them more substance but because they are different from the 'complete hero' we
often encounter in works of fiction.[45]

The 'complete hero', or in Boak's terms the 'richly human
character', purports to be a duplication of a real human being and
the truth of this kind of character lies in his realisation of his
human counterpart. Such a blurring of the ontological gap
between fiction and reality corresponds to an ideology which sees
the world as a static phenomenon to be represented in fiction. Such
a replication can occur only within the *status quo* which accommodates a static conception of the literary act. The Realist novel
(Balzac, Flaubert), for example, is caught in an insurmountable
paradox because it avoids the very problems with which it
proposes to deal. The tragedy of an Emma Bovary or a Père
Goriot vanishes behind the serenity of that world the writer has so
objectively described to us. After Emma Bovary and Père Goriot
disappear we can still feel secure, because the world in which they
have evolved remains in existence for the reader's self-assurance.
The reader can say: they pass but I am still here! Balzac or
Flaubert, in effect, do not ask why, for that would involve a
reappraisal of reality which in turn might threaten the *status quo*.
After all, Emma Bovary commits suicide not because there was
something wrong in her socio-political reality but because she
could not control her passions, or because there was a flaw in her
character!

But if the socio-historical reality is dynamic, it cannot be replicated (unless we force duplication on it) as a whole, be that whole
an individual or a group. What, therefore, is the ontological status
of Malraux's protagonists? Can we talk of pure absences? Indeed,
the character as a well-rounded entity with an identity card is non-
existent in Malraux's fictional world. His protagonists are personages — personae — incarnated roles. In his study of Laclos's
Liaisons dangereuses Malraux indicates in a nutshell his conception
of characterisation, the basic postulate being that the writer's
purpose is not the creation of 'full entities', complete beings with
psychologies and personalities but 'faire agir des personnages en
fonction de ce qu'ils pensent'.[46]

Les personnages ont ceci de particulier qu'ils accomplissent

des actes prémédités, en fonction d'une conception générale
de la vie.

Avec eux le héros finit et le personnage significatif commence. Il y a dans tout personnage significatif au moins trois
éléments: d'abord la conception d'un but de l'homme, puis la
volonté de l'atteindre, puis la mise en système de cette
volonté.[47]

Ces personnages existent à peine physiquement et n'ont pas
de biographie.[48]

There is no doubt that Malraux's signifying personage has an
autonomous life since he acts freely in accordance with his world
view; he is independent to the extent that he signifies an idea,
incarnates an ideology. At the same time this personage is
Malraux's own extension because Malraux provides him with his
field of play, the idea to incorporate. It should be noted that the
signifying personage is not an abstraction; it is not a pure idea.
Between the personage and the idea, there is the role. In other
words, we are not dealing with an absence but with a partial
presence; the personage does not coincide with the idea because
fiction, being a scene that demands performances, cannot accomo-
date abstracted ideas. In Malraux's view of the form, fiction
requests the signifying personage in order to move the idea forward; because fiction constitutes the description of situations, a
personage is needed to carry out the actions the situation calls for.
The signifying personage is the body of the idea — the minimum
physicality incarnation requires. The signifying personage is not
fact but value. In contrast to the *nouveau roman*, Malraux's novel is
not a novel of absence; it is the novel of a necessary active
presence.

The signifying personage exists in the present only; not only are
we not exposed to his past but he himself probes his past, if he does
so at all, in function of a present preoccupation.[49] The reader is
exposed to that present only, to one point of view at a time; if he is
to recreate the text, the reader must of necessity enter the consciousness of the personage. (The first scene of *La Condition
humaine*, for example, exposes the reader precisely to what Tchen
is experiencing at the moment: we see with Tchen the street lights
through the window and the shadow of the cat in the room; we feel
the wound Tchen inflicts to his arm and the nausea caused by it.)
Malraux is no doubt influenced by film techniques, for in film too
the viewer is exposed to one point at a time. When the present of a

given scene in the Malrucian world becomes past, when the action of a given moment is consumed, then we move to another present.[50] This is not to say that we are confronting here a situation of fragmentation; the lack of connectedness among the scenes of *L'Espoir* or the novels on China is apparent because the scenes do not follow one another in time though they belong to the same reality being portrayed, be it the Spanish Civil War or the Chinese Revolution. And this complex reality affects various personages in various settings. Again, these scenes and settings follow one another in the book because the book is linear in its physical nature; but in Malraux's fictional universe they occur in simultaneity in a multiplicity of times and settings.

> Le champ de vision du lecteur est restreint à celui du personnage principal, de la même manière qu'au cinéma, le champ de vision du spectateur est celui de la caméra: la caméra, comme le personnage, est toujours en situation dans le monde.[51]

Malraux's novel of situation, then, makes all psychological considerations irrelevant. Though autonomous in their actions, his heroes must be, by definition, extensions of himself, incarnations of his ideas. Identical to him, they have no past and nothing to look back to. We should not even use the word 'hero'; like the word 'character', it connotes a well-rounded entity, a finished product, an artificial construct.

> Je ne crois pas vrai que le romancier doive créer des personnages, il doit créer un monde cohérent et particulier, comme tout autre artiste. Non faire concurrence à l'état civil, mais faire concurrence à la réalité qui lui est imposée, celle de la 'vie', tantôt en semblant s'y soumettre et tantôt en la transformant pour rivaliser avec elle.[52]

But is not tailoring one's life story to that of the world an exercise in bad faith? Is this not the ultimate in mythomania? Does Malraux disappear from the centre of his story in order to assign to himself the centre of world events? Cecil Jenkins finds the *Antimémoires* lacking in structure and intention. He claims that Malraux 'is in effect trying to apply a fictional aesthetic to a work of memoirs, and in some sense obliged thereby to treat himself as a fictional character' and that 'through being drawn into writing above the self, he has not quite done himself justice.'[53] Rima Drell Reck also believes that Malraux's approach is elitist and that 'despite the strikingly active, historical quality of his novels and of his life, Malraux remains committed to a lifelong meditation on action and art as supra-historical phenomena.'[54]

It seems that these two critics have missed Malraux's point in the *Antimémoires*. He is not writing 'above the self', and action and art are not 'supra-historical phenomena' in his world. What is at stake here is the essence of literature itself, its definition and purpose. With *Antimémoires* as the crowning of his fiction, Malraux is advancing a new conception of literature — a literature that negates psychology; in other words, the negation of the accepted practice of literature. With the rejection of memory, introspection and psychology (all of which point to the same reality in Malraux's view of the literature of yesterday), he is making a statement on what literature ought to be. For given the impossibility of knowing oneself, introspection and psychology become futile: how can one claim to know the Other when one does not know oneself! The Other as a closed entity is non-measurable, a pure unknown. The only realm of exchange and communication is action, for in action the dialectics of the moment is all that counts. And action, in turn, means freedom from memory: not forgetfulness as temporary amnesia (where the possibility of control is still given to the past over the present), but forgetfulness as a radical act eradicating the residues of the past and forcing the present over consciousness. The present is, in essence, a ceaseless beginning, and man renews this present through his continual metamorphosis. Man, the anonymous and impersonal man, the artist of ancient cultures and civilisations, everyman, is the generator of metamorphosis.

Le processus créateur de l'artiste implique le besoin de dépasser la représentation dont il se nourrit, et il est de conquête et non de soumission.[55]

L'art est un anti-destin.[56]

Notre art me paraît une rectification du monde, un moyen d'échapper à la condition d'homme . . . Dans ce qu'il a d'essentiel, notre art est une humanisation du monde. (NA 128)

To Malraux, art is non-mimetic; it recreates the world in ever-renewed forms. Style is an existing structure which the artist penetrates; it is the artist's own realm of action. Art is an anti-destiny because it rebels against destiny in its re-creation of an autonomous reality which is parallel to the world without duplicating it. As Malraux indicates in *Les Voix du silence*, the historical process of artistic creation is dialectical. An artist is always born to a cultural reality, to a particular epistemic configuration, which he assimilates in order to achieve signification and transcendence. The artistic act is inscribed within an artistic discourse the parameters of which the artist must transcend through the creation of new forms via the permutation of the old ones.[57] Malraux's views on art are consistent with his own literary creation; it would therefore be wrong to assume that he functions within the Realist tradition or within the prevalent autobiographical tradition. It is clear that he transcends both and creates new forms which are more adequate to the expression of our historical situation. His views on the critical activity counter all traditions of positivistic criticism; his conception of the colloquy points to a critical activity based on group effort and dialogue.

> The Colloquy has at its disposal a much wider field, its methods applying to more than the individual life. It selects events as well as people: Mao's Long March, Hiroshima, the assassination of President Kennedy, all follow one another like the acts of tragedy conceived on a planetary scale . . . How can we fail to see that we are working out a new method of grasping the individual which is not that of individualism? Its method seems to be to substitute for well-regulated lighting a vast number of snapshots, bits of film, shadow images. It owes much to journalism and audio visual aids. Its values are not those of biography. A biographer's dream is to exhaust all the possibilities offered by his model . . . Individualism takes the individual both for its subject and its object . . . The Colloquy, being rather like a hunter on the scent, escapes those who use it as a method. Less superficial than it might appear, it regards its pluralistic approach as important, and is careful not to confuse it with eclecticism. The pluralism of a Colloquy surrounds its subject, picks him out, loses him, like the beams of an anti-aircraft searchlight on the track of an aeroplane. The provisional element introduced by metamorphosis meets the element of chance introduced by the Colloquy.[58]

This passage sums up Malraux's views of literary criticism as an activity; his conception of the Colloquy advances a new view of the critical activity which counters the traditions of positivistic literary criticism. The Colloquy negates the individual act of the critic centreing on the individual life of the writer. Since an individual life overflows its immediate parameters into an infinity of ramifications, the Colloquy attempts, by a process of approxima-tion, to cover, at least partially, some of these ramifications. Because the author is caught in a network of relations — style, form, culture, country, historical period, ideology, etc. — he can never be exhausted. He exists in these relations only; hence the absurdity of any attempt to grasp the 'writer' or his 'work'. The pluralistic approach of the Colloquy coincides with Malraux's comprehensive and dialectical outlook on phenomena. Like the Malrucian novel, the Colloquy is open-ended; it deals with subjects-in-situations, with the movement of events.

Antimémoires,[59] then, competes with life; it creates a coherent world through a series of permutations of the material world. Again, it is not a historical reconstruction, but a relating to the world through the act of fiction which in itself is biographical. Fiction as an act of relation opposes the spontaneity and satisfac-tion of the 'story' as it is or was lived. Fiction means the inten-tional creation of situations where different consciousnesses meet each other and the world, and not the creation of linearly developed monadic individuals. Fiction is a statement of value, and the intentionality of value transcends biographical spon-taneity. Literature, then, is the biography of situations pertaining to the human condition. *Antimémoires* is such a depiction through its selection of three of the most instrumental historical events in our century — Ghandi at the head of the Indian masses on the salt march against the British Empire, Mao at the head of his armies crossing the Ta-tu river, and the annihilation of masses of human beings and their values in the Second World War: the entrance of two huge nations on the scene of modern history, and the degrada-tion and humiliation of multitudes because of the loss of faith in human values. The choice of two nations of the East is not gratuitous: it counterbalances the individualism of the West. In the East man is (still) an integrated member in the group, and not an alienated, self-sufficient entity torn from its supportive structures.

But despite the horrors and tragedies recounted by camp survivors and the eulogy to Jean Moulin, the martyred Maquis commander, in the last section of the book, *Antimémoires* remains a celebration of man throughout his historical vicissitudes. Malraux emphasises repeatedly the sacred dimension of human life. Whether he speaks of the old religions and cultures or of recent historical events, Malraux relates to the sacred in man — that part of man which cannot be annihilated by torture or degradation. 'Or il restait assez d'humanité, même aux prisonniers agonisants pour deviner que la volonté de vivre n'était pas animale, mais obscurément sacrée' (AN 587). And this sacredness has nothing whatsoever to do with metaphysics. It is man's ability to prevail in his ongoing metamorphosis of old structures in the creation of new forms. Not by chance does Malraux end the volume with a final visit to the Lascaux caves, for in these caves human destiny throughout the ages is enacted. It is in these caves that history is played out. The Lascaux caves are the dwellings of primitive man, the location of his art; they also provide storage for the arms of the Resistance fighters. An 'incomprehensible bond' links the animals on the walls with the crates of weapons. On the final page these caves are being restored for visitors, turned into a museum.

> Est-ce au sortir d'un tel lieu, sous un firmament semblable, qu'une sorte de gorille chasseur comme les fauves et peintre comme les hommes comprit pour la première fois qu'il devait mourir? (AN 569)

7

Conclusions

At the term of this study it would seem impossible to conjecture as to the future of autobiography as a central literary practice in Western society, for any discursive formation is apprehensible only within a retroactive, negational process. The formulation of any discursive mutation must of necessity posit a historical span; we can come to terms with an epistemic shift only after it has taken place: after a discursive elaboration has emerged, consolidated and finally ceased to function as a dominant practice. We know negationally that the medieval hierarchical conception of subjectivity has exhausted its operational activity by the end of the Renaissance precisely because there emerged new practices (i.e. rational methodic activities geared toward possession and dominion) which displaced the hierarchical model, and these practices are 'unlike' the ones that medieval man was incorporating and to which in turn he contributed. And if, as Wittgenstein says, the limits of our language are the limits of our world, a consciousness discursively 'different' from ours will be needed to ascertain the operative efficacy of the centralising and territorialising subjectivity of the discourse of modernism.

Thus, while Malraux transgresses the generic structure (and thereby helps to demystify it), the autobiographical practice retains the form of a product — the self, a commodity with an exchange value. And the saleability of the self in our society makes autobiography a productive literary form, overtaking the whole field of literature. Every other politician, actor and media person writes his or her life story, not to mention literary autobiographies. One no longer has to await a ripe old age to undertake this task; autobiography seems to be waiting for the man rather than the man for the autobiography. This literary form constitutes a mere fragment of a wider social movement which promotes the self; and the massive trend towards the (re)establishment of the irreducible self is inscribed within a much wider social praxis. The burgeoning literature of self-awareness (which is part of the even larger phenomenon of 'self-help' literature) conforms to the same ideological presuppositional structure; like autobiography, it offers the healthiest and shortest cut to self-knowledge, through multiple processes of introspection and examination of the self or some part thereof. This is a further movement towards the internalisation of the life process, and the separation of the individual from the social context in which he is born and which nurtures his consciousness. This trend aims at the amelioration of the individual to the detriment of his life-supports, his social milieu, and the others who make it up. The self in this literature[1] remains the exclusive property of its owner, an object on which one can operate.

In effect, then, while the demystifying intention of this book is geared to the level of the signifier — that is, the forms of expression that the concept of self adopts in the Western literary tradition — the aim has been the signified itself, the social organisation which makes for the possibility of these forms of expression. The assumption is that the demystification of a given form provides an adequate critique of the social intertext filtered through that form. If autobiography consists of a myth, this myth (for ideological reasons pertaining specifically to the free market) is inserted into the social text as a natural phenomenon: 'everyone has a self' is an evident statement, for common sense dictates that every autobiography refers to a self, to a pre-given structure outside the text, to an essence, to Man.

The self, it is thus claimed, exists before language, and the transparency of language allows for the pure referentiality of the literary text. So the myth of autobiography involves two related postulates: that the self is inside each one of us, and that it is a pre-given structure, a finished product, and a free one at that (for freedom is the *sine qua non* of exchange relations). The emphasis in the prevalent ideology has been on the structure of the self and not on its structuration, where structuration means a process of production. But if the self is created in and through language, it can never be a finished product; it cannot be analysed or described since the description itself is in ceaseless movement.

At stake therefore is the ideological confirguation which determines the creation of the self as a natural phenomenon. If we take

Rousseau as an example, we see that the confessions as a mode of expression conform to the ideology of the contract, that they are inscribed within his theory — the eighteenth-century theory — of the social contract. The *Confessions* as a mode of expression translate a set of social statements which one can extract from the social world — the beliefs and paradigms at the bottom of our very sociality, for the politics of liberalism starts in eighteenth-century revolutionary France.

> The difficulties of modern liberal-democratic theory lie deeper than had been thought, the original seventeenth-century individualism contained the central difficulty, which lay in its possessive quality. Its possessive quality is found in its conception of the individual as essentially the proprietor of his own person or capacities, owing nothing to society for them. The individual was seen neither as a moral whole, nor as part of a larger social whole, but as an owner of himself. The relation of ownership, having become for more and more men the critically important relation determining their actual freedom and actual prospect of realising their full potentialities, was read back into the nature of the individual. The individual, it was thought, is free inasmuch as he is proprietor of his person and capacities. The human essence is freedom from dependence on the wills of others, and freedom is a function of possession. Society becomes a lot of free equal individuals, related to each other as proprietors of their own capacities and of what they have acquired by their exercise. Society consists of relations of exchange between proprietors. Political society becomes a calculated device for the protection of this property and for the maintenance of an orderly relation of exchange.[2]

The possessive dimension of the self can be achieved only if it is spatialised, made into an object, and its temporal dimension is annihilated; in order for the self to be possessed freely, it must be an object, for ownership has to do with having and not being. Consequently one does not talk about production but about 'characteristics', 'qualities', 'adapability' — that is, internal features which presumably originate within the individual. In short, ownership of the self dictates the introduction of atomisation and reification into the social structure. As suggested, the relationships existing within this social structure conform to the market conditions which prevail therein: they are contractual. Equality and freedom in our society are necessary formal conditions for the realisation of the social contract; they negate, in effect, man's definition as social, as sharing genuinely in a communal life with fellow humans. This equality and freedom operate on a division within, and separateness without, of selves from one another and on the roles such as social structure imposes on its subjects. Atomisation and reification are at the heart of our praxis of seriality. And seriality, as Sartre demonstrated, permeates all the domains of our life-world and most basically our dealings with one another.

> La série quelle qu'elle soit et en tout état de cause se constitue à partir de l'unité-objet et, inversement, c'est dans le milieu sériel et à travers des comportements sériels que l'individu réalise pratiquement et théoriquement son appartenance à l'être commun. Il y a des conduites sérielles, il y a des sentiments et des pensées sériels; autrement dit, la série est un mode d'être des individus les uns par rapport aux autres et par rapport à l'être commun et ce mode d'être les métamorphose dans toutes leurs structures.[3]

Seriality has engulfed us to the extent that we see it as part of our very nature: it is forced upon consciousness as inevitable. In this book we have investigated the parameters of a major expressive form of this seriality: the ways in which it manifests itself in the autobiographical conception of selfhood. For autobiography as a discursive practice is both a process of production of meaning and at the same time a process of structuration of a subjectivity. Autobiography, then, is not and cannot be the description of a finished reality, for reality itself is a process of production: all autobiography does is produce the subject of seriality. And the demystifying activity corresponds to the negational dimension of conciousness; it is a critical effort directed against the reification of the individual and the ossification of the institutions (whatever they may be) which provide that individual with a subjectivity. Negation is inherent to the social praxis; it is a part of that process whereby social forms evolve from preceding ones. (The society of the future remains an ever-moving target, for any institutional structure tends to stagnate and is ultimately transcended.)

It might appear that the claims made here are similar to the assertions of R. D. Laing.[4] Laing, no doubt, argues for the same socio-historical motivations behind the phenomenon of alienation; he sees in the social ego a repressive apparatus and grounds all our anxieties in the social praxis. However, Laing distinguishes between true and false madness, arguing for the social benefits of true madness as if it contained some integrative power, as if it were a welcome change from the ego capitalist society has forced upon us. But Laing idealises madness and, in effect, takes it out of the social realm. For while he argues very forcefully for the praxical reasons behind madness and mental illness, he posits an inner and an outer world — the inner self and the external ego — the one corresponding to the magical, the mystical and the demonic in man, and the other to our warped social egos. And the alternative to alienation is a flight from the social ego into the deepest recesses of the true inner self.

> True sanity entails in one way or another the dissolution of the normal ego, that false self completely adjusted to our alienated social reality: the emergence of the 'inner' archetypal mediators of divine power, and through this death a rebirth, and the eventual re-establishment of a new kind of ego-functioning, the ego now being the servant of the divine, no longer its betrayer.[5]

The metaphysical import of such a statement is quite evident. Contrary to what Laing claims, the dissolution of the ego yields only another ego. Laing's mystification is as strong as the autobiographical myth of the self. Madness is not a safety valve for normalcy but a hopeless (helpless) challenge against repressive reification. Laing fails to see the ideological dimension of the repressive apparatus called the self, which has to do with purely material and historical phenomena; idealising madness may allow one to escape the repressive apparatus, but not negate it. There is no division in man between inner and outer: if the schizophrenic does not make sense, it is not because he hovers between the inner and the outer but because he questions the sense-making process offered him by an engulfing hegemonic mode.[6] It is this questioning activity that allows us to learn (in this Laing is correct) from the exercise of madness.

The relationship between autobiography and madness was hinted at but not dealt with here because the main concern of this study has been with the proprietal dimension of selfhood (its centralisation and territorialisation), which constitutes one of the two vectors which underlie the presuppositional structure of industrial capitalism (its Oedipal dimension). The second vector (the Ulyssean dimension) is toward the decentralisation and deterritorialisation of this same self through the fluidity of the capitalist mode of production (its *perpetuum mobile*). It remains to be seen how the self is a repressive apparatus, and the forms of expression that repression adopts in autobiography. In other words, the conclusions of Deleuze and Guattari in *Anti-Œdipe* ought to be investigated in the realm of autobiography. Such a study would complement the one offered here, and would provide further clarification on the translation of social contradictions in the individual subjectivity.

L'axiomatique sociale des sociétés modernes est prise entre deux pôles, et ne cesse d'osciller d'un pôle à l'autre. Nées du décodage et de la déterritorialisation, sur les ruines de la machine despotique, les sociétés sont prises entre l'Urstaat qu'elles voudraient bien ressusciter comme unité surcodante et re-territorialisante, et les flux déchaînés qui les entrainent vers un seuil absolu. Elles recodent à tour de bras, à coups de dictature mondiale, de dictateurs locaux et de police toute-puissante, tandis qu'elles décodent ou laissent décoder les quantités fluantes de leurs capitaux et de leurs populations. Elles sont prises entre deux directions: archaisme et futurisme, néo-archaisme et ex-futurisme, paranoia et schyzophrénie. Elles vacillent entre deux pôles: le signe despotique paranoiaque, le signe-signifiant du despote qu'elles tentent de réanimer comme unité de code; le signe-figure du schyzo comme unité de flux décodé, schyze, point-signe ou coupure-flux. Sur l'un elles font garrot, mais elles s'écoulent ou s'épanchent par l'autre. Elles ne cessent à la fois d'être en retard et en avance sur soi.[7]

Notes and References

Chapter 1

1. See, for example, Wayne Shumaker, *English autobiography, its emergence, material and form* (Berkeley, University of California Press, 1954), and Philippe Lejeune, *L'Autobiographie en France* (Paris, Armand Colin, 1971).

2. Lejeune, *L'Autobiographie en France*, p. 14.

3. Elizabeth Bruss, *Autobiographical acts* (Baltimore, Johns Hopkins University Press, 1976).

4. Philippe Lejeune, *Le Pacte autobiographique* (Paris, Seuil, 1975).

5. John Searles, *Speech acts* (Cambridge Univeristy Press, 1969).

6. Hans Robert Jauss, 'Littérature médiévale et théorie des genres', *Poétique*, no. 1 (1970).

7. Ibid., p. 82.

8. Bruss, *Autobiographical acts*. pp. 5–6.

9. Ibid., p. 7.

10. Emile Benveniste, *Problèmes de linguistique générale* (Paris, Gallimard, 1966). See Chapter V, 'L'Homme dans la langue'.

11. Lejeune, *Le Pacte autobiographique*, p. 20.

12. Ibid., p. 26.

13. Ibid., p. 21.

14. Benveniste, *Problèmes de linguistique générale*, p. 254.

15. Ibid., p. 260.

16. Ibid., p. 261.

17. Lejeune, *Le Pacte autobiographique*, p. 36.

18. Stephen A. Shapiro, 'The dark continent of literature: autobiography' in *Comparative Literature Studies*, no: 5 (1968), p. 425.

19. Ibid., p. 435.

20. Roy Pascal, *Design and truth in autobiography* (Cambridge, Mass., Harvard University Press, 1960), p. 19.

21. Ibid., p. 78. See also pp. 185–95 regarding fictional techniques in autobiography.

22. Ibid., p. 195.

23. Roy Pascal's basic credos are to be found in his article, 'The autobiographical novel and the autobiography', *Essays in criticism*, vol. 9 (1959). 'The very form of the work of art seems to have something insincere about it which is inappropriate to the autobiographer's purpose' (p. 135). Representation and referentiality are the key to the delineation between autobiography and its subgenres; 'such a shaping of the work is, of course, necessarily involved in the very concept of the novel . . . the autobiography has its points of reference outside the work, in real life, in the non-fictionality of the author' (p. 148).

24. *New Literary History*, vol. IX, 1 (Autumn, 1977), pp. 2–26.

25. Ibid., pp. 2–3.

26. Ibid., p. 9.
27. Ibid., p. 26.
28. John Sturrock, 'The new model autobiographer', *New Literary History*, vol. IX (1977–8), p. 51.
29. For a substantial analysis of this concept in literature, see Edward Said, *Beginnings* (New York, Basic Books, 1975).
30. Gertrude Stein, *The autobiography of Alice B. Toklas* (New York, Vintage Books, 1960).
31. John Searle, 'The logical status of fictional discourse', *New Literary History*, vol. VI (1974–5), p. 327.
32. Walter J. Ong, *Rhetoric, romance and technology* (Ithaca, Cornell University Press, 1971), p. 167.
33. See Ong's *Ramus, method and the decay of dialogue* (Cambridge, Mass., Harvard University Press, 1958), pp. 306–14.
34. 'At this point Ramus' concept of method becomes particularly interesting because of the fact that this standard description of method is highly reminiscent of printing processes themselves, so that it enables one to impose organization on a subject by imagining it as made up of parts fixed in space in the way in which words are locked in a printer's form.' Ong, *Rhetoric, romance and technology*, p. 183.
35. And this preoccupation with textuality focuses on a movement 'from work to Text . . . attempts to present the articulations of the "theory" of this change of perception by which the literary object (which is clearly not an "object") moves from that of a formal, complete, organic whole to that of a "methodological field", a concept whose very premise implies the notions of activity, production and transformation'. Joshua Harari, 'Critical fictions/critical factions' in *Textual strategies: perspectives in post-structuralist criticism* (Ithaca, Cornell University Press, 1979), p. 38.

Chapter 2

1. Eric Auerbach, *Mimesis* (Princeton University Press, 1974), p. 23.
2. For an elaboration on this concept, see Jean-Pierre Faye's masterful study of the antisemitic problem in his *Migrations du récit sur le peuple juif* (Paris, Belfond, 1974). This concept is most adequate for the description of recurring narrative patterns in history. It should be noted, however, that 'migration' is a dynamic concept; that is, it is dependent upon the mutations that take place in the historical process. It is not the continuity or consistency of a given narrative pattern (for history is made up of narrative patterns) which is being sought — for that would mystify the historical reality — but, rather, the transformations that take place within a recurring narrative pattern or concept. Cervantes's *Don Quixote* may be looked at as a transformation of the Christian biblical narrative, for example.
3. 'Neo-Platonism lends itself particularly well in certain areas to his purpose. First, it helps him to understand and accept the Christian belief in God as an incorporeal and intelligible Substance by convincing him of the reality of the invisible, universal, and eternal Platonic forms. The

Forms are Christianized by being conceived as thoughts existing in the mind of God and St Augustine believes that the *ordo universi* revealed in Scriptures is identical with the imperfect realization in this world of the Platonic Ideas.' G. L. Keyes, *Christian faith and the interpretation of history: a study of St Augustine's philosophy of history* (Lincoln, University of Nebraska Press, 1966), p. 106.

4. For an overview of the available criticism, see the introduction to Robert J. O'Connell, *St Augustine's Confessions: the Odyssey of a soul* (Cambridge, Mass., Harvard University Press, 1969).

5. St Augustine, *The Confessions* (New York, Doubleday, 1960), p. 43. Further references will be made in the body of the text, initialled 'AC'.

6. The contradiction between form and content in Augustine can arise only after there is an autobiographical model, a tradition; if Augustine is compared to Rousseau, for example, then his writing lacks formal coherence. It is clear that in Augustine's time this contradiction was non-existent, since there was no autobiographical model available; the horizon of expectancy was different from ours today. No doubt the Augustinian discourse inserts itself within some already existing literary tradition but there is no one known model which is presumed to have constituted an intertext, although one may find micro-autobiographical texts even in the biblical narrative.

7. Two antagonistic attitudes coexist in the Augustinian text: on the one hand, man's wilful aspiration towards redemption and, on the other, a sense of predetermination and helplessness. Here we encounter the mixture of two traditions: the one, the notion that man is a free and rational agent; the other, that he is a created product in the hands of the Creator. The input of both traditions is quantitative and non-exclusive; at certain historical moments a greater share of God's contribution is required, at others, man can do with his rationality alone. By the eighteenth century when a wave of atheism swept certain groups in French society (specifically, the writers and philosophers), rationality had to do with man's ability to assume the social contract by transcending his primitive instinctual drives and egocentrism. This fetishisation of Reason will be dealt with subsequently.

8. James F. Anderson, *St Augustine and being* (The Hague, Martinus Nijhoff, 1965).

9. 'For the difference between Manichean and Christian was that, while the one saw the life task in learning to separate what had unjustly been condemned to coexist, the soul and the body, the other saw the salvation in reuniting in one healthy whole what man by his own fault had permitted to be torn asunder.' K. J. Weintraub, *The value of the individual* (Chicago, Univeristy of Chicago Press, 1978), p. 45.

10. 'Augustine always associated this pilgrimage home with an upward motion. Man has fallen out of place, away from the light into darker regions; his weight always endangering to fall back even further', ibid., p. 38. Notice the relationship between darkness and heaviness, light and lightness. The Christian imbrication on this idea is interesting for in the early Christian view to see the light meant to do away with the body, to become weightless, ethereal.

11. 'L'aspiration à Dieu n'est pas un état d'âme ou une exigence

simplement subjective, mais un statut ontologique, connaturel à l'homme, dont l'état "naturel" est donc celui d'un être créé avec une destination dont l'accomplissement transcende tous ses actes et l'ordre de la nature.' M. F. Sciacca, *St Augustin et le néo-platonisme: la possibilité d'une philosophie chrétienne* (Paris, Editions Béatrice Nauweleerts, 1956), p. 49.

12. 'Augustine makes similar remarks about the relationship between ontology and epistemology. Augustine's ontology consists of an hierarchical structure of reality with God, its creator, at the apex and the world of bodies at the lowest. His epistemology finds man beginning with sensation but attempting to climb by way of reason to the eternal ideas in the mind of God. Augustine conceived of God as both the source of human existence and the goal of human knowledge.' Ronald H. Nash, *The light of the mind: St Augustine's theory of knowledge* (Lexington, University of Kentucky Press, 1969).

13. St Augustine, *The political writings*, ed. H. Paolucci (Chicago, H. Regnery, 1962), p. 5.

14. Such an assumption necessitates the total passivity of consciousness: 'Truth is found and not made, and the human mind is subject to it.' M. C. D'Arcy, 'The philosophy of St Augustine', in M. C. D'Arcy *et al.* (eds), *A monument to St Augustine* (London, Sheed & Ward, 1930), p. 168.

15. Philippe Sellier, *Pascal et St Augustin* (Paris, Armand Colin, 1970), p. 202.

16. This manipulation of material reality is true of all theocentric systems and takes concrete form in the multiple icons which the system forces upon the perceiving consciousness. The icon, literally, permeates the horizons of the subject who, when manipulated, exists in the icon and not in the world.

17. 'En somme, tendance à absorber l'ordre naturel dans l'ordre surnaturel . . . tendance à absorber le droit de l'Etat dans celui de l'Eglise.' H. X. Arquillière, *L'Augustinisme politique* (Paris, Vrin, 1955).

18. Bernard Groethuysen, *Origine de l'esprit bourgeois en France* (Paris, Gallimard, 1927), p. 17.

19. Augustine, *The political writings*, p. 39.

20. Ibid., p. 42.

21. 'Put briefly, Augustine's political theory is based upon the assumption that political activity is merely symptomatic: it is merely one way in which men express orientations that lie far deeper in themselves.' Peter Brown, *Religion and society in the age of St Augustine* (New York, Harper & Row, 1972), p. 35.

22. Ibid., p. 41.

23. Auerbach, *Mimesis*, p. 73.

24. Henri Irréné Marrou, *L'Ambivalence du temps de l'histoire chez Augustin* (Paris, Vrin, 1950), p. 71.

25. R. A. Markus, *Saeculum: history and society in the theology of St Augustine* (Cambridge University Press, 1970), p. 84.

26. J. J. O'Meara, *The young Augustine* (London, Longman, 1954), pp. 17, 19.

27. In contrast to this interpretation, Christopher Dawson claims that Augustine holds a dynamic conception of the historical process: 'If man is not the slave and creature of time, but its master and creator, then history

becomes a creative process. It does not repeat itself meaninglessly; it grows into organic unity with the growth of human experience. The past does not die; it becomes incorporated in humanity. And hence progress is possible, since the life of society and of humanity itself possesses continuity and the capacity for spiritual growth no less than the life of the individual.' 'St Augustine and his age' in M. C. D'Arcy *et al.* (eds), *A monument to St Augustine*, p. 71. No doubt Dawson himself speaks from within the Augustinian discourse; for how can history become a creative process if it has a beginning and an end. Man's mastery over the historical process necessitates original lack.

28. Paul Henry, SJ, *St Augustine on personality* (New York, Macmillan, 1960), pp. 3, 6. In the archaic perception of things there was no division between the personal and the impersonal. This division will be instituted with the development of the concept of property.

29. Walter Ullman, *The individual and society in the Middle Ages* (Baltimore, Johns Hopkins University Press, 1966).

30. Colin Morris, *The discovery of the individual 1050–1200* (London, SPCK, 1972).

31. Paul Delaney, *British autobiography in the seventeenth century* (London, Routledge & Kegan Paul, 1969), p. 168.

32. Ullman, *The individual and society*, p. 36.

33. Evelyn Brige Vitz, 'Type et individu dans l'autobiographie médiévale', *Poétique*, vol. 1, 1975, p. 431.

34. Ernst Cassirer, *The philosophy of the Enlightenment* (Princeton University Press, 1961), p. 39.

35. Ullman, *The individual and society*, p. 56.

36. Carl Becker, in *The heavenly city of the eighteenth century philosophes* (New Haven, Yale University Press, 1974), sees the similarities between Scholasticism and the Enlightenment; he claims that the eighteenth century is closer in world view to the thirteenth century than to our own: 'I think the Philosophes were nearer the Middle Ages, less emancipated from the preconceptions of medieval Christian thought, than they quite realized or we have commonly supposed' (p. 29). Becker's interpretation that 'the Philosophes demolished the heavenly city of St Augustine only to rebuild it with up-to-date materials' (p. 31) is indicative of his own bias; he chooses to read the thirteenth century in the eighteenth. Despite their striking similarities, we cannot reduce the one to the other; after all, the eighteenth century gave birth to capitalism. Becker would like to do away with the irreversible, ongoing movement of the historical flow.

37. Groethuysen, *Origines de l'esprit bourgeois en France*, p. 118.

38. Ibid., p. 184.

39. Eric Khaler, *The inward turn of narrative* (Princeton University Press, 1973), p. 14.

40. Lejeune, *L'Autobiographie en France*, p. 43.

41. Delaney, *British autobiography in the seventeenth century*, p. 170.

Chapter 3

1. The *Historia calamitatum* appears as the first letter in the correspondence of Abelard and Heloise. The Bibliothèque de Cluny edition, *Lettres d'Héloise et d'Abélard* (Paris, Armand Colin, 1959) is used in this study; references will be initialled 'A'.

2. *Discours de la méthode* (Paris, Vrin, 1966). The *Discours* is classified as an autobiography by a number of critics although it has been studied mainly in terms of its philosophical content. Indeed this text satisfies all the definitions dealt with in Chapter 1. P. Lejeune includes it in his list in *L'Autobiographie en France*; Hiram Caton builds his whole thesis on the autobiographical aspects of the *Discours* in *The origin of subjectivity: an essay on Descartes* (New Haven, Yale University Press, 1973), p. 30. But the *Discours*'s major impact is not limited to its autobiographical form; its content is as crucial in that it establishes for the first time an inalienable bond between rationality and individuality. This relationship will prevail (and still prevails) in all social theories of the Enlightenment for it will be argued that through his Reason man makes a choice to join his fellow men in a social contract based on equality.

3. Mary M. McLaughlin thinks that Abelard had a different purpose in mind — namely, that the letter was directed at Heloise: 'whether or not he meant his letter for a particular recipient, it seems unlikely that so elaborate an apology was not designed for the kind of circulation that did, evidently, bring it to Heloise's hands.' 'Abelard as autobiographer: the motives and meaning of his *Story of calamities*', *Speculum*, 42 (1967), p. 468. D. W. Robertson, on the other hand, claims that 'Abelard undoubtedly wrote it not to console some anonymous friend, but to supply the beginning of a basic document for his new order.' *Abelard and Heloise* (New York, Dual Press, 1972), p. 118.

4. See Jacques Monfrin, 'Le Problème de l'authenticité de la correspondance d'Abélard et d'Héloise' as well as John F. Benton, 'Fraud fiction, and borrowing in the correspondence of Abelard and Heloise', *Pierre Abélard, Pierre le Vénérable, les courants philosophiques, littéraires et artistiques en Occident au milieu du XIIe siècle* (Paris, Editions du Centre National de la Recherche Scientifique, 1975). The problematic of authentification constitutes a central preoccupation of most books on this correspondence; there is an aspiration on the part of the critics to set the record straight. See, for example, the introductory chapters of Étienne Gilson, *Héloise et Abélard* (Paris, Vrin, 1938) and Robertson, *Abelard and Heloise*.

5. Edward W. Said, 'On originality' in Monroe Engel (ed.), *The uses of literature*, Harvard English Studies IV. (Cambridge, Mass., Harvard University Press, 1973).

6. M. McLaughlin, 'Abelard as autobiographer', p. 488. This view is shared by J. Ramsey McCallum: 'The new theory sets the emphasis upon the free employment of *ratio*, the conceptual and investigating activity of the intellect. There is a shaking loose from submission to *a priori* and dogmatic illumination.' *Abelard's Christian theology* (New York, Richwood Publishing Co., 1976), p. 42.

7. J. G. Sikes, *Peter Abelard* (Cambridge University Press, 1932), p. 60. For a substantial analysis of the controversy over Abelard's

rationalism, see Jean Jolivet, *Arts du langage et théologie chez Abélard* (Paris, Vrin, 1969), pp. 337 – 63. Jolivet himself postulates synthesis between faith and reason in Abelard: 'Il faut donc mettre au rang des erreurs historiques l'opinion qui fait d'Abélard un précurseur du rationalisme: il ne l'est ni d'intention, ni de fait; logicien avant tout, il a contribué à la théologie systématique, nullement à une séparation de la raison et de la foi' (p. 348).

8. Julius R. Weinberg, *A short history of medieval philosophy* (Princeton University Press, 1964), p. 75. Abelard himself spells out his predilection for argumentation and rationality over authority: 'Ainsi dans toute science la controverse a sa place, que ce soit à propos d'un texte ou à propos d'un point de doctrine, et, chaque fois qu'on s'affronte en une discussion, exposer la vérité d'une raison a plus de force que produire une autorité.' Jean Jolivet, *Abélard: choix de textes* (Paris, Seghers, 1969), p. 138.

9. See Jonathan Rée, *Descartes* (London, Allen Lane, 1974), p. 25.

10. G. Paré, A. Brunet and P. Tremblay, *La Renaissance du XIIe siècle: les écoles et l'enseignement* (Paris, Vrin, 1933), p. 281. About Abelard's method in *Sic et non*, see pp. 281 – 92.

11. Leif Grane, *Peter Abelard: philosophy and christianity in the Middle Ages* (New York, Harcourt Brace, 1964), p. 22.

12. Jolivet, *Abélard: choix de textes*, p. 120.

13. Meyrick H. Carré, *Realists and nominalists* (Oxford University Press, 1966), pp. 37 – 8. Carré thinks that Abelard's new approach to universals constitutes an elaboration on the Nominalism of Roscelin: 'Universals, then, are neither *voces* nor *res*, neither words nor things. Here Abelard introduces his own modification of the Nominalism of Roscelin. Universals are sermones, concepts. The *vox* of Roscelin is a mere physical occurence, a displacement of air. But the word means something. The word "flower" is not merely a physical event; it refers to a general nature. But this general nature is arbitrarily selected. The human mind imposes itself upon a natural order as the sculptor fashions the stone to form a statue. Universal terms, sermones, imply a judgement about things, the judgement, namely that many different things have common qualities' (p. 60). But, it seems to us, Abelard's contribution to the problem of universals is, rather, a negation of Realism and not an elaboration on Nominalism; the attempt is made to establish the ontological status of the individual and do away with the Realist reduction of the particular to the universal (that is, in the social context, to challenge the universality of the church). Abelard's partial marginality is inscribed within this problematic of the universal versus the particular.

14. Jean Largeault credits Abelard with a cultural dimension to knowledge, 'Cette différence entre le naturel et l'institué est fondamentale dans la distinction vox-sermo. Le langage a un caractère de donnée culturelle (invention humaine, convention), il n'est pas une substance. Quoique les mots dans leur ensemble se rapportent aux choses et soient orientés vers elles, leur domaine a ses lois propres.' *Enquête sur le Nominalisme* (Paris, Béatrice-Nauverleerts, 1971), pp. 88 – 9. This is an attempt at reading the latest theories of knowledge into Abelard. The twelfth century marks the beginning of individualism and of methodised (albeit rudimentary) and

internalised conceptions of knowledge and not the social construction of knowledge.

15. G. Verbeke, 'Introductory Conference: Peter Abelard and the Concept of Subjectivity' in *Peter Abelard: proceedings of the international conference, Louvain, May 10–12, 1971* (The Hague, Martinus Nijhoff, 1971), p. 8.

16. 'Pécher est une chose, accomplir le péché en est une autre, et la première peut être entière sans la seconde; une bonne intention est une chose, un acte bon en est une autre; et puisqu'il s'agit là de deux biens radicalement distincts dont chacun se suffit à soi-même, il est impossible de les additionner. On peut donc commettre un acte matériellement coupable dans une bonne intention, ou un acte matériellement coupable dans une intention mauvaise.' Gilson, *Héloïse et Abélard*, p. 106.

17. D. E. Luscombe, *Peter Abelard's ethics* (Oxford University Press, 1971), p. 5.

18. In the medieval world, there was hardly any room for coexistence of the hegemonic and the marginal. Of interest is the fact that marginality in the High Middle Ages was limited to the scientific discourse: Giordano Bruno, Copernicus and Galileo paid a dear price for it.

19. For a contextualisation of the discursive practices of madness and criminality, see Michel Foucault's books: *L'Histoire de la folie à l'âge classique* (1961) and *Surveiller et punir* (1975).

20. The body as absence bears a relationship to the concept of seriality; the marginality (i.e. madness) of an Artaud or Rousseau is the refusal of that self provided by society. Marginality is a challenge to reification for there is no doubt that a body can equal an object only when it is conceived of as a point on a series of objects sitting beside one another and oblivious to one another. (Sartre's example of a group of people waiting for a bus in *Critique de la raison dialectique* (Paris, Gallimard, 1960), pp. 308–15, is a case in point). But the apex of reification of self will be reached with mass production; the complexity of the human is now reduced to a vacuous picture on the TV screen, to a tube of toothpaste. The ever-growing process of reification brings into focus the stereotypification of the human phenomenon to its bare physicality; all models repeat one another, without presence or fullness of human content. Self is an abstracted otherness, not the Otherness one meets in a sane social praxis which conditions one's own self-definition, but a sterile quantity of detached features that is forced upon consciousness through its own inertia. The blatant papier-maché effect of all commercial advertising erases the specificity of the human likenesses which are presumably represented on the screen. The human being now equals the product.

Chapter 4

1. 'Expérience ontologique et déduction systématique dans la constitution de la métaphysique de Descartes', *Cahiers de Royaumont* (Paris, Editions de Minuit, 1957), pp. 14, 21.

2. Ibid., p. 27. This article is a recapitulation of the argument Alquié develops in *La Découverte métaphysique de l'homme chez Descartes* (Paris, PUF, 1950). Alquié's static view is more prominent in his statements about history; the historical process is reduced by Alquié to individual consciousness: 'La conscience est mesure de toutes choses, et du Monde où elle est prise, sans pourtant prétendre expliquer toute chose, et le Monde lui-même. Mais ceci n'autorise pas à la subordonner à l'histoire, ˈ l'expliquer toute par son temps, ce qui est d'abord la croire abusée. Car tenir une philosophie pour conditionée par l'histoire, c'est négliger le projet qui en est l'âme, et qui est de découvrir une vérité indépendante de l'histoire, parfois même la vérité de l'histoire' (p. 345).

3. *Descartes selon l'ordre des raisons* (Paris, Editions Montaigne, 1968), p. 18.

4. Ibid., pp. 99, 235.

5. This is true of most books on Descartes produced in the past few decades. L. J. Beck's *The metaphysics of Descartes* (Oxford, Clarendon Press, 1965) and *The method of Descartes* (London, Oxford University Press, 1952) conform to this category, the assumption being that Descartes must be 'explained'. Anthony Kenny's *Descartes: a study of his philosophy* (New York, Random House, 1968) focuses on the same concerns: doubt, the onto-logical argument, reason and intuition, mind and body — in short, Descartes's own preoccupations. Martinus Versfeld is a typical example of a critic who negates the Cogito while sharing its very ideological presuppositions: 'The method employed by Descartes in metaphysics is suitable for investigating selected tracts of reality, but not for answering the question: what is the ultimate structure of reality? The result is that Descartes' metaphysics becomes an investigation of the character of a part of the real; namely, the self. The result is the inevitable reduction of metaphysics to psychology. Descartes could seem to himself to be a metaphysician because he assumes that the self contains the universe in idea, so that by contemplating the part of the real called the self, one was inquiring into the ultimate character of the real.' *An essay on the metaphysics of Descartes* (London, Methuen, 1940), p. 85. This critique of the method follows the ideology of the method to its extreme. Versfeld accuses Descartes of being a reductivist, of reducing metaphysics to psychology while himself postulating an 'ultimate structure of reality'. So the Cogito is not enough to account for Versfeld's metaphysics.

A different kind of mystification can be found in Marcelle Barjonet-Huraux's view of Descartes who, she claims, is a materialist, on the grounds that he devotes more pages in the *Discours* to blood circulation than to the existence of God, and that he based the body/soul relationship in the pineal gland: 'La conscience n'est donc pas, en définitive, la mesure du psychisme. Celui-ci prend sa source ailleurs qu'en elle, dans l'organique; il est en rapport constant avec le milieu, les circonstances, dont il subit les aléas et la conscience paraît au moins autant déterminée par l'ensemble des réactions du sujet corporel qu'elle ne les détermine.' *Descartes* (Paris, Editions Sociales, 1963), p. 75. This is a reduction of Descartes's metaphysics to his physics. Descartes's recourse to the pineal gland is the point at which his whole philosophy falls apart, but it does not make of him a materialist. Spinoza will pick up the Cartesian problematic at this point and claim that thought and extension do not meet in man but constitute two of the infinite number of God's attributes.

6. See, for example, the volume on Descartes in the 'Modern studies in philosophy' series (New York, Anchor Books, 1967). Most articles in this volume revolve around epistemological problems, that is, a logical verification of the Cartesian argument. 'Truth', 'certainty', 'scepticism' are some of the notions used by these critics. The basic concepts are never put into question and never is there an attempt at questioning the ideology which motivates the Cartesian argument.

7. Ibid., pp. 122, 123.

8. A. J. Ayer, *The problem of knowledge* (Harmondsworth, Penguin, 1956); more specifically, Chapter II, 'Scepticism and certainty'.

9. 'L'idée profonde de Descartes, sous-jacente à la méthode, c'est qu'il y a un rapport direct entre le loisir et l'invention, c'est dans le loisir, toujours, qu'il s'est exercé aux sciences, dans le divertissement des voyages. C'est dans la retraite solitaire, délivré, encore une fois, des soins et des passions, qu'il trouve sa métaphysique et élabore sa physique. C'est à loisir qu'il contemple les merveilleux attributs de Dieu; c'est faute de loisir que les hommes reçoivent des idées trompeuses; c'est à loisir qu'on doit lire et relire sa philosophie; c'est pour garder le loisir et cultiver son esprit qu'il ne souhaite pas d'emploi.' Roger Lefèvre, *L'Humanisme de Descartes* (Paris, PUF, 1957), p. 136. Lefèvre's humanistic approach to Descartes is itself inscribed within the Cartesian discourse, for while recognising Descartes's static approach to the social order and his promotion of meditation and 'divertissement' as a foundation of social organisation, he concludes: 'On découvre que le Cartésianisme est, et a voulu être — répondant à son époque afin de la dépasser — un effort d'amélioration de la nature par la culture, un appel à l'épanouissement de la liberté, une ascension du vouloir individuel, et collectif, vers l'universel et vers Dieu. D'un mot, un humanisme' (p. vii).

10. Despite the disparities that have been noted between Descartes and Augustine, there seems to be more in common between them than meets the eye. Etienne Gilson points to the basic similarities between the two and cites key passages in Augustine the content of which could easily be ascribed to Descartes. 'Reason is leading the discussion with Augustine: "You who wish to know yourself, do you know at least that you are? — I know it. — How do you know it? — I don't know. — Are you a thing that is simple, or that is composed? — I don't know. — Do you know whether you are moving or not? — I don't know. — But you know that you think? — Yes, I know that. — Consequently, that you think at least is true. — It is true. — You know therefore that you are, that you live and that you think." *Soliloquies* Book II, Chapter 1. "First I ask you, in order to begin with what is most evident, whether you are or not? And in this you cannot fear to be deceived in your answer, because in case you did not exist, you could not possibly be deceived." *On free will*, Book II, Chapter 3. "If I am wrong, I am, for he who does not exist, cannot be deceived; thus from the very fact that I am deceived, it follows that I am. How then could I possibly be deceived in believing that I am, since it is an obvious thing that I am so long as I am deceived." *The city of God*, Book XI, Chapter 26.' Etienne Gilson, *The unity of philosophical experience* (New York, Scriber's,

1937), p. 155. Gilson is of course looking for the unity of his *philosophia perennis*, but the fact remains that whoever attempts to demystify Descartes must look back at Augustine, and this presents quite a problem in our perception of ruptures in this historical phase that encompasses Augustine and Descartes and their respective discursive intertexts. Arguments can be made for the absence of ruptures altogether, as well as for a break in the twelfth century with Abelard. The approach here has been to conceive of this change in terms of an imbrication; that is, Abelard and Descartes 'add' something to the old structures; they do not transgress them.

11. 'Le temps ne doit pas être considéré comme un développement, ni comme la mesure de quelque chose qui est passage de la puissance à l'acte et par conséquent développement, ni comme une puissance héterogène à la suite des instants et plus profonde qu'elle. Il est cette suite même tour à tour terminée par chaque instant.' Jean Whal, *Du rôle de l'idée de l'instant dans la philosophie de Descartes* (Paris, Vrin, 1953), p. 11.

12. For an analysis of the concept of seriality, see F. R. Jameson, 'Seriality in modern literature', *Bucknell Review*, vol. VIII, no. 1 (1970) as well as J.-P. Sartre, *Critique de la raison dialectique* (Paris, Gallimard, 1960), pp. 306–77.

13. Gilbert Ryle, *The concept of mind* (Harmondsworth, Penguin, 1949), p. 15. See especially the first chapter which deals with 'Descartes' myth'.

14. T. Spoerri's article 'La Puissance métaphorique de Descartes' in *Cahiers de Royaumont* (Paris, Editions de Minuit, 1957) dwells on the relationship between Descartes's philosophy and its historical context in terms of three organising metaphors which permeate the *Discours*: the path, the house and the machine. The path connotes slow and careful walking, 'jamais Descartes ne court, ni ne grimpe, ni ne saute, ni ne vole. Cette marche a une direction, elle va tout droit . . . derrière tout cela il y a l'angoissant instinct de sécurité: il ne faut pas tomber' (p. 281). This security is further developed in terms of the house metaphor; Descartes, indeed, talks repeatedly about solid foundations. Finally, the machine metaphor, hypostasised by the clock, provides a view of Descartes's mechanistic approach to extension. Spoerri divides between the palaeo-technic and the neotechnic dimensions of the machine metaphor: 'Dans cette insistance mécanique se révèle la loi même de l'époque de Descartes . . . [deux âges] Le premier est caractérisé par une mécanique de contact, le second par l'action à distance. Le premier a comme dimension fonda-mentale la *res extensa*, l'étendue, la continuité spatiale et temporelle; l'autre, l'espace stellaire, les champs magnétiques, le vide intranucléaire' (pp. 284–5). Spoerri, however, deals with the Cartesian metaphoric dimension in positive terms and claims that the security and continuity connoted by these metaphors has to do with God's disappearance from the picture. This is debatable. But these metaphors can be fruitful if they are given a social meaning. The slow walking and the fear of falling, the security in the house (property) and the link and continuity among the various parts of the machine all point to Descartes's fear of change. A machine that operates on matter from a distance introduces a gap which creates an anxiety the seventeenth century could not possibly know because, ultimately, God was the filler of all gaps. So Spoerri cannot be justified in postulating two machines; the seventeenth century knows

one machine only, the mechanistic machine.

15. Henri Gouhier, *Essais sur Descartes*, (Paris, Vrin, 1949), p. 275.

16. Geneviève Rodis-Lewis in *La Morale de Descartes* (Paris, PUF, 1957) claims that Descartes has a social consciousness. Her mystification of Descartes clouds any possibility of coherence in her understanding of his philosophy. On p. 97 she says: 'si l'âme se saisit d'abord métaphysiquement comme un moi isolé ce n'est donc qu'une étape, et la morale cartésienne n'est pas un individualisme', but on this same page she quotes Descartes: 'mettre en évidence les véritables richesses de nos âmes, ouvrant à chacun les moyens de trouver en soi-même, et sans rien emprunter d'autrui, toute la science qui lui est nécessaire à la conduite de sa vie.' Her Cartesian bias, however, comes through more clearly in *L'Individualité selon Descartes* (Paris, Vrin, 1959), and the words speak for themselves: 'C'est donc un harmonieux accord de toutes les facultés humaines que poursuit une philosophie qui puisse élever notre nature à son plus haut degré de perfection' (pp. 240–1). But despite her bias, Lewis clarifies an interesting relationship between Descartes and his predecessors which supports Gilson's claim as to the influence of Augustine on Descartes. 'L'individualité est donc une propriété de tous les esprits, en tant qu'ils sont libres et conscients. C'est pourquoi Descartes est si spontanément fermé à la notion d'une pensée impersonnelle: le fondement ultime de l'individualité est l'unité et l'unicité de Dieu . . . L'individualité de l'homme est donc liée à son essence, et à "sa forme qui est l'âme": ainsi la formule traditionnelle qui attribue l'individualité à la forme prend dans le cartésianisme une valeur très profonde' (p. 234). The Cogito is, then, the other side of the soul.

17. Frederick Broadie, *An approach to Descartes' meditations* (London, Athlone Press, 1970), pp. 48–9. Although Broadie's assessment of the meditative activity in Descartes seems to be correct, one can detect some kind of dualism in his claim as to the relationship between awareness and action. Certainly, Descartes cannot deduce one from the other for action involves physicality and Descartes separates between thought and extension. But awareness and action cannot be divided, to be aware of one's being-in-the-world is to be acting in the world. The eradication of dualism necessitates a rejection of any separation between mind and matter, cognition and action.

18. Hiram Caton sees in Descartes a social activist of a special kind: 'His new "legislation" is not directly political; like the law of the New Testament, it may be introduced by a private individual. The new law is the politics of man's auto-emancipation from his enslavement to nature: it is the politics of progress.' 'Descartes' rhetoric seems clearly designed to weld the self-interest and indignation of the multitude into a powerful force that will "overturn" those states and institutions that attempt to frustrate the public work that Descartes would set in motion. It easily translates into the Enlightenment battle for science and humanism against the dark powers of superstition and despotism.' *The origin of subjectivity: an essay on Descartes* (New Haven, Yale University Press, 1973), pp. 63, 64. Caton wants to see in Descartes a saviour of humanity and a social revolutionary. This is a misreading of Descartes; one wonders to what 'multitude' Caton is referring.

19. Gilbert Ryle claims that the shift occurs from 'conscience' to 'consciousness'. 'The theologian's privacy of conscience became the philosopher's privacy of consciousness, and what has been the bogy of Predestination reappeared as the bogy of Determinism.' *The concept of mind*, p. 24.

20. Gouhier, *Essais sur Descartes*, p. 271.

21. Descartes further elaborates on his social theory in a letter to Elizabeth: 'Les lois communes de la société, lesquelles tendent toutes à se faire du bien les uns aux autres, ou du moins à ne point se faire de mal, sont ce me semble, si bien établies, que quiconque les suit franchement, sans aucune dissimulation et artifice, mène une vie beaucoup plus heureuse et plus assurée que ceux que cherchent leur utilité par d'autres voies.' Quoted by Lefèvre, *L'Humanisme de Descartes*, p. 136.

22. Marcelle Barjonet-Huraux indicates that as early as 1596 there are movements towards mass production and saleability of labour on a wide scale and especially in the field of textiles; see her *Descartes*, p. 29. This phenomenon is not exclusive to France; in 1651, Hobbes will claim in his *Leviathan*, Chapter 24: 'a man's labour also is a commodity exchangeable for benefit as well as any other thing.' (New York, The Liberal Arts Press, 1958), p. 197.

Chapter 5

1. 'Pour le dix-huitième siècle, comme pour le dix-septième, l'existence apparaît comme devant être sans cesse sauvée du non-être. Il n'y a qu'une différence, mais radicale. Cette existence continuée ne l'est plus par une création divine continuée. La conservation de l'univers et de la créature n'est plus conçue aussitôt comme l'effet immédiat de l'acte créateur. Celui-ci se situe infiniment en arrière, en le moment lointain et quasi fabuleux qui fut le moment premier des choses. Mais de l'instant actuel le Dieu créateur et conservateur est absent. L'acteur principal n'est plus sur la scène.' Georges Poulet, *Etudes sur le temps humain*, vol. I (Paris, Plon, 1972), p. 25.

2. *Les Confessions* (Paris, Garnier, 1964), p. 781. All further references will be made in the body of the text initialled 'C'.

3. Jean Starobinski, *La Transparence et l'obstacle* (Paris, Gallimard, 1971), the most comprehensive work on Rousseau to date, builds his entire thesis on this seemingly insignificant anecdote.

4. *Emile ou de l'éducation* (Paris, Garnier, 1939). Further references will be made in the body of the text initialled 'E'.

5. 'Rousseau lui-même ne croit pas que l'homme naturel se détruise au fond de l'homme social. La nature, qui est un absolu, demeure inaltérable . . . Si l'homme social est un monstre, c'est moins par son essence même que par sa structure, qui n'est pas homogène . . . L'homme du monde se compose de l'être profond et d'un masque, qui cache le premier sans l'effacer. Si l'on prend un masque, c'est moins pour se dissimuler que pour se reconnaître: on veut ressembler à tout le monde, et par là on se rassure.' Robert Mauzi, *L'Idée du bonheur dans la littérature et la pensée*

françaises du dix-huitième siècle (Paris, Armand Colin, 1969), p. 91. This monumental work constitutes a comprehensive study of the major problems of eighteenth-century French thought. In this passage Mauzi seems to suggest that somehow the mask, in Rousseau, is a necessity, a counterbalancing opposition to the real self. That is, Rousseau postulates a dialectic between the social mask and the real-natural self and without this negational structure the real self would vanish, without this necessary duality man would lose his deep uniformity. This is, of course, quite an optimistic reading of Rousseau although Mauzi does not negate the notion of depth itself. This reading is shared by many critics who claim a dialectical movement in Rousseau between the inside and outside. However, this is a dialectic that originates in the inside since the primary oppositional term is the natural self. A true dialectical structure must be external; that is, in the adjustment the subject makes via the ongoing data he receives from the outside in his being-for-the-other. I am not what 'I am', Rousseau would have us concede, but I am what 'I am not' and 'What I am being in my continual being-for-the-other'. The gap between the natural and the social self remains unbridgeable.

6. *Discours sur l'origine de l'inégalité* (Paris, Garnier-Flammarion, 1971), p. 140. Further references will be made in the body of the text initialled 'IN'.

7. 'La philosophie a donc pour premier office de chercher l'homme au-delà de ce que "ses progrès ont ajouté ou changé"', mais elle est, elle-même, un de ses progrès.' Henri Gouhier, 'Nature et histoire dans la pensée de Jean-Jacques Rousseau', *Annales Jean-Jacques Rousseau*, vol. 33, p. 9.

8. 'Rousseau aime à se placer au point zéro de l'histoire ou sur son seuil, au moment où elle n'est pas encore engagée sur la pente de l'irréversibilité. Non seulement il se tient à distance de l'histoire, mais il n'attribue aux faits et aux circonstances qu'une importance secondaire; les axiomes et les relations lui importent plus que les évènements, toujours marqués du sceau de la relativité.' Marc Eigeldinger, *Jean-Jacques Rousseau: univers mythique et cohérence* (Neuchâtel, La Baconnière, 1978), p. 20.

9. Henri Gouhier, *Les Méditations métaphysiques de Jean-Jacques Rousseau* (Paris, Vrin, 1970), p. 14.

10. Ernst Cassirer, *The question of Jean-Jacques Rousseau* (New York, Columbia University Press, 1963), p. 50.

11. Claude Lévi-Strauss, 'Jean-Jacques Rousseau fondateur des sciences humaines' in *Jean-Jacques Rousseau* (Neuchâtel, La Baconnière, 1962), p. 245.

12. There is a similarity between Descartes's naked self and Rousseau's self; they both claim universality since both selves can exist only in a state of non-difference; they both conform to pure repetition. This is of course a discursive phenomenon for it is the same conception of self that is being consolidated.

13. 'La disparité sociale et la séparation psychologique vont de pair . . . Cette déchirure ne passe pas seulement entre l'homme civilisé et son prochain, elle passe à l'intérieur de chaque conscience: nous sommes séparés de nous-mêmes, nous avons perdu l'unité.' Jean Starobinski, 'La

Pensée politique de Jean-Jacques Rousseau' in *Jean-Jacques Rousseau* (Neuchâtel, La Baconnière, 1962), p. 87. We must emphasise, though, that the alienation within oneself must be understood against the background of the lost innocence of natural man; it is not the alienation that ensues from the lack of coherence among the roles that the subject must play in society. Rousseau himself, on occasion, caught a glimpse of the contradictory demands made on man by society. 'Ce qui fait la misère humaine est la contradiction qui se trouve entre notre état et nos désirs, entre nos devoirs et nos penchants, entre la nature et les institutions sociales, entre l'homme et le citoyen; rendez l'homme à lui-même et vous le rendrez heureux autant qu'il peut l'être. Donnez le tout entier à l'état ou laissez le tout entier à lui-même, mais si vous partagez son cœur vous le déchirez; et n'allez pas vous imaginer que l'état puisse être heureux quand tous ses membres pâtissent.' 'Fragments politiques', *Œuvres complètes*, vol. III (Paris, Gallimard, 1964), p. 510.

14. The manipulative statement of the rich man achieves a better expression under Rousseau's biting cynicism; in another context, Rousseau makes the rich man divulge his schemes: 'Vous avez besoin de moi, car je suis riche et vous êtes pauvre; faisons donc un accord entre nous: je permettrai que vous ayez l'honneur de me servir, à condition que vous me donniez le peu qui vous reste, pour la peine que je prendrai de vous commander.' *Discours sur l'économie politique, Œuvres complètes*, vol. III, p. 275.

15. The primacy of property in Rousseau's social theory is supported by an expressive key passage in his *Discours sur l'économie politique, Œuvres complètes*, vol. III, pp. 262–3. 'Il est certain que le droit de propriété est le plus sacré de tous les droits des citoyens, et plus important à certains égards, que la liberté même; soit parce qu'il tient de plus près à la conservation de la vie; soit parce que les biens étant plus facile à usurper et plus pénibles à défendre que la personne, on doit plus respecter ce qui se peut ravir plus aisément; soit enfin parce que la propriété est le vrai fondement de la société civile, et le vrai garant des engagements des citoyens: car si les biens ne répondaient pas des personnes, rien ne serait plus facile que d'éluder ses devoirs et de se moquer des lois.' Here we see clearly the correspondence between property and selfhood, the one being the guarantor of the other.

16. Georges Poulet, *Etudes sur le temps humain*, vol. I (Paris, Plon, 1972), p. 211.

17. Pierre Burgelin, *La Philosophie de l'existence de Jean-Jacques Rousseau* (Paris, Vrin, 1973), p. 152.

18. Marcel Raymond, *Jean-Jacques Rousseau: la quête de soi et la rêverie* (Paris, José Corti, 1962), p. 24.

19. B. Munteano, *Solitude et contradictions de Jean-Jacques Rousseau* (Paris, Nizet, 1974), p. 22.

20. Robert Mauzi, *L'Idée du bonheur dans la littérature et la pensée françaises au dix-huitième siècle* (Paris, Armand Colin, 1969), p. 121.

21. *Les Rêveries du promeneur solitaire* (Paris, Garnier, 1960), p. 68. Further refences will be made in the body of the text initialled 'R'.

22. Rousseau cannot plan ahead; this is why a passing whim becomes a most urgent matter. 'L'incertitude de l'avenir m'a toujours fait regarder

les projets de longue exécution comme des leurres de dupe. Je me livre à l'espoir comme un autre, pourvu qu'il ne me coûte rien à nourrir; mais, s'il faut prendre longtemps de la peine, je n'en suis plus. Le moindre petit plaisir qui s'offre à ma portée me tente plus que les joies du Paradis' (C 162).

23. Biographical criticism on Rousseau increases by the day. (See, for example, Lester G. Crocker, *Jean-Jacques Rousseau*, 2 vols (New York, Macmillan, 1968, 1973); Frances Winwar, *Jean-Jacques Rousseau: conscience of an era* (New York, Random House, 1961); George H. Havens, *Jean-Jacques Rousseau* (Boston, Twayne Publishers, 1978).) These critics have one central aim: to set the record straight, to find the unity behind Rousseau's disorganised plurality. Jean Guéhenno, the most quoted critic on Rousseau, wants to bridge the gap between what Rousseau thought he was and what he was in reality; he rewrites the *Confessions* but with more details, sometimes down to the day or even the hour. A passage from his book which gives an adequate summary of this ideology of the biography: 'Le plus grand artiste n'a que peu de nouveau à dire. Il n'est qu'une grande intuition, mais cette intuition a un caractère d'éternité, vaut en dehors de tous les temps. Quelque chose d'éternel, qui avait toujours été obscurément senti mais n'avait jamais été vu ni dit, se trouve, à un moment du temps et avec une singulière intensité, saisi par lui, tout voué qu'il soit lui-même à la mort. Le critique n'a rien fait encore sans doute tant qu'il ne s'est pas approché du génie, dont il analyse l'œuvre et la vie, tel qu'en lui-même enfin l'éternité l'a changé. Mais peut-être la seule voix du génie a-t-elle cette vibration éternelle, et c'est à lui-même toujours qu'il faut finale-ment revenir.' *Jean-Jacques Rousseau* (Paris, Gallimard, 1962), p. 14.

24. Starobinski, *La Transparence et l'obstacle*, p. 207.

25. What about Thérèse Levasseur, the companion of Rousseau's life and mother of his children? Starobinski suggests that their relationship remains on the level of the senses and the body, the immediacy of which conforms to the sensuality of natural man. It is a 'basic' relationship in which reason takes no part. Indeed, Rousseau speaks of her as a 'supplé-ment', a replacement. She could not possibly threaten his unity. We recall that Rousseau enjoyed sharing Thérèse's simple-mindedness and stupidity with his friends. She could not fill the role of the much-dreaded Other.

26. Munteano, *Solitude et contradictions de Jean-Jacques Rousseau*, p. 86.

27. Marcel Raymond makes a stronger claim: 'C'est donc au seuil du néant, au point où la conscience affleure à peine, où la respiration du moi paraît s'anéantir dans une respiration cosmique, que tout est donné à l'homme.' *La Quête de soi et la rêverie*, p. 217. To R. Mauzi, 'L'absolu existentiel est aussi vide qu'il est plein. Il consiste en une négation: la negation du temps, le refus de la vie et de tous les sentiments qui l'accompagnent.' *L'Idée du bonheur*, p. 297. Mauzi sees the deficiencies of Rousseau's negational structure in its direction towards the inside; this condition of recuperation within total loss is functional to the elimination of desire. If the object is annihilated, the subject becomes its own object (which is what autobiography is all about), which means the total conservation of existential energy, the coincidence of self with self.

28. 'Devenu écrivain pour démontrer qu'il ne fallait pas l'être, il

continue à l'être pour montrer qu'il ne l'est pas.' Georges May, *Rousseau par lui-même* (Paris, Seuil, 1973), p. 58.

29. This contradiction is well elaborated by Claire Solomon Bayet in her book *Jean-Jacques Rousseau ou l'impossible unité* (Paris, Seghers, 1968). Uttering the word already constitutes a distance from the truth (and *a fortiori* writing it) but Rousseau has no choice since 'La vérité, il faut pour qu'elle soit réalisée, qu'elle soit dite; et c'est de la dire, c'est-à-dire de la médiatiser et par là de la trahir, qui la fera vraie' (p. 28). This is the case, paradoxically, because truth reveals itself in what negates it; that is, in appearance and injustice, just as natural man is hidden behind the masks of civil man.

30. Starobinski, *La Transparence et l'obstacle*, p. 283.

31. All references will be made to *Œuvres complètes* (Paris, Gallimard, 1964), in the body of the text initialled 'SC'.

32. Rousseau's own critique of Hobbes should not be taken too seriously because he owes him (together with eighteenth-century French social theorists — another indication of the discursive development of the concept of the social contract) the basis of his own system, which is quite evident in the *Discours*. M. Davy in 'Le Corps politique selon le Contrat Social de Jean-Jacques Rousseau et ses antécédents chez Hobbes' in *Etudes sur le contrat social de Jean-Jacques Rousseau* (Paris, Publications de l'Université de Dijon, vol. XXX, 1964) retraces Rousseau's main arguments to Hobbes, the crucial commonality between the two being that: 'Selon Hobbes, comme selon Rousseau, la première et unique source de tout pouvoir se trouve en chaque individu' (p. 89). There is little doubt that the duality of People and Prince harks back to Hobbes, but the crucial difference is that Hobbes tilts the balance in favour of the Prince while Rousseau does in favour of the People.

33. 'Ainsi Rousseau a rejeté toutes les explications courantes de la sociabilité: elle n'est ni d'origine divine, comme le voudraient les théologiens, ni inscrite dans la nature humaine, comme le pensaient Diderot et la plupart des Encyclopédistes, ni fondée sur les développements de la vie familiale, ni imposée par le plus fort, ni due à une convention entre un roi et des individus qui accepteraient à s'assujétir à son autorité.' Louis Millet, *La Pensée de Rousseau* (Paris, Bourdas, 1966), p. 97.

34. 'On se trouve en présence d'un pacte de caractère exceptionnel par lequel une collectivité considérée comme une seule personne conclut un engagement réciproque avec ses membres pris individuellement.' Robert Derathé, *Jean-Jacques Rousseau et la science politique de son temps* (Paris, Vrin, 1970), p. 225.

35. The theologico-metaphysical dimension of the General Will is well outlined by Hans Barth in his article 'Volonté générale et volonté particulière chez Jean-Jacques Rousseau' in *Rousseau et la philosophie politique* (Paris, PUF, 1965). Barth believes that, in essence, this General Will must be innate since it is not functional to human trial and error: 'La voilà présente tout à coup, de manière surprenante; sans recourir à personne, elle prend le commandement qui lui revient comme à un être échappant à tout empire humain et s'élevant au-dessus de tout pouvoir qui prétendrait disposer d'elle dans le monde. Les interprètes qui en viendraient à méconnaître le fondement métaphysique et théologique de la

volonté générale, commettraient une erreur impardonable' (p. 41).

36. For a clarification of this point, see Derathé, *Jean-Jacques Rousseau et la science politique de son temps*, pp. 232–3.

37. For an overview of these two trends, see Derathé's opening chapter in *Jean-Jacques Rousseau et la science politique de son temps*, as well as Pierre Burgelin's introduction to his *La Philosophie de l'existence de Jean-Jacques Rousseau*.

38. *Rousseau: totalitarian or liberal* (New York, University of Columbia Press, 1956), p. 75. Chapman, however, opts for Rousseau's liberalism by claiming that individual autonomy is the key to Rousseau's political and moral theory. 'Here is no atomistic theory of man's relation to society. Rather, it is a theory which, while giving weight to man's dependence on his society, sees in him capacities for autonomy and responsibility and demands that he exercise them' (p. 155). We must mention here that these two trends are sometimes seen as a struggle within Rousseau himself between two subjective tendencies. This trivialisation of Rousseau's social theory is carried best by critics who reduce everything to mere psychologism. See for example, William H. Blanchard, *Rousseau and the spirit of revolt: a psychological study* (Ann Arbor, University of Michigan Press, 1967). Blanchard sees in the mixture of totalitarianism and liberalism in Rousseau's social theory a conflict between his liberal ideals and his sadomasochistic desires. 'Rousseau was a liberal at war with himself, a man trying to convey a message of freedom to mankind while a dark shadow within him whispered a cousel of submission' (p. 134).

39. Cassirer, *The question of Jean-Jacques Rousseau*, p. 55.

40. Ibid., p. 63.

41. Robert Derathé, *Le Rationalisme de Jean-Jacques Rousseau* (Paris, PUF, 1948), pp. 4–5.

42. Ibid., pp. 25–38.

43. Ibid., p. 5 footnote.

44. Cassirer, *The question of Jean-Jacques Rousseau*, p. 82.

45. Derathé, *Le rationalisme de Jean-Jacques Rousseau*, p. 15.

46. Derathé, *Rousseau et la science politique de son temps*, p. 148.

47. 'La pensée de Rousseau est révolutionnaire, avant tout parce qu'elle est née d'une opposition fondamentale et irréductible envers un ordre existant.' B. Groethuysen, *Jean-Jacques Rousseau* (Paris, Gallimard, 1949). Groethuysen sees in Rousseau the only redeeming thinker of the Revolution (see his other book, *Philosophie de la révolution française*); we believe this to be an overstatement. Rousseau certainly said no, but at the same time he ran away to the woods. Rousseau was far from a believer in revolutions although he felt they were inevitable; in his Réponse au roi de Pologne Duc de Lorraine regarding the first *Discours*, Rousseau says: 'Il n'y a plus de remède, à moins de quelque grande révolution presque aussi à craindre que le mal qu'elle pourrait guérir, et qu'il est blamable de désirer et impossible à prévoir' (IN 95).

48. For an elaboration on this logical circularity, see Pierre Burgelin, 'Le Social et le politique chez Rousseau' in *Etudes sur le contrat social de Jean-Jacques Rousseau* (Paris, Publications de l'Université de Dijon, vol. XXX, 1964). As to the infinite regression we are pointing to, Derathé seems to be engaging in it while attempting to protect Rousseau's theoretical

weaknesses: 'Selon Rousseau, ce n'est pas le contrat qui est à l'origine des premières relations sociales. Ce serait même plutôt l'inverse . . . C'est donc en réalité le développement de la sociabilité qui a rendu nécessaires les établissements politiques.' *Rousseau et la science politique de son temps*, p. 177. If sociability is prior to the contract, what do we need a contract for — the social is already there! This is an attempt to blur Rousseau's primary postulate which is the zero point, the pure beginning.

49. 'For Rousseau, inequality of property is a matter of no moral significance, a fact which man can accept as much as he must put up with the unequal distribution of bodily strength, skills, and mental gifts . . . The state does not guarantee to each individual an equal share of possessions; it is exclusively concerned with securing an equal measure of rights and duties,' Cassirer, *The question of Jean-Jacques Rousseau*, p. 60. If this is true then how is Rousseau going to compensate for natural inequality with civil equality? (Bodily strength and skills are natural.) It is surprising that Cassirer does not see in this a major flaw in Rousseau's system, for if there is no material equality then what does freedom mean?

50. Jacques Dehaussy, 'La Dialectique de la souveraine liberté dans le contrat social de Jean-Jacques Rousseau', in *Etudes sur le contrat social*, p. 139. Dehaussy indicates the ideological presuppositions behind this logical flaw which is germane to eighteenth-century French thought. The lack of logical rigour is due to 'cet individualisme, qu'il partage avec ses contemporains, et qui veut que la propriété (et surtout la propriété ou, tout au moins, la possession de la terre) constitue en quelque sorte, l'expansion spatiale de la personbalité humaine, nécessaire pour que celle-ci acquière sa pleine indépendence' (p. 140).

51. 'Tout droit consiste dans l'application d'une règale unique à des gens différents, à des gens qui, en fait, ne sont no indentiques ni égaux. Par suite, le "droit égal" équivaut à une violation de l'égalité, à une injustice.' Galvano della Volpe, 'Critique marxiste de Rousseau' in *Etudes sur le contrat social*, p. 503.

52. Dehaussy, 'La Dialectique', p. 140.

53. John Charvet, 'Individual identity and social consciousness in Rousseau' in *Modern studies in philosophy: Hobbes and Rousseau*, ed. M. Cranston and R. S. Peters (New York, Doubleday, 1972), p. 466.

54. 'L'aliénation totale de chaque associé avec tous ses droits à toute la communauté n'aboutit pas dans la doctrine de Rousseau à la suppression des droits naturels de l'individu, mais il s'agit d'un artifice pour les convertir en droits civils.' Derathé, *Jean-Jacques Rousseau et la science politique de son temps*, p. 229.

55. 'Natural man is human in possessing individuality for himself, but this he possesses independently of the existence for him of any other consciousness, so that this individual identity is determined for himself by himself alone without the intrusion of others on this identity. It is thus not beginning as a mere animal that natural man is to be developed by circumstances into civilized, social man, but as a being already inhabiting a human world characterized by the existence of only one human being in it.' John Charvet, *The social problem in the philosophy of Rousseau* (Cambridge University Press, 1974), p. 17. This book constitutes an in-depth analysis of Rousseau's social problem. Charvet, however, does not refer to all the autobiographical writings which confirm Rousseau's consistency with

regard to the problem of mediation. Nor does he see ideology as the motivating factor behind this social theory; he merely indicates the logical flaws in Rousseau's argumentation.

56. 'What has taken place is not an identification between myself and his suffering self, but rather a separation of his needs as suffering body from himself as person and then the appropriation of these needs as mine . . . There is merely oneself and the extension of oneself in the body of another. Nowhere is there another for me.' Charvet, ibid., p. 92.

57. Mauzi, *L'Idée du bonheur dans la littérature et la pensée françaises du dix-huitième siècle*, p. 650.

Chapter 6

1. *Le Miroir des limbes* (Paris, Gallimard, 1976) is made up of two related parts: *Antimémoires* carries the narrative till the end of 1965; *La Corde et les souris* picks up the narrative in March 1966 and ends with Malraux's final sojourn in hospital. *La Corde et les souris* is made up of *Les Chênes qu'on abat*, *Oraisons funèbres*, *La Tête d'Obsidienne*, *Lazare*, and *Hôtes de passage*, which were all published separately in book form by Gallimard. References will be respectively initialled 'ML', 'AN' and will be made to the Gallimard edition of 1967.

2. See, for example, Michael Riffaterre, 'I have been reading Malraux's *Antimémoires*', *Columbia Forum*, Winter 1968, pp. 30–5. Riffaterre focuses on the repetition of the fiction in *Antimémoires* without indicating what motivates this repetition.

3. *La Tentation de l'Occident* (Paris, Grasset, 1926). Hereafter initialled 'TO'.

4. *La Voix royale* (Paris, Gallimard, 1930). Hereafter initialled 'VR'.

5. *La Condition humaine* (Paris, Gallimard, 1946). Hereafter initialled 'CH'.

6. Mayrena was a real-life character who built his own kingdom among the native tribes of the Sedang region in Indochina before the First World War, and tried to cede it in turn to France, England and Germany who were competing for spheres of influence in the region. Of interest in this section of *Antimémoires* is the blurring of boundaries between fiction and reality. Malraux meets Clappique, a character in one of his novels; an equivalence is here established between the ontological status of Malraux and Clappique. Clappique, in turn, makes a fictional narrative of the real life-story of Mayrena. Is Clappique's story of Mayrena to be trusted? Malraux refuses us any delineation or clarification, the message being that all these narratives are both real and fictive.

7. *Le Temps du mépris* (Paris, Gallimard, 1935). Hereafter initialled 'TM'.

8. *Les Noyers de l'Altenburg* (Paris, Gallimard, 1948). Hereafter initialled 'NA'.

9. *L'Espoir* (Paris, Gallimard, 1937). Hereafter initialled 'E'.

10. See in this connection Walter Langlois, *André Malraux: the Indochina adventure* (New York, Praeger, 1966). Langlois devotes his book to Malraux's two-year stay in Indochina in the twenties as it shaped his

literary career. Aside from Langlois's biographical attempts, there are important excerpts from the local papers and especially *L'Indochine enchaînée* which Malraux edited. See also Jean Lacouture, *André Malraux: une vie dans le siècle* (Paris, Seuil, 1973). Lacouture argues that Malraux's biographical inexactitudes are compensated for by the quality of his writing, and that if Malraux was not present in all the places he describes, 'il est vrai que ses visions refont un monde aussi vrai que le vrai, et que son Asie rêvée s'impose presque aussi fort qu'une Asie vécue' (p. 115). Lacouture, evidently, holds to the categories of truth and fiction. Malraux will no doubt be overtaken by biographers as more data and documents become available, mainly because Malraux, and any man of action, calls for interpretation. In a sense biography, as the duplication of a lived experience, defeats its purpose since it never establishes the 'truth' which is its basic postulate. Biography is merely the creation of a fiction, and all 'great' men call for more than one biography.

11. Germaine Brée, 'The *Antimémoires* of André Malraux', *Contemporary Quarterly*, vol. 11 (1970), p. 237.

12. Emile Lecerf, in his book *André Malraux* (Paris, Editions Richard-Masse, 1971), focuses on Malraux's lack of interest in style *per se* and his use of style not as form but as content. Indeed, the literary form, as Malraux conceives it, is itself value: it incarnates an ideology. And this has to do, as Lecerf suggests, with Malraux's synthetisation of the novelistic tradition. 'Chez Malraux, le style n'existe pas en soi. Il n'est que l'expression, souvent rocailleuse, d'un potentiel émotif. Ce déplacement de l'intérêt résulte de toute une technique du roman; alors que le roman français est analytique, le roman de Malraux est synthétique' (p. 26). Also, 'les romans de Malraux sont écrits dans un langage et dans une pensée dialectiques. La dualité inhérente au langage et à la pensée analytique est dépassée' (p. 126).

13. 'Malraux seems to think of metaphor as an essential falsification. Ellipsis, on the other hand, is not the curtailment in the expression of a thought, but a revelation, for Malraux thinks of it as a direct juxtaposition without any explanation, "not of two words but of two facts". No matter how unrelated two facts are, they are both present at a scene and are a part of the truth of that scene.' Charles F. Roedig, 'Malraux on the novel (1930–1945)', *Yale French Studies*, no. 18 (Winter, 1957), p. 41.

14. Malraux always finds adequate tools to express some of this complexity; here, it is a newspaper and telegrams, in *L'Espoir*, telephone conversations, in *Les Conquérants*, radio announcements and notes on billboards.

15. We must differentiate here between History with a capital 'H' and history with a small 'h'. Malraux refers in this passage to History as the time structure which makes up the past, the existing, the possible and the probable — the process which encompasses all phenomena. History with a small 'h' refers to a particular reading of history; that is, to an ideological configuration, and histories — the productions of a given set of consciousnesses in given moments in time — are engulfed by History. Malraux's emphasis on the irreducibility of the historical process is well expressed by Walter Berger in *Les Noyers de l'Altenburg*: 'Il y a une évidence à laquelle nous sommes en effet soumis . . . sans laquelle ni l'idée de patrie, ni celle

de race, ni celle de classe sociale ne seraient ce qu'elles sont. Nous y vivons comme les civilizations religieuses vivaient en Dieu. Sans elle aucun de nous ne pourrait penser. C'est notre propre domaine: c'est l'histoire' (NA 139).

16. The Colloquy of Altenburg may be seen as a sterile discussion among intellectuals but if we look closely at the structure of the book, we realise that it counterbalances the other episodes, that is, the gas attack of the first war and the prison of the second. In effect, the Colloquy which hypostatises dialogue is there to constitute an equilibrium: it is the meditation on the action.

17. An important but often neglected book is Jeanne Delhomme's *Temps et destin: essai sur André Malraux* (Paris, Gallimard, 1955) which constitutes a purely philosophical treatise on Malraux. Delhomme's book, which defies my classification, stands on its own and provides a stimulating though abstract existential view on Malraux's text. Here are her views on the concepts of original lack, on memory and on art: 'Une absence première, totale, irrémédiable, impossible à combler et à escamoter; c'est cela l'origine, l'absence absolue d'origine, derrière le monde, derrière la vie, derrière l'histoire, il n'y a que les forces de l'absence qui n'est absence de personne, absence de rien' (p. 25). 'La mémoire est sa présence à soi en tant qu'elle ne cesse de se créer dans l'instant et que cette création est approfondissement de soi' (p. 137). 'Séparé sans séparation, étranger sans étrangeté, l'univers de l'art ne se superpose pas à l'univers à l'univers sensible pour constituer un univers second et surajouté; il n'y a pas deux mondes, il n'y en a qu'un, c'est le monde de l'art, l'anti-monde qui est le seul monde, anti-temps qui est le seul temps' (p. 173).

18. Joseph Hoffman, *L'Humanisme de Malraux* (Paris, Librairie Klincksiek, 1963).

19. Thomas Jefferson Kline, *André Malraux and the metamorphosis of death* (New York, Columbia University Press, 1973).

20. Lucien Goldmann, *Pour une sociologie du roman* (Paris, Gallimard, 1964). James W. Greenlee, *Malraux's heroes and history* (Dekalb, Northern Illinois University Press, 1973), p. 4. See also David Wilkinson's *Malraux: an essay in political criticism* (Cambridge, Mass., Harvard University Press, 1967), p. 6. 'His concern is not with the essence of being or the nature of the universe, but with the position of man in time and among men, with man in history, with man in the social order.'

21. R. M. Alberes, 'André Malraux and the "abridged abyss"', *Yale French Studies*, no. 18 (Winter, 1957), p. 47.

22. F. E. Dorenlot, *Malraux ou l'unité de la pensée* (Paris, Gallimard, 1970), p. 41.

23. It should be noted here that the non-event can take place only within a non-metaphysical, non-theistic system. The non-event makes for the differentiation between historical transcendence and metaphysical transcendence postulated by Malraux and Augustine respectively. In God's great book there are no non-events for everything is predetermined. But if we agree with Malraux that the world is made of forgetfulness, then everything is possible for man, only then freedom and action become possible. 'En effet, si Dieu n'existe pas, s'il n'existe pas de nature transmise de siècle en siècle l'homme n'es rien *a priori* et, par conséquent, peut

tout. Toute reflexion sur la gratuité de l'existence fait conclure à la liberté.' Dorenlot, ibid., p. 63.

24. Consider, for example, Hong and Tchen, the revolutionaries; Perken and Garine, the adventurers; Clappique, the drifter; Kyo and Manuel, the militants; and the artist in *Les Voix du silence*. There are other important roles: Gisors, the opium addict who incarnates the role of the dreamer; Ferral, the opportunist and economic manipulator of both coloniser and colonised; the anarchist as incarnated by Puig; the devout Catholic as represented by Ximenès. The roles referred to are the ones to which Malraux devoted most of his fiction. Also, the dreamer shares a lot with the drifter; Clappique is the other face of Gisors. Ferral's thirst for power is also shared by the various adventurers.

25. 'Even some characters who refuse all value to politics, such as Clappique and Ferral in *La Condition humaine*, are forced by the situation to see themselves politically and, if only for a while, to give some political form to their lives.' Catherine Savage, *Sartre, Malraux, and Aragon as political novelists* (Gainsville, Fla., University of Florida Press, 1965), p. 8. We cannot agree with Savage's basic claim that in Malraux 'political action is a dispersion rather than a purposeful channelling of efforts and desires' (p. 9) and that his political novels succeed because they are 'anti-political' (p. 15). Savage's ideological bias, which is shared by the liberal-humanist critical writers on Malraux, comes through in the following passage: 'Certainly, the more we have to turn to external criteria in order to assess and criticize, the farther we get from the ideal of art as we are now accustomed to viewing it' (p. 15).

26. 'Devenu le prisonnier d'un univers qu'il a lui-même créé, Clappique s'évanouit, balloté par le destin contre lequel il avait pensé pouvoir se réfugier dans l'éphémère liberté d'un univers imaginaire.' Hoffmann, *L'Humanisme de Malraux*, p. 166.

27. *Les Conquérants* (Paris, Gallimard, 1928), p. 62. Hereafter initialled 'CO'. Joseph Hoffmann sees the adventurer as a heroic figure in whom the forces of life oppose the forces of death. He seems to have overlooked this passage, perhaps because his main concern is with the metaphysical dimension of Malraux's novel. To Hoffmann, the adventurer incorporates the 'opposition en l'homme entre ce qui est subi et ce qui est voulu: sa part la plus haute — le courage et la volonté d'affronter — s'impose difficilement mais victorieusement à sa part la plus basse — l'instinct de conservation, la peur.' *L'Humanisme de Malraux*, p. 140. Another passage which supports my claim: 'Je n'aime pas les hommes. Je n'aime pas les pauvres gens, le peuple, ceux en somme pour qui je vais combattre' (CO 68).

28. There is an interesting relationship, in Malraux's world, between eroticism and action; both provide the adventurer with a frenetic thrill. Claude Mauriac devotes half of his book, *André Malraux ou le mal du héros* (Paris, Grasset, 1946) to this relationship: 'L'amant de Malraux a tendance à considérer la femme comme un objet, mais il veut, au même moment, qu'elle reste une personne humaine' (p. 96). 'L'amour physique, pour André Malraux, consiste, nous l'avons vu, dans la recherche simultanée de la plus grande dépersonnalisation et de la plus grande personnalisation possibles: devenir autre pour prendre de

soi-même une conscience aigue' (p. 109). Malraux has devoted considerable attention to this dialectic of the look in *La Condition humaine*: the
relationship between Ferral and Valérie constitutes an extensive analysis
of this problematic. 'Un être humain, pensa Ferral, une vie individuelle,
isolée, unique, comme la mienne . . . Il s'imagina elle, habitant son
corps, éprouvant à sa place cette jouissance qu'il ne pouvait ressentir que
comme une humiliation' (CH 99). 'En somme il ne couchait jamais
qu'avec lui-même, mais il ne pouvait y parvenir qu'à la condition de
n'être pas seul . . . oui, sa volonté de puissance n'atteignait jamais son
objet, ne vivait que de le renouveler; mais n'eût-il de sa vie possédé une
seule femme, il avait possédé, il possèderait à travers cette chinoise qui
l'attendait, la seule chose dont il fût avide: lui-même' (CH 188). It is clear
then that the adventurer and the lover in Malraux's fiction share the same
predicament: in the exercise of their own power they want to meet the
Other, whether another human being or a social situation, on their own
terms and not on the Other's terms. For an extensive analysis of the look
as a social phenomenon, see Jean-Paul Sartre, *L'Etre et le néant* (Paris,
Gallimard, 1945), pp. 428–84.

29. The word 'revolutionary' is used here in talking about Hong and
Tchen because this term is prevalent in the critical literature. In effect,
however, they are anarchists who oppose any kind of order and promote
destruction for its own sake, to the extent that their own selves are consumed in the process. The frenzy of such an undertaking, in Malraux's
words, borders on mysticism. 'Mais il sentait, comme tout mystique, que
son absolu ne pouvait être saisi que dans l'instant. D'où sans doute son
dédain de tout ce qui ne tendait pas à l'instant qui le lierait à lui-même
dans une possession vertigineuse' (CH 123).

30. The commitment of the militant comes forcefully through in one of
Malraux's most powerful scenes: the cyanide episode. Katow who is about
to be burnt alive in a locomotive gives away his cyanide to two of his
comrades, thus sacrificing himself in death. Geoffrey T. Harris, among
other critics, claims in his book, *André Malraux: l'éthique comme fonction de
l'esthétique* (Paris, Minard, 1972) that 'l'action, thème central des cinq
romans, aboutit soit à une défaite total, soit à une victoire équivoque'
(p. 34). The deaths of Katow and Kyo, then, are failures of the revolutionary cause. However, reading failure in Malraux's novels of action is a
short-sighted view for Malraux merely indicates the end of an episode in
an ongoing historical process; the book is open-ended and the story
continues. Souen and other young revolutionaries will continue the
struggle. The book ends on old Gisors's note: 'Oui, sans doute, les
hommes ne valaient-ils que par ce qu'ils avaient transformé. La Révolution venait de passer par une terrible maladie, mais elle n'était pas morte.
Et c'étaient Kyo et les siens, vivants ou non, vaincus ou non, qui l'avaient
mise au monde' (CH 269).

31. In *L'Espoir*, Garcia says: 'L'Apocalypse veut tout, tout de suite; la
révolution obtient peu — lentement et durement. Le danger est que tout
homme porte en soi-même le désir d'une Apocalypse. Et que dans la lutte,
ce désir, passé un temps assez court, est une défaite certaine, pour une
raison très simple: par sa nature, l'Apocalypse n'a pas de futur' (E 119).
The apocalyptic view is opposed in this novel to the discipline and

planning as exemplified by Manuel and Garcia: 'J'appelle discipline l'ensemble des moyens qui donne à des collectivités combattantes la plus grande efficacité' (E 117).

32. Jean-Paul Sartre, introduction to Roger Stéphane's *Portrait de l'aventurier* (Paris, Editions Sagittaire, 1950), pp. 16–17. This book constitutes a comprehensive analysis of the figure of the adventurer. Stéphane sees in solitude the main motivation of the adventurer: 'la dérision commence ici: parti pour fuir la solitude, l'aventurier va la rencontrer à chaque moment de son destin' (p. 97). Stéphane's main claim is in the historisation of the phenomenon 'adventurer'; it is clear that there is no room for the adventurer in our times because 'l'ère des aventures individuelles est close depuis que l'action des forces collectives s'est ouvertement substituée à la prise de l'individu. Un homme seul, audjourd'hui n'a pas de chance de marquer l'histoire' (p. 42).

33. Erving Goffman, *The presentation of self in everyday life* (New York, Anchor Books, 1959), p. 253.

34. Ibid., p. 238.

35. Ibid., p. 76.

36. This is the point at which self becomes a repressive apparatus and madness sets in, for the individual's ultimate weapon against role imprisonment is to go out of bounds. Artaud, for example, refused the self he was given: he is not, in his own words, the son of his mother or father, or Antonin Artaud, the writer and theatre critic: he is his own father and mother and Christ, etc. For a substantive analysis of the relationship between schizophrenia and capitalism, see Gilles Deleuze and Félix Guattari, *Anti Œdipe: capitalisme et schizophrénie* (Paris, Editions de Minuit, 1972).

37. *L'Evénement*, September, 1967. Quoted by Lacouture in *André Malraux: une vie dans le siècle*, p. 399.

38. W. M. Frohock in *André Malraux and the tragic imagination* (Stanford University Press, 1952), points to the existing relationship between individualism and the memory processes. Memory here means that process an individual uses to recapture something that is non-existent, since the time-gap always creates a further distance from the lived experience and in effect one does not recall but one creates a new experience. Memory in the end coincides with creative imagination. 'Individualism places men in unhappy straits. There is nothing on which to found a new conception of man except the consciousness each man has of himself. And here we totter, Malraux says, on the brink of the absurd, for there is no way for man to know himself. The instruments we use in judging others cannot be brought to bear. Even our memory is conditioned, and what we remember of our own acts is private, and dependent on all the forces which condition our memory. There is no way of examining our past lives which does not employ subjective and thus completely undependable means' (p. 32).

39. 'Psychologiquement, Malraux refuse d'élucider l'homme par l'inconscient, parce que ce serait ouvrir la porte à toutes les incertitudes, à toutes les lâchetés. De même intellectuellement, il refuse de recourir à l'irrationel pour expliciter le mystère de l'existence.' Dorenlot, *Malraux ou l'unité de la pensée*, p. 222.

40. Jean Carduner, *La Création romanesque chez Malraux* (Paris, Nizet, 1968), p. 56.

41. 'C'est ici que la critique accuse Malraux en général: le personnage romanesque semble se dissoudre, ce n'est pas lui qui parle, c'est Malraux lui-même qui se sert de son personnage pour examiner ses idées, en faire son porte-parole. L'auteur s'asservit son personnage au lieu de le laisser vivre; Garine, c'est une marionette qui parle avec la voix de Malraux.' Carduner, *La Création romanesque chez Malraux*, p. 30.

42. Denis Boak, *André Malraux* (London, Oxford University Press, 1968), p. 1. In her book *André Malraux: the conquest of dread* (Baltimore, Johns Hopkins Press, 1960), Gerda Blumenthal makes a similar if more sophisticated claim. Malraux, or the eternal writer, to Blumenthal, writes in order to conquer the demons within, to solve a personal problem: 'This has throughout the ages been one of the achievements of art: to exorcise the powers of night and deliver the artist and those of his time and situation from their grip and fascination' (p. 7). 'Political action is of the moment and suffers tragic and inevitable degradation in time; in smiting one face of Saturn, it resurrects another, possibly, no less hideous. In artistic creation, through the mystery of style, darkness is not merely challenged, it is transfigured' (p. 12).

43. Boak, *André Malraux*, p. 83.

44. Similar arguments are used by W. M. Frohoc in his critique of *La Condition humaine*; the lacuna left by an incomplete characterisation, to Frohoc, makes of this novel a document more than a work of art. 'It will survive more by its value as a document than as a piece of literature, and by its appeal to the comprehending intellect rather than to the emotions. Its confusion, its loose ends, its diffuseness, may even increase its documentary interest.' *André Malraux and the tragic imagination*, p. 125. Again, the measuring stick is the traditional novel of character. Frohoc fails to see that the 'loose ends' and 'diffuseness' are intentional, there to counter the mimetic conception of literature which flourished throughout the Classical Age.

45. It is clear that the fiction Malraux is negating is that which conceives of the novel not as process but as object; the preoccupations of such a conception of the novel correspond to the aesthetics of pleasure. The work is an object to be enjoyed at leisure. Purely aesthetic concerns are there of course to mask a chaotic reality the writer wants to avoid. Charles F. Roedig understands Malraux's conception of the novel as a form which widens our consciousness of social experience. 'The value of the work will not be in the novelist's private experience of the subtlety of his tale, but rather in his choice of events drawn from the common experience and reported with his "tone" reflecting the impact of that experience.' 'Malraux on the novel (1930–1945)', p. 41.

46. André Malraux, *Le Triangle noir* (Paris, Gallimard, 1970), p. 30.

47. Ibid., p. 32.

48. Ibid., p. 40.

49. What can we say of Tchen's meditative passages throughout *La Condition humaine*? Do they not point to at least a partial psychologisation? Geoffrey T. Harris, in his *André Malraux: l'éthique comme fonction de l'esthétique*, makes a claim which supports mine: 'Paroles non énoncées,

paroles quasi articulées, les pensées de Tchen, tant dans la fond, diffèrent à peine du mot parlé et ce procédé est utilisé tout le long du roman' (p. 44).

50. The reader of Malraux's novels ought to be aware of the dates and times in which the stories occur; we are always exposed to specific moments in the day or dates in a given month. However, times are not treated equally by Malraux; certain moments explode with action while others are forgotten. The spacing of the action itself is a necessity, for the novel, or a whole fictional world, could not possibly cover the events of one day in a revolution let alone a whole revolution or war, but Malraux must give the reader a historical perspective. The action in *L'Espoir*, for example, is represented as a panorama of unrelated scenes within a chronological order: it covers the period from 17 July 1936, the date of the uprising, to 18 March 1937 when a Republican victory takes place at Guadalajara. The novel is open-ended and does not cover the rest of the war. Malraux published it *in medias res* to create a sense of emergency; he used it as a propaganda tool for the Republican cause.

51. Carduner, *La Création romanesque chez Malraux*, p. 74. 'Another scene follows, taking place elsewhere, with other characters. There is no resumé of what took place in the interval, everything narrated occurs in the present and is experienced as it unfolds. No explicit narrative connects these scenes.' Alberes, 'André Malraux and the "Abridged Abyss"', p. 50. It is clear that the absence of narration coincides with Malraux's intentional lack of omniscience which is compensated for by devices like a given angle of view, hearing, expressive gestures, dialogues, letters, telegrams, to mention but a few — all techniques of exteriorisation.

52. A note by Malraux in Gaetan Picon, *Malraux par lui-même* (Paris, Seuil, 1968), p. 38.

53. Cecil Jenkins, *André Malraux* (New York, Twayne Publishers, 1972), p. 147.

54. Rima Drell Reck, 'The Antimémoires: Malraux's ultimate form' in *Kentucky Quarterly*, vol. 15, no. 1 (1969), p. 162.

55. André Malraux, *Les Voix du silence* (Paris, Gallimard, 1952), p. 622.

56. Ibid., p. 637.

57. 'A style as such is not consciously created where nothing existed before. First, the artist must accept the forms of a predecessor, then he must rebel against the limitations he finds in them, then overturn them by introducing a large or small number of new forms, and a new mode.' David Wilkinson, *Malraux: an essay in political criticism* (Cambridge, Mass., Harvard University Press, 1967), p. 141.

58. André Malraux in Martine de Courcel's *Malraux: life and work* (New York, Harcourt Brace Jovanovitch, 1976), p. 231.

59. '*Antimémoires*: l'opposition aux Mémoires comme procédé au réalisme de l'introspection comme exemple, la dissociation de la mémoire et de la chronologie, des confessions et de la sincérité, de la lucidité et du lyrisme invitent à chercher plus loin que dans l'ordre de succession des événements, la soumission de la psychologie aux secrets, la fidélité à l'aventure héroïque, la chaîne et la trame d'un texte où s'entrecroisent le souvenir de la fiction et la fiction comme souvenir, le réel comme imaginaire et le possible comme vrai; roman d'un passé et re-présentation

d'un futur, reconnaissance *de soi* et pressentiment *d'un* soi, dénonciation de l'équivoque du temps contesté par la simultanéité de l'espace où, la figure d'une nation, se déposent la vie des peuples, leur histoire, leur activité, leur passivité, procès du lieu que défait la durée des civilisations, le livre d'André Malraux relève d'une mémoire *prophétique* qu'amplifie une imagination *historique*, imagination à rebours et mémoire à l'envers qui s'exercent *sans modèle*, tirant de ce qui fut ce qui sera, ce qui sera de ce qui fut.' Jeanne Delhomme, 'Des Mémoires à la mémoire' in *Critique*, no. 248 (January, 1968), pp. 48–9.

Chapter 7

1. For an overview and critique of this literature, see Edwin Schur, *The awareness trap: self-absorption instead of social change* (New York, McGraw Hill, 1977). 'Only a leisure class can afford to devote so much time, energy and money to self exploration . . . It is to such a class and its typical problems that the movement's basic appeal is directed. And far from inciting a break with our dominant patterns of competitive consumption (as some awareness-oriented idealists had hoped would happen), the ''new consciousness'' has itself become a commodity. It is being heavily promoted, packaged, and marketed, much like any commercial item. While the movement provides middle-class consumers with an attractive new product, attention is diverted from the more serious social problems that plague our society — poverty, racism, environmental decay, crime, widespread corporate and governmental fraud' (p. 7).

2. C. B. MacPherson, *The political theory of possessive individualism* (London, Oxford University Press, 1962), p. 3.

3. J.-P. Sartre, *Critique de la raison dialectique* (Paris, Gallimard, 1960), p. 316. Sartre differentiates between the domain of pure praxis, the genuine praxis of communal living, and the domain of the 'pratico-inerte' which constitutes the structure of seriality. It is clear that seriality is not in our nature and that it is an ideologically motivated phenomenon forced upon consciousness by the creation of material supports within the social organisation. 'Le groupe se définit par son entreprise et par le mouvement constant d'intégration qui vise à en faire une praxis pure en tentant de supprimer en lui toutes les formes de l'inertie; le collectif se définit par son être, c'est-à-dire en tant que toute praxis se constitue en lui comme simple exis; c'est un projet matériel et inorganique du champ pratico-inerte en tant que multiplicité discrète d'individus agissants se produit en lui sous le signe de l'Autre comme unité rééle dans l'Etre, c'est-à-dire comme synthèse passive en tant que l'objet constitué se pose comme essentiel et que son inertie pénètre chaque praxis individuelle comme sa détermination fondamentale par l'unité passive, c'est-à-dire par l'interpénétration préalable et donnée de tous en tant qu'Autres' (pp. 307–8).

4. R. D. Laing, *The divided self* (Harmondsworth, Penguin, 1965); *The politics of experience* (Harmondsworth, Penguin, 1972).

5. *The divided self*, p. 119.

6. In *The politics of experience*, Chapter 5, Laing speaks of the mystical

dimension of schizophrenic experience, thus shifting the borders of normalcy to the realm of madness. But Laing remains a victim to the same ideology he rejects; his basic contradiction can be phrased as 'negational idealism', not far from Rousseau's experience. Rousseau said no and ran to the woods to seek his true self; Laing says no and reaches into the deepest recesses of his being to encounter that self. Laing seems to forget that the inner is a transformation of the outer.

7. Gilles Deleuze and Félix Guattari, *Anti-Œdipe: capitalisme et schizophrénie* (Paris, Editions de Minuit, 1972), pp. 309–10.

Index

187